PUCK
HEAVEN

PUCK HEAVEN

Minnesota State Boys' Hockey Tournament Trivia

Jim Hoey

author of *Minnesota Twins Trivia*
and *Minnesota Vikings Trivia*

NODIN PRESS

Design and Layout: John Toren
Cover photo by Kyle Oen

Abbreviated photo credits accompany the photographs. Many of them were provided by the Minnesota State High School League (MSHSL) and the United States Hockey Hall of Fame Museum in Eveleth.

ISBN: 978-1-935666-28-8

Second printing, revised 2015

Library of Congress Control Number: 2011940575

Nodin Press
530 North Third Street
Suite 120,
Minneapolis, MN
55401

Every effort has been made to ensure the accuracy of the information contained in this book. If you notice an error or omission, please notify us and we'll correct it for the next edition. In addition, if you have information or material that would befit this publication, please contact me and I will include it in an updated version. Thank you and now relish in the glory of the Minnesota State Boys' High School Hockey Tournament!

-Jim Hoey, ajehoey@comcast.net

To all those who have contributed in any way over the years to making the Minnesota State Boys' High School Hockey Tournament a truly magical event.

ACKNOWLEDGEMENTS

I would like to thank all of the people who have been so helpful and have supported my efforts in compiling this book and to those who gave me suggestions and counsel, with special kudos to Tom Johnsen, Tom Novitzki, Kyle Oen, Luke Olson, and William Troumbly. To my wonderful wife Ann and son Eddie, my appreciation is endless for accepting my passion for this project and for your love and understanding in allowing me the time to complete it.

A special thanks to my publisher and friend, Norton Stillman, for his guidance and direction in publishing this book and to John Toren for his fine work with design, layout, and technical expertise and to Kyle Oen for his cover photo. My gratitude extends to the Minnesota State High School League, Vintage Minnesota Hockey and the U.S. Hockey Hall of Fame for their permission in allowing me to use their photographs and to all the individuals and photographers who also did so.

Background and resource materials were gleaned from several sources, including the archives of the Minnesota State High School League, the Minnesota State Historical Society, the St. Paul Public Library, *Skate for Goal* by Gary L. Phillips, *Minnesota State High School Hockey Tournament History* by Art Solz, Jr., *A Complete History of the Minnesota Boys and Girls High School Hockey Tournament 1945-2000*, yearly supplements by Doug Johnson and Maggie Kirchoff of *Let's Play Hockey*, and *Frozen Memories* and *More Frozen Memories* by Ross Bernstein.

Finally, I am indebted to all the former players, coaches, and others who were and have been involved in the Minnesota State Boys' Hockey Tournament for their input. No doubt, there is a unique bond among the individuals who have made it so special. I am humbled and honored to have had the opportunity to work on such a project and sincerely hope that you will enjoy this unique perspective of a truly special yearly event and renowned tradition.

Contents

Introduction

Personal Perspectives

Few traditions are more a part of the fabric of Minnesota life than the State High School Boys' Hockey Tournament. Since the inaugural event in 1945, it has captured the imagination of the state's populace and perhaps no other prep tournament in the nation quite encapsulates the excitement, glamour and allure than the hockey tournament here in the State of Hockey. Every year, there is new inspiration that hearkens back to decades of pride and tradition built by generations of players, coaches, and fans. Since its inception, schoolboys from around the state have created marvelous memories for themselves, their high schools, and the millions who pilgrimage each year to the tournament or witness it on television.

Mention the State Boys' Hockey Tournament to any long-time Minnesotan and the odds are strong that the person will regale you with stories about their grandfather, father, son, husband, uncle, cousin, brother-in-law, friend or neighbor and their exploits in the state tournament. There is sentiment, excitement, and heart-felt sincerity in their voice because this event is so ingrained in our identity. Hockey in our state is a passion for so many and the Tournament, as they say, has a special place in the culture of our state, just like the State Fair and the cabin "up-north."

Stories and anecdotes about the State Boy's Hockey Tournament are as enduring as mosquitoes on a Minnesota lake in July and discussions and arguments about who were the best players in certain eras and who were the best teams are ubiquitous. The grand tradition and lore of the state hockey tourney was constructed on the skills and abilities of winter wunderkinds like John Mayasich and Willard Ikola and on the coaching genius of fellows like Oscar Almquist and Larry Ross. It was continued by skating heroes like Tim Sheehy and Craig Norwich and bench-masters like Tom Saterdalen and Mike Randolph.

As instrumental as the players and coaches have been in carving out this special niche in our midst, perhaps its place in our hearts and psyches emanates just as much from the epic and historic games that are etched in the minds of the hockey community.

Alas, it is the drama of those unforgettable games of yesteryear and the incredible memory of those who played in or witnessed those contests which prompted the publishing of this book.

Whenever this author is involved in a conversation about the tournament, it is always amazing to learn about the minute details of a game that are relayed by the teller of the tale, which is only matched by their incredible zeal in talking about a particular player or team. On a myriad of occasions over the years, I have been asked about specific games, players, coaches, or situations and have been struck by the degree of animation in their observations and their loyalty and bond to the tournament.

For more than thirty years I was employed as a social studies teacher, but sports, especially hockey and baseball, has been a passion of mine from an early age. An affinity for statistics and a joy for writing, combined with a deep interest in history and ice hockey, has resulted in the book you hold in your hands, a trivia book on the state high school hockey tournament. In assembling this volume, it has been fun and energizing recalling memories of the sport and the tournament as both a player and fan. My hope is that this book will help the readers rekindle the past as they peruse these pages and that it will serve as a source for them as they reminisce about a truly great sporting phenomenon. For the uninitiated and the youth, may this serve as a source of history.

Little towns across the state and nation are often noteworthy for a particular identity and so it is with Taconite, my hometown, a town founded in 1907 on the western end of the Mesabi Range. The tiny iron-mining hamlet, whose population has numbered between 310 and 350 people for most of the last 100 years, is almost synonymous with the sport of hockey. A warming-shack full of trophies in Taconite's city hall is tribute to its proud puck history. Anyone driving into the town's main street can see the outdoor rink prominently featured in the center of the village and might even witness a Zamboni resurfacing the natural ice (at least in winter!).

Other iron-mining communities along northern Minnesota's two iron ranges are also closely linked to the sport. With its location not far from the Canadian border and cold temperatures for four to five months a year, it wasn't really surprising that hockey become an integral part of life in places like Eveleth (50 miles northeast), which later became the home of the U.S. Hockey Hall of Fame, and to other cities like Grand Rapids and Hibbing.

Hockey has been intertwined with the pulse of Taconite just as the town's development was correlated to the whims of the mining industry. Most of the town's male residents at least tried to play the game. Old-timers testify that hardly a man who ever lived in the town hadn't played in his youth. In 1920, a Canadian immigrant named Ambrose Hoey, my grandfather, migrated west from Niagara Falls, Ontario and introduced the game that would bring the village much of its glory, pride, and tradition. Hoey organized the first team as immigrant families from Europe arrived in town to begin an abiding connection to the game.

By the late 1920's, burgeoning families were watching their youngsters play hockey for long stretches from November through March. Many a boy put his skates on at home, skated on the ice-covered streets to the rink, and returned home for lunch and/or supper, only to return once again until the lights went out on the rink. Much of the socialization of Taconite's young people took place on the ice and in the warming house. The kids scraped and shoveled the rink, too, helping their skating legs.

Prior to WWII, the Taconite team participated in a senior hockey league with a lineup that was strictly made up of residents of the little village, a tradition that would last for decades. The talent on the team was exceptional. One player, a gentleman named Jimmy Hodgins, was an outstanding player who had the chance to play pro hockey. Instead, he decided to stay home to help the youth learn the game. He was the town clerk, owned the local pool hall and served as a highly-respected and influential youth coach. Hodgins died in Italy in 1943 fighting for his country.

From the end of WWII to the late 1960s, Taconite was a force in senior hockey in Minnesota. A talented group of players who had grown

Taconite youth hockey players, 1962

up with the game reached their prime and won six straight Arrowhead League titles, competing against teams from Duluth, Eveleth, Hibbing, Virginia, and Grand Rapids, among others. Many of the players were attending Greenway High School in nearby Coleraine, but the school didn't sponsor hockey until the 1953-54 season.

One of those players was Jim "Slimmy" Troumbly, my mother's brother, who was the leading scorer for the U.S. in 1950 when the Americans finished second in the world tournament in London. He was playing senior hockey at the age of 14 and played at an exceptional level into his 40s and was an icon on the western end of the Iron Range.

"Slimmy" was one of seven Troumbly brothers who competed for the Taconite Hornets and he was the person who originated the nickname. His brother Ken was a former Gopher captain and one of the founders of the Minnesota Amateur Hockey Association, the forerunner of Minnesota Hockey. My father, Ed, was a defenseman for those teams in the 1940's and 1950's. One of the few players who was not born and raised in the town later in that era was Rube Bjorkman, the Roseau High, Gopher and Olympian, who was serving as the head coach for Greenway at the time. Taconite was twice a state champ and won one national title and also finished second once and third twice in national tournaments. Taconite's senior team regularly outdrew Greenway High in attendance until the late 1960s.

With literally half the town related to us in some fashion, our first house was situated about 100 feet from our outdoor rink. My cousin and best childhood friend, Bobby Lawson, lived next door and we spent most of our winter at the rink. My dad wouldn't let me use a stick at the rink until I learned to become a better skater. Maybe that's why I never became a great puck-handler! Our first official youth level was the...Small Fries, before the term Ponies or Squirts became fashionable. We didn't have many organized practices and we usually played games outdoors as our indoor rink (now called Hodgins-Berardo Arena) was not built until 1962. Jim "Chick" Berardo had been a standout goalie for Taconite and had a tryout with the Detroit Red Wings and was serving as the arena manager and sometimes goalie coach when he died at age 49 during my senior year. During the construction of the arena, I often remember my uncles working on the building up until the time they had to lace up their skates for that evening's senior-league contest.

As for coaching, we had veterans from the community who had played the game but there was little strategy or skill development or the rigid practice regimen common today. We just played and were expected to play hard and be creative. Because we were a small town, we were lucky to have 10 guys on our teams so we played a lot and many of us got to play a level up, which really picked up our game because of the increased speed and size of the older boys. Our mettle was that we played for hours every day and we would often play with just half the ice surface and there might be 25 kids playing in that small of an area. You had to learn how to pass the puck and if you kept it, you had to be a pretty expert stick-handler. There were no whistles, no coaches, no scoreboard, and no fans. We made up our own rules. We just played and then played some more.

Long before youth hockey became so organized, we rarely traveled as Small Fries or Pee Wees. We played the other small communities that made up School District 316—Bovey, Coleraine, Marble, Calumet, Pengilly, and Cloverdale. After the indoor facility was built, we played some of our games inside but otherwise, we played outdoors. Taconite, because of its long hockey background, had a head start over the other towns, and usually we won at least two of the three levels (the other being Bantams). As Pee Wees and Bantams in the mid-1960s, certain guys were selected to play on a so-called "All-Star" team, where we would play occasional games against teams like Hibbing or Eveleth before the playoffs.

Basically, kids who played hockey at Greenway High School in Coleraine during that era had to learn how to get along and find chemistry with players from all the little mining towns cited above who had been rivals through eighth grade. As Pee Wees, Taconite beat Calumet in a best-of-five series and they were tough because they had a kid named Mike Antonovich and he was good....real good. Perhaps that was the high school coach's toughest challenge, how to bring together players from different towns who went to different elementary schools until they shared junior-high classrooms together in Bovey and senior-high classrooms in Coleraine.

Growing up, I played defense until I was 10 but because I was smaller, the switch was made to forward. I was supposedly a hard-working and aggressive player with decent skills but was certainly no star. It was fun to play with cousins and buddies and we enjoyed competing with the older kids at the rink, who made you earn your stripes and challenged you to improve your game. By the time I was a Bantam, we had six younger Hoey boys playing the game. Getting to practice was easy, as every Mom and Dad didn't have to drive their sons to practices or games.

We either walked one block from our new house built in 1960 or jumped in somebody's dad's car for a ride to Coleraine to play indoors. One time, we piled 14 kids into Pecky Guyer's car, whooping and hollering all the way there and back. No kidding!

When Greenway started their high school hockey program, they played their games at our rink in Taconite and my uncle Luke Hoey, who lived with us, was on the team. Later, they would play adjacent to the football field in Coleraine, with the ore dumps providing the back-drop.

I recall seeing my mom's twin brothers, Ronald and Donald, pumping in goals by the boat-load for the Raiders. Both earned scholarships at the "U" after the 1959 season but both returned home at the Christmas break, never to return, and went to work for Troumbly

Brothers Construction, which was headed up by siblings "Slimmy," "Bucko" (Vernon), and Ken.

As a strong Catholic family, we had to sacrifice something impor-tant for Lent and February always posed a challenge as the state hockey tournament was now being broadcast on TV.

Dad decided we would give up TV but there was one caveat: we would definitely watch the hockey tourney. In '62, we were doubly excited as Greenway earned their first berth in the tournament with Bjorkman coaching and star forwards Mike Tok and Jack Stebe and goalie John Lothrop. As a nine-year-old watching on television, I was watching one of Taconite's own, Johnny (X) Carpenter, a big defenseman who had skated on the same familiar surface as me. Greenway jumped out to a 4-0 lead and beat Minneapolis Washburn 5-2 in the first round.

GHS was a deep and talented team but Iron Range Conference rival International Falls was our next foe in the semifinals and they had exciting and talented forwards named Keith Christiansen and Jim Amidon and a little goalie called "Lefty" Curran. They beat us 3-2 in a game we could have won. Stebe and Jim Barle scored for us but Curran finished with 31 saves. In the third-place game, Doug Woog of South St. Paul scored the game-winner in a 2-1 loss for the Raiders as goalie Jim Metzen had 34 saves to Lothrop's 21.

Though our new arena had only natural ice, it helped build our program. We loved the hard ice surface, even though we had to wear long-johns for much of the winter. While the Hornets were now play-ing at the rink, the crowds for the high school games were now picking up and onto the scene came an Alberta native to coach the team, Grant Standbrook, as Bjorkman moved up to the college ranks to coach at Rensselaer Polytechnic Institute in New York State.

Standbrook had played at UMD and he was a revolutionary. In the mid-1960s, he was already deep into off-ice training and weight-lift-ing, both of which were uncommon at the time. Watching the varsity and B-squad teams practice, there was no doubt that he put a premium on conditioning with his fast-paced workouts and puck movement. As a Bantam at the time, you wanted to play for him because he exuded confidence and his style of play was upbeat, with an emphasis on quick, short passes and aggressive forechecking.

In eighth grade, Mr. Standbrook was my science instructor. He was a dynamic teacher, always dressed impeccably and constantly energizing. Standbrook was a man of discipline and it was obvious he practiced what he preached. The hockey players wondered what he thought of us as players. One morning, I found out. The previous night, our Greenway All-Star Bantam team had lost to Eveleth in a playoff game in Hibbing. Late in the game, I took the heel of a stick above my right eye and needed eight stitches. Arriving in class hoping to get some sympathy from my mentor, what with the large bump my red badge of courage, I was encouraged when Standbrook sauntered over before class as some classmates discussed the loss. As I awaited his words of compassion, he asked me if I was all right and I said, "Yeah." He nodded and retorted, "Heard you had your head down." Yup.

Greenway made their way to state again in 1966 with Bob Tok and Kent Nyberg as the scoring stars but International Falls was in the midst of their great run and ended up winning their fourth state title in five years. Our Raiders lost 4-2 in the first round as Roseau's star center, Bryan Grand scored all four goals. We hammered White Bear Lake 10-4 for fifth place. However, Standbrook resigned to take over as head coach at Dartmouth and was replaced by another youthful coach, Bob Gernander, a Duluth Denfeld graduate who had been both a hockey and baseball star for the Hunters and was once drafted by the Los Angeles Dodgers.

As a freshman in 1966-67, we were still in junior high in Bovey but many of us would be trying out for the B-Squad. In those years, about half of the squad was made up of freshmen and the other half sophomores. We didn't have any artificial ice and no access to cars, so the only workouts prior to the tryouts were done by playing football, running, or weightlifting. I didn't play much on the football team but I did lead calisthenics and was in good shape. One problem developed the night before tryouts. I tried on my skates and they were too small. Dad left work at the mine early to get me some new skates at Ray's in Grand Rapids and I got to the rink a bit late for the scrimmages. There were 65 kids trying out for two teams and the squads were usually limited to 15 to 17. The new skates were not comfortable over the three days of tryouts but I still felt I would certainly "make the cut" after what I felt was an adequate to solid effort.

Perhaps I didn't know it at the time but a life lesson was in the offing. Our assistant coach, Paul Rygh, rounded up all the freshmen and sophomores and read off the list of players who made the B-Squad. My heart started to pump as he read off the names of the no-doubters—my cousin Bobby, Tom Peluso, Bobby Lynch, Jim Kosak, Eugene Gustason, and others. He finished the list and my name wasn't one of them. Bam! It felt like an anvil had dropped from the ceiling and hit me in the head. As I staggered out of the room, Kosak, a consummate guy and a good friend, came over to try and console me. A few others told me that I should be on the team. My assumption had always been that I would play for Greenway and maybe even play in college. Was it all over?

For several weeks, I lingered around our outside rink in Taconite but was imagining what was going on at practice four miles away in Coleraine. School was something I always enjoyed but there was definitely despair in not playing with my friends and former teammates. The varsity started off well and the B-Squad had talent, too, and there was a lot of buzz surrounding our hockey program. However, I wasn't a part of it and it hurt. Midway through the season, I was at the rink and Bobby Lawson walked from the after-school activities bus. Instead of walking to his house exactly opposite the east end of the rink, he scurried over onto the ice and said he had something to ask me. "Delford Saxhaug has quit the team and coach Rygh wants to know if you would like to join the team", he said. Shocked but elated at my good fortune, I blurted out, "Of course." We both smiled, he went home to eat supper and then joined me later at the rink.

A bit out of shape, I was overjoyed to be on the ice the next day and quickly adjusted to my new situation. We won most of our games and then got to sit and watch our "A-squad", as we called it then, perform with precision. Coach Gernander made a smooth transition with his new charges. Taconite's own Ken Lawson was a standout defenseman and his brother Gary was a smart centerman. We had three talented lines, a rarity at the time, with differing styles but they could all pass adroitly. My neighbor, Mike "Sluggo" Meade was adept around the net

and could score goals and good-guy Mike Adams, a steady defenseman with a good shot, was also on the varsity. Another long-time rink-
rat, Bill "Cotton" Guyer was a teammate on the B-squad.

Calumet's own Mike Antonovich, our sophomore dynamo, was
a marvel as the offensive sparkplug and he seemed to always shine
in the big moments. Dartmouth-bound Jeff Kosak from Coleraine
was the captain and a fine all-around player and Bill "Pie" Joy was
the goalie. The bus rides were always entertaining and the team could
best be described as a bunch of characters, nearly all with at least one
nickname. One unforgettable trip brought us to Fort Frances, Ontario,
where we faced International Falls, which still didn't have an indoor
facility. Duluth Cathedral had just snapped their 66-game winning
streak but it was still a challenge to beat them. For me, it was a task
just to get over the boards, which were about head high. I got as tired
trying to climb up the boards as I did playing a shift on the ice.

After an exciting victory over the legendary Larry Ross, we had
to be escorted out of the building as the Broncos' supporters were not
happy. At the border, we were detained for well over an hour. Why? Our
bus driver, Ed Linser, was asked if we had brought anything back from
the border that we didn't have as we entered Canada and he said, "Yeah,
a victory"! It was a great line and we all howled with laughter but the
border agent wasn't pleased. Guess he was a Broncos fan. Finally, we left
the frigid north behind but filled with great optimism for the future.

Our season, of course, ended with the regular season, but the varsity was on a mission. Some of the key contributors were back from
the '66 state entrant, like Mick Metzer of Pengilly, George Delich of
Bovey, and Mike Barle of Coleraine. Hibbing had a great team with
the likes of Bob Collyard, Bill Baldrica, and Mark Barbato but we
defeated them by a single goal in both the district and regional finals.
The 1-0 win in Hibbing's Memorial Building for the Region 7 title
was one of the most dramatic games I have witnessed (from the upper
row, nonetheless).

Greenway faced Mpls. Roosevelt in the first game of the '67 tournament. Steve Hall was a stalwart for the Teddies. After a slow start,
the Raiders eventually took a 5-1 win with five different players scoring, an indication of how balanced the team was. After watching the

first round on our black and white Setchell-Carlson TV, I was on one of the fan buses the next afternoon as our Raiders were to face rival Hibbing in the semifinals for the fifth time that memorable season. As freshmen, we were on the bus with the high school kids, which was an education in itself. It was an exhilarating ride, with cheering and singing most of the way as well as fending off some verbal jabs and jousts from the upperclassmen.

We arrived late in the afternoon into downtown St. Paul, by far the largest city most of us had ever encountered. We pulled up right alongside the Auditorium and rushed inside. Wow! We were in the big time now. Unfortunately, Baldrica and Collyard put the hated blue-clad rivals ahead 2-0 as we got off to another slow start. However, midway through the second period, the Raiders passing game was in high gear and Mike Adams and Antonovich scored to tie it. Seated in the upper reaches of the stands behind one net, the Greenway fans were up and out of our seats, especially when the human fire-hydrant, Mick Metzer, scored to put us ahead in the third period. Baldrica scored to tie it but Taconite's Gary Lawson scored with 34 seconds left, beating Andy Micheletti, to give us our fourth one-goal win over the Bluejackets.

As we drove back into the night, St. Paul Johnson beat No. St. Paul 5-4 in overtime to earn a title berth. Saturday morning, we headed back to St. Paul on the bus and the students were fired up and energy wasn't a problem. We got there in time to see Hibbing beat North St. Paul to earn third place. Johnson was tough with the talented brother tandem of Ron and Doug Peltier and goalie Terry Del Monte. Though Johnson took a 1-0 lead after one period, it was apparent that our team was peaking at the right time. Ken Lawson, Jeff Kosak, and Jim MacNeil each scored to give us a 3-1 lead entering the final 12 minutes. The Governors scored with 1:18 left and it was nail-biting time. No fear. Antonovich calmly scored the final goal with 10 seconds left to make the final 4-2. Bedlam. Our northern contingent exploded with joy. Hugging and screaming, we witnessed our boys in the hogpile on the ice. What a moment!

We stayed to watch the awards ceremony, which included the naming of Antonovich, Metzer, Ken Lawson, and Bill Joy to the all-tournament team. While they were certainly worthy, it was no doubt, a true team effort that earned our school's first state hockey champion-ship. Though it was late; it was a spirited ride home, to be sure. Despite the early-morning arrival back home, it seemed like the entire popula-tion of our district was present for the caravan that welcomed the team back on Sunday afternoon. A celebration took place at the high school auditorium and I had never witnessed more happy people in my life; at least, not until dealing with the mob following Game 7 when the Twins copped their first World Series title twenty years later.

Six players from the title team returned for the '68 season, includ-ing captain Ken Lawson and the inimitable Antonovich. There were openings to make the varsity, surely, and our B-squad had some tal-ented kids to fill the vacuum. With the state title, a lot of attention was coming Greenway's way so there was a lot of speculation on who would make the grade. I was just concerned about making the B-squad roster. Tryouts for the varsity would take place on the slow ice surface in the cavernous Hibbing Memorial Building. As a sophomore now attending the high school in Coleraine, coach Gernander encouraged me to go out for the A-squad. I'm glad he did as I wasn't planning on it. Sure, it would help secure my spot on the Bombers (B Team)!

After the final day of tryouts, players were told to report to a spe-cific locker room for the cut announcement for the varsity. I stayed behind because I truly didn't think I had a shot to make the team. I was confident that I had played well enough to secure a place on the second line on the B-squad as there were some solid junior and senior forwards who had looked good in the workouts and scrim-mages. As the players filed out of the room, one of our managers, Tony Jasper, came over to tell me that I was one of three sophomores who would be playing on both the A-squad and the B-squad, at least to start the season. One was Eugene Gustason, another Taconite guy, and my buddy Jim Kosak. I was shocked! We were fortunate, really, as we got to practice with both teams every day and got into terrific shape.

Two weeks later, the Iron Range Conference jamboree was held in Hibbing and though they were not full-length games, they were still useful exhibition games. It was surreal to put on the dark green jersey with the number 4 on the back. With me being 5' 5" and 115 pounds, the purple and gold fellows playing for International Falls looked pretty imposing and the silver fox, Larry Ross, was on the bench for the Broncos. Wow! I watched from the bench, learning the ways of top-level high school hockey from close up. With four seconds left in the shortened contest, I was sent out to play right wing. My heart pumped as my nerve-infested body wobbled out for the face-off for the uneventful few ticks remaining. I managed to stay upright.

Expectations were high for our club, even though we had several positions to solidify. Taconite's Kenny Lawson was the unquestioned leader on and off the ice. Terry Casey of Bovey was the senior starter in goal with Cloverdale's Mike Rantala as the back-up. On defense, Coleraine's Mike Holland was back as a steady performer. Dave "Moose" Prestidge was a physical specimen and and a newcomer as a junior from Lawrence Lake, the rural area just north of Taconite. My cousin Bobby Lawson, a sophomore, was sure to be a budding star as an all-around defender.

At forward, Antonovich was joined by fellow Calumet resident Jim Stephens, a smooth skater and finesse player. Cloverdale's Tom Peluso was opposite Stephens on the wing, another 10th-grader with a wicked snapshot and the confidence to be a star. Peluso was quickly nicknamed exactly that, "Star", by the seniors. On the second unit was Lawrence Lake senior center, Sandy "Jughead" Markovich, who had been on the B-squad the previous year. Two other seniors, Dave Stangl of Coleraine and Mike "Sluggo" Meade of Taconite, played on the wings.

In the days of 12-minute periods, players on the third line didn't see much ice time. There were six of us who found part-time duty on the third unit. Coleraine's Gary Moorhead was a speedy junior wing and my cousin, Billy "Bucko" Troumbly was a slight but crafty junior wing. Eugene Gustason and Jim Kosak got less time than the others but both were multi-sport athletes with talent. Yet another Taconite guy, junior wing "Cotton" Guyer was a gutsy, hustling forward. Yours truly also played both forward spots on both the "A" and "B" teams.

The forwards worked diligently with Paul Rygh, who had won a state title as an all-tournament wing at Roseau and later won an NCAA title with North Dakota. This was just his second year as an assistant and he was up to the task. He was a sound tactician and was particularly adept at both instruction and counsel. "Rygher" was rather quiet but was always a gentleman and he was super working with the younger, less-experienced players.

The head coach, Bob Gernander, wore a crew-cut and was nicknamed, "Marsh", as he took after Duluth sportscaster Marsh Nelson. We trusted him, as he had already won a state title in his first year as a coach and he could mix it up with the guys, too. We didn't realize it then, but these two coaches weren't much older than we were, but they were competent and prepared. They had to prove themselves on the ice, too, as they both played for the Taconite Hornets, so their players had ample opportunity to see them in action. Rygh was a strong skater with great touch while Gernander was a stay-at-home defenseman who could block a shot and always seemed to make the intelligent play. A review of the coaches' performance was always forthcoming the next day at practice, with teasing certain to follow in addition to the playing critique.

The Raiders had strong support at our rink, which was called the West Range Arena at that time. We shoehorned 2,300 fans into the building. For the biggest games, one had better pick a spot in the bleachers by the end of the first period of the "B" game or your sight lines might be limited. All the onlookers had to dress warmly, as the big doors behind each of the goals were opened to the frigid outside air. It was chilly for everyone, including the goal judges, who stood literally on the back of the net. We cruised through the regular season with a great record (19-1) and I got a ton of ice-time practicing three hours a day and normally getting to play two B-squad periods and two periods of varsity. However, my varsity experience was scanty and I was not on either the power-play or penalty-kill squads.

However, the team had to trim its roster from 18 to 15 for the playoffs so Gustason, Kosak, and I became alternates. We were to still practice with the team but wouldn't be in uniform on game days. It was okay with us, as we felt privileged to still be a part of the team and looked forward to our junior season, when we would play a bigger role. Reporting to practice the next day, there was a surprise. Gary Moorhead had decided to quit the team and play in our outstanding Pep Band instead. Huh! I couldn't believe it. The kid was a great trumpet player, but to give up a chance of a lifetime? I was selected to replace him and was placed at center between "Cotton" and "Bucko" for the duration of the post-season. We had been a combination for quite a few games and while offensively-challenged, we skated our butts off and rarely were scored upon. We relished playing together and had a lot of laughs, to boot. We were given a nickname but I will refrain from revealing it, though you can surmise it wasn't a compliment.

In District 28 action, we downed neighboring Grand Rapids 6-1 but then fell to Hibbing 2-0 with Andy Micheletti recording the shutout for the Bluejackets. In those days, the four district finalists were allowed in regional play so there was hope. In Region VII play, we beat Cloquet 6-3 before dispatching Hibbing 4-1 in the semis to avenge the earlier loss. In the finals at the year-old Duluth Arena, we faced International Falls. They were still the gold standard for excellence in high school hockey and Larry Ross was still the man. Though the rough ice made for a slower tempo game, it was evenly-fought and regulation ended in a scoreless tie with Terry Casey and Dave Doris dueling. We were downcast as Rick Toninato scored in the second overtime to send the Broncos to state. We weren't crestfallen, however. Region III, anyone?

In those days, the Region VII and VIII runner-up faced off against each other to determine the state qualifier representing Region III. It was called the "Back-Door" and we took advantage of it, downing Thief River Falls 4-1. That's right; we had lost twice in the post-season and still earned a berth in the state tourney. We knew that we could be a formidable foe but we were slated to play top-ranked Mounds View in the opening game of the tournament.

On the Tuesday prior to the tournament, there was a feverish pep-fest and send-off in the high school auditorium, where the students were delirious with excitement in the hope that the team could win back-to-back state crowns. As we sojourned to St. Paul, we were just as excited to be going to the Cities as we were to play in the tournament. There were hijinks on the bus, as usual, and if there was tension, we didn't know it. We arrived in downtown St. Paul and pulled our gear off the bus and sauntered into the Lowry hotel, adjacent to the St. Paul Hotel and just a block from the Auditorium.

All the teams were housed in the Lowry and each was designated for a different floor, based on their region number. As we carried our duffel bags and jerseys into the hotel, there was a lot to take in; especially the shoeshine boys, the barbershop, and the elevator. I had never been on one and it was quite a contraption. The short, elderly African-American gentleman who operated the crank to control the carriage had to estimate the speed of the elevator to determine when to slow it down so the bottom of the carriage would be level with the floor. It was so fascinating for us that we rode it as much as possible, sometimes having to take a huge step up or take a big jump down.

My roommate was Mike Rantala, who became my best friend on the team. After we got settled in, we had a meeting in a really posh room to inform us of the agenda and the coaches told us about their expectations for our behavior and that we were here to win, above all else. We would be given some freedom, but we should make sure we didn't walk too much on the sidewalks in order not to get shin splints.

On the day before the tournament, we practiced on the St. Paul Auditorium ice and we were a bit surprised at the fine quality of the ice, more fitting for an up-tempo style of play. Prior to our workout, we were able to walk around and see the sights downtown. A bunch of us hung out together and we managed to sneak in a viewing of *Bonnie and Clyde* at a nearby theatre.

In between, we attended a banquet for all the teams at the St. Paul Hotel. Everybody was in a sport coat and it was a great event, with all the players and coaches being introduced. Our squad was seated right next to the head table and my cousin Bucko and I overhead some guy on the dais complain that 90 percent of the high school kids play with their head down. I turned to Bucko and said, "This guy doesn't know what he is talking about." A few seconds later, the same fellow got up to speak after being identified as the main speaker. His name was Glen Sonmor, head coach of the Minnesota Gophers. Gulp!

Some of the players took the opportunity to take in the North Stars game versus the Montreal Canadians at the Met Center out in

Bloomington while others stayed around the hotel. On Thursday morning, we had a meeting to discuss our first-round opponent, Mounds View, and we were all ears as a Twin Cities hockey guru told us about their tendencies. We knew they were good because they beat us in the state bantam tourney three years earlier. The Mustangs had skill and size, with twins Brad and Bart Buetow playing at 6'5" and well over 200 pounds, real giants for hockey at that time. They were top-ranked and a very fearsome foe.

With locker rooms being inadequate at the Auditorium, we actually dressed in our hotel rooms and walked with the fans to our quarterfinal game with Mounds View no more than an hour before the game was to begin. It was strange but neat to converse with the fans about our team.

When we got to the rink, we put our skates on not far from our bench, behind a large curtain and got a short pep talk and final instructions from Gernander. It was surreal to be out on the ice that you had witnessed only on TV and there were 8,334 people watching. Prognosticators figured the opening game could be one of the best games of the tournament and they were right. Both teams scored twice in the first stanza, with Tim Tyson and Bart Buetow scoring for Mounds View and Dave Stangl and Jim Stephens for us. No question, Mounds View was as good as any team we had played that year. As for our third line, we got out for a couple short shifts and didn't get scored on. There was no scoring in the second period but Mounds View had the better of the play but Terry Casey was solid in goal with 11 saves.

Midway through the third, Mike "Stinky" Antonovich, raced out of the penalty box, took a pass from Stephens and beat Mike Schuett to give Greenway a 3-2 lead. However, Bart Buetow scored with 15 seconds left in regulation with Schuett off for a sixth attacker. In overtime, Stangl scored the game-winner at 4:31 in a goal-mouth scramble. It was bedlam in the stands for our fans as we poured onto the ice to congratulate Stangl for putting us in the semifinals.

On our way out of the Auditorium within 15 minutes of the end of the game, I was stunned to see a guy selling newspapers with photographs and an article on our game. We were elated, of course, and now we had time to kill before playing on Friday night. We would face St. Paul Johnson and fiery head coach Lou Cotroneo, who we saw down International Falls 7-4 on our hotel room television sets. In the evening session, Minneapolis Southwest beat Roseau 4-2 and South St. Paul upended Edina 6-2.

We ate all of our meals in the hotel together as a team and seeing as all the teams were staying at the same hotel, we got to see players from all the teams. The north versus south mentality was still strong at the time and we got to know guys from Roseau and International Falls and we rooted for each other. Now we were the only northern team left and we were sure they were pulling for us.

Johnson, which had a strong following from the "East Side," had another powerful team, led by Doug Peltier, Scott Frantzen, and Phil Anderson. We got off to a strong start, with Tom Peluso and "Jughead" Markovich giving us a 2-0 lead. Kenny Lawson and Jim Stephens both scored and we had a seemingly-safe 4-1 lead with nine minutes left. However, Casey was making some great stops for us as the Governors pressed the play. Bob Giannini tallied and then John Horton scored his second goal in a 44-second span to make it 4-3 with six minutes left. We held on for dear life as Casey finished with 34 saves in a great performance and Gary Swanson had 26 for Johnson.

South St. Paul tipped Minneapolis Southwest 2-0 in the other semifinal and the stage was set. There was a lot of sentiment for the Packers, for two reasons. Head coach Lefty Smith had announced that he was taking the Notre Dame job for the next season and the Packers hadn't won in any of their other 14 trips to the tourney to that point. The Packers were led by goalie Mark Kronholm, Joe Bonk, Dale Abram, and Ken Madden.

Our club was a pretty loose outfit and there was no recognizable extra tension on Saturday, February 24, 1968 with Greenway trying to become the third team from the Iron Range Conference to win consecutive state crowns (joining Eveleth and International Falls). We were expecting another close contest in the title game and it was tied 1-1 after two periods with Stangl scoring for us in the first period and George Tourville for the Packers in the second. However, we had the edge in play entering the final 12 minutes. Suddenly, it was an avalanche of goals as our top line went beserk. Peluso scored 37 seconds into the period to give us the lead. Less than a minute later, Stephens tallied, and then Antonovich pumped in two in a minute and it was 5-1 as we scored four goals in 3:38. It was clear, we were going to win the state title and in style, too.

As the third line, we figured we would get a big chunk of playing time in the final eight minutes or so. "Bucko" almost made it 6-1 when he hit the post with a 25-foot wrist shot that bounded off into the corner. When we got to the bench, I was so excited he almost scored, I must have told him 20 times that he hit the post and that if he would have scored, "Cotton" and I would have also had assists. Soon thereafter, Peluso scored his second goal to make it a five-goal lead with 4:28 left. As he raised his stick to celebrate, it struck Stephens in his left eye and he appeared seriously hurt as he lay crumpled on the ice. Our whole bench stood, worried about his status.

Amidst this somber moment came one of the most hilarious moments of my life. Our bench was located near the blue line on the end of the rink where Stephens was injured and the line of Troumbly-Hoey-Guyer was seated at the far left end of that bench. After a loud thud, we turned our heads quickly to our left to find our beloved trainer, Mike Orlovich, (also known affectionately as Uncle Dudley) collapsed under the weight of a whole section of seats, the type with the scissors that fold up. In his hurried response to get out to help poor Stephens, Mike had tried to hurtle out the gate but fell with only his upper torso not ensconced in the wooden chairs.

Realizing the seriousness of the health concerns of our teammate on the ice, we looked at each other blankly. We started to smirk and giggle, covering our faces. We looked back to find Mike struggling to get out of the grip of the seats. We tried to stop from laughing but it was just too darn funny. We didn't want to show disrespect to our teammate or to Mike but then most people couldn't see what we were seeing. Even the fans nearby were laughing hysterically by now. The coaches looked over to see why we were laughing and we tried to explain but it was to no avail. We didn't play again that night and understood why.

After 30 seconds or so, we tried to get Mike out of his predicament but it just seemed to get worse. Mike was a humble but proud man and the look of determination on his face will never be forgotten. The set of seats that he was caught up in was heavy, and we were all struggling because Mike was squirming around like a fish. Some of his bag had spilled out onto the ice and he managed to pull himself further toward the gate and actually had part of his head out the open area to the rink. Some of the fans caught eyes with us and we were all doubled over, unable to control ourselves. We knew Mike wasn't hurt but he was cursing like a sailor and it all made for one unbelievable situation.

Finally, after what seemed an inordinate amount of time, some arena personnel arrived and started barking orders to everyone. Soon, Mike was freed just at about the time Stephens was being carried off the ice. Orlovich, truly one of the nicest gentleman I have ever known, acted as if nothing ever happened, which made it even funnier. Stephens, by the way, wasn't able to finish the game; he was treated and recovered in a short time.

When the game finished, we had a convincing 6-1 win and the 1968 state hockey crown. Not bad for a team that had been beaten twice in the post-season and shut out in both games, to boot.

We raced onto the ice, almost knocked over Lou Nanne, and managed to not injure ourselves in the madhouse that is a hockey hogpile. Soon, we clapped as Stangl, Kenny Lawson, Casey, and Antonovich were all named to the all-tournament team. Then, they presented our captains with that marvelous piece of hardware, the first-place trophy.

After the hugs and back-slapping ended, we headed back to the hotel to clean up and go into the night. Our group (Gustason, Kosak, Troumbly, Rantala, manager Tony Jasper, and I) celebrated by stuffing our faces at White Castle. Do you know much $13 would buy for one guy in 1968? We paraded around downtown for awhile and then headed back to the hotel, where we commiserated with players from other schools amidst all kinds of tomfoolery.

On the ride home back to the Iron Range, a tired but happy group of teenagers reviewed the events of the past several days with great fondness as the first-place trophy awaited all the well-wishers in the caravan that ensued through our hometowns. We headed to the Schofield Memorial Gymnasium in Coleraine for a welcome back celebration. It was the second such event in 12 months and there was hope we could add to it in future seasons. A few weeks later, we were invited to attend the NCAA hockey tournament at the Duluth Arena. We got to see Tim Sheehy play for Boston College and Ken Dryden play goal for Cornell. Denver, with rugged Keith Magnuson and goalie Gerry Powers, beat North Dakota 4-0 in the finals.

As a junior in 1968-69, I had grown to 5'7" and about 140 pounds and was hoping to play a much bigger role on the team. We would have an inexperienced defense as John Pearson and Mark DeMarais of Coleraine and Dan Travica of Bovey would prove their promise in joining holdovers Bobby Lawson and Moose Prestidge. Plus, we had Antonovich and Peluso back, two of the top scorers in the state. Carter Pierce, a transfer from International Falls, would be battling Mike Rantala for the starting nod in goal.

When the season started, I played right wing on the top line with Antonovich and Peluso and got plenty of scoring opportunities. It was a treat to play with players of that caliber and our season was going well, as we went 13-2 in our first 15 games. The coaches made a move to shift me to center on the second unit with junior Bobby Lynch of Calumet and Pearson, who moved up to play forward. Cotton Guyer moved up to play on the first unit. Another line had my cousin Bucko, sophomore Jim Peluso, and either Jim Kosak or Eugene Gustason. The changes made us a better team and I was still one of the main penalty-killers, which was my favorite part of the game. While Antonovich was a revelation on the ice for us and our undisputed star, this team had a great chemistry and was a more balanced squad than the previous year.

We had a shot to win the always-tough Iron Range Conference and did so, finishing the regular-season 17-3. In District 28 play, we hammered Chisholm 8-3 but then Hibbing beat us 4-1 for the second straight season in the finals. Yet again, we were given another shot in Region VII play and Cloquet went down to the tune of 11-1. In probably our best game of the year, we avenged the earlier loss less than a week later with a convincing 5-1 win over Hibbing in a game played in Virginia. We eked out a 3-2 win over Eveleth in Hibbing to earn the

The Greenway Raiders team photo, 1969-1970

regional title as GHS had earned a fourth straight berth in the state tournament.

The 1969 tournament would be played in March for the first time and at a new venue, the Metropolitan Sports Center in Bloomington. After another festive send-off at school, we headed off to the Cities with "Hey Jude" and other Beatles hits blaring over the radio.

Besides playing on the same ice as the NHL North Stars, the high schoolers would be playing in front of crowds twice the size of the ones at the St. Paul Auditorium. The soothsayers were saying that this tournament was wide open, with strong teams from Edina and Minneapolis Southwest, along with northern powers such as Greenway, Roseau, and Warroad. A rematch of the '68 final would take place in the second game of the evening session in the first round when we skated against South St. Paul, which had Kronholm back in goal and Terry Madland, Gene Mortel, and Ken Madden as their top play-makers.

Our friends from Roseau (4-1 over Harding) and Warroad (4-3 over Minneapolis Southwest) had earned their way to the semifinals in the afternoon and Edina handled Mounds View 5-0 in the first night game. With about 15,000 people in the stands, it was a bit intimidating for the players but the ice conditions and the warmth of the building were more of a concern. There was water standing on one end of the rink and the ice was very slow, making it difficult to make a crisp pass and it was difficult to breathe in the hot air, even in the warm-up.

South St. Paul scored early in the game and Kronholm had 14 stops as the Packers took a 1-0 lead. In the middle stanza, Greenway scored three goals in a 1:53 span with Antonovich, Hoey, and Tom Peluso all tallying to grab a 3-1 lead. However, the Packers made a strong third-period push and goals by Mortel and Mike Neska tied it 3-3. South St. Paul took a late penalty and with Greenway on the power-play, Ken Madden scored shorthanded with a goal that took a bad bounce and got by Rantala with 19 seconds left. As the horn sounded, we bowed our heads and trudged upstairs to the locker room amid a lot of tears.

We had just blown a two-goal lead in the third period and got blind-sided. Give the Packers credit, they earned it. Now, we were relegated to consolation play. We also had the unenviable task of determining who we would root for in the first semifinal on Friday—Roseau or Warroad.

We were on speaking terms with guys from both teams and even rode the bus out to practice at the Met Center with Warroad, who had just two seniors. But one of them was Henry Boucha, who had been playing with the Warriors since eighth grade and was already an idol in our parts.

We had beaten Warroad 3-2 at our rink midway through the season and we knew that Roseau had talent in guys like John and Robbie Harris and Dale Smedsmo and Earl Anderson.

No doubt, once you leave championship-round play, there is not the same enthusiasm in one's game and there are whole lot less people watching you play. We returned to the ice about 12 hours later and beat Mounds View 4-1 or maybe I should say Antonovich beat them because he scored all four goals, two in both the first and third periods.

Our entire team then watched the Warroad-Roseau semifinal with angst as we didn't want either team to lose. Alan Hangsleben, an outstanding sophomore defender who also wowed the crowds with his great skills, scored to put Warroad ahead with an assist to Boucha. Those two studs on defense rarely left the ice. With Warroad leading 2-1 in the third, Boucha scored to give them a two-goal cushion and they held on for a 3-2 win. Edina drilled South St. Paul 7-1 so the

David versus Goliath title match was set for Saturday night.

In the fifth-place game, we faced Minneapolis Southwest, with Brad Shelstad in goal and his talented brother Dixon at center. Both Antonovich and Peluso scored for us as regulation ended in a 2-2 tie. Guess who scored the overtime winner for Greenway? Yup, Antonovich, with assists to Peluso and Guyer just 33 seconds into the extra session. At least we picked up the consolation trophy and both Antonovich and Peluso were all-tournament.

Perhaps Antonovich's best moves came that night as he was leading the cheers for Warroad in his Greenway High letter-jacket. With most of the crowd already rooting for the tiny school from the northern border, Boucha was checked into the glass behind the net and was carried off the ice with a ruptured eardrum. Edina led 3-2 at the time and later increased it to 4-2 but Warroad rallied with two goals from Frank Krahn to tie it. The excitement in that building was electric as Antonovich whooped up the crowd. In overtime, Skip Thomas scored to beat Jeff Hallet to give Willard Ikola's boys their first of many state titles.

The 1969-70 season brought some new uniforms for the Raiders, artificial ice, and the promise of an explosive offense. Wendell Grand, another Roseau graduate, joined us as an assistant coach. Now up to about 5'8" and 155 pounds, I was no longer a shrimp. Tom Peluso was our captain and Bobby Lawson and I were the alternate captains. Bobby Lynch centered Peluso and me while Jimmy Peluso was between Jim Kosak and Eugene Gustason. Newcomers at forward included Calumet senior Rick Helmer, Marble junior Brian Aimonetti, Pengilly's Joe Miskovich, Cloverdale's Doug Michaels, and my cousin Tim Lawson, a talented eighth-grader.

Bobby Lawson spearheaded the defense corps, along with Pearson, Travica, and DeMarais and Lawrence Lake's Dan Strand. Rantala was secure as the starting netminder with cousin Mike Troumbly as the back-up.

We started off with a bang, going 13-0 and ranked number one in the state. We had a big and physical team and were aided by the new rule that allowed body checking all over the ice for the first time.

We didn't lose until Hibbing beat us 4-1 at their place but we came
back quickly to dispose of St. Paul Johnson easily by the tune of 8-2
at our rink and Lou Cotroneo came in to tell us how good we were. A
great Eveleth team team later tied us 3-3 and then rival Grand Rapids
surprised us 8-6 late in the season. However, we showed resolve by
handling a fine Warroad team 8-4 the next night. We finished 17-2-1
playing a rigorous schedule and we could score goals.

In district play, we pounded Duluth Central 7-0 in Virginia before
dispatching International Falls 4-3 in Eveleth. Back at Virginia's great
ice surface, we drilled Duluth Denfeld 9-2 to take the district title. In
Region VII play, we hated playing in the slush at the Duluth Arena
and we battled a deep Duluth East club, but we were lucky to win 4-3
in overtime on Bobby Lynch's goal and the strength of Rantala's strong
play in goal. In the finals, we took on Mike Polich and star defensemen Dennis Fearing and John Perpich. Hibbing won 5-4 to take the
region crown.

We had to go to Thief River Falls to play Bemidji for the Region
III berth and won 6-1, playing one of our best games of the year. We
were rated second in the state and we were a threat to score six or seven
goals every night but we were fortunate to be in the tourney again.
Thank God for the "Back Door"!

When you are coming to the tournament for the third straight
season, you count your blessings knowing how fortunate you are to be
there. Despite the fact the attention and recognition is nice, you know
how to deal with all the hoopla and all the distractions. The 1970 state
tourney would go down as one of the most competitive and memorable in state puck annals. Edina and Minneapolis Southwest were
both undefeated and had coaches in Ikola and Dave Peterson who
were titans in the game. Hibbing was big and talented and Warroad
had a slew of good forwards.

The teams were housed at the Curtis Hotel in Minneapolis and we
even took cabs out to the Met Center for practice the day after arriving
in town. We had stopped at Williams Arena to practice and got a visit
from Antonovich, who was now playing for Sonmor at the "U". We
and many others felt we were one of the favorites to win it all, though
we had shown a recent propensity for defensive breakdowns.

Undefeated Southwest was nearly upset in the opening game but rallied from a 3-0 third-period deficit to nip North St. Paul 4-3 on Paul Miller's overtime goal. Hibbing advanced with a 4-0 win over White Bear Lake. Playing in the first game of what would turn out to be one of the most exciting nights in tourney lore, we faced St. Paul Johnson. The Governors had lost eight games during the season and even though we easily handled them by six goals in our mid-season game up in Coleraine, this was the state tournament and there is no such thing as not taking your opponent seriously. Cotroneo was a competitive guy and they had two fine defenseman in Les Auge and Bob Peltier.

Neal Barrette scored early to give his Johnson club the lead but they had lost one of their star players when Mark Kroll broke his collarbone on the first shift. The ice was much better than the previous season but we got off to a sluggish start until Bobby Lawson tied it near the end of the first period. In the final two periods, we picked up our game and started to pepper shots at Johnson goalie Doug Long, who was pulled in our first meeting. Long had 12 saves in the middle stanza but only Johnson's Tom Holm scored to give his team a 2-1 lead after two periods.

Early in the final period, Bobby Lynch tipped in a Tom Peluso shot to tie it and then Joe Miskovich pounced on a turnover and scored unassisted to give us a 3-2 lead two minutes later.

Jim Metzger countered for Johnson at 4:21 for a 3-3 tie but the Raiders began to carry the play. Peluso had several great chances only to be stoned by Long, who had 36 saves as regulation ended. Before the first five-minute overtime, we felt we were the better team but just needed a way to get one past not just Long but their shot-blocking defenders.

Unfortunately, we got into penalty trouble in overtime. Eugene Gustason took a penalty and then Lawson got another and we faced a 3 on 5 penalty-kill. I played up top with two men down and knew that one mistake could mean disaster. Rantala only faced a couple of shots and we were able to kill off both penalties as Johnson outshot us 4-3 during that first overtime.

In the second overtime, we outshot the Governors 8-3. On one shift, I had a lot of net to shoot at from 15 feet but hit the left post. Peluso kept bearing down on Long but to no avail. In the third overtime we outshot them 6-1, and in the fourth it was 6-2; it seemed like it was just a matter of time before we would score and Rantala was playing well in goal for us. As first-line players, we got plenty of ice time but we were getting tired. Could we just find a way to win and fast, because we had two more games to win a state title?

In the locker room between one of the overtimes, Antonovich came in to bolster our spirits. It was too bad his eligibility was up! By the end of the fourth overtime, I knew we would be playing in the second-longest game in state tourney history when the fifth extra-session began.

We had played 15-minute periods in the regular season, so we were only 11 minutes past that total. In the fifth overtime, our line was on the ice when disaster struck. There was a goal-mouth scramble and Fran McClellan wacked at his own rebound in front of Rantala and the puck managed to wobble across the goal line. Johnson had upset us 4-3 at 3:24 of the fifth overtime.

It was over. Dejected and exhausted, we shook hands with the Governors and Long, who had set a new record with 61 saves, including 25 in overtime.

We climbed slowly up to our locker room, which was absolutely quiet and somber. It was interrupted only by sobs. It seemed like forever before we took our skates off. True sadness.

Guys tried to console one another but it was impossible and the coaches acknowledged the efforts of each of the player's one by one. We had played well and valiantly but we had lost.

How could we lose to a team we had beaten by six goals? It was agonizing to know I would never wear the "green" for Greenway High again. I thought we might be good enough to have won three or four tourneys in a row but it wasn't to be. It hurt, real bad.

As Edina and Warroad began a game that would go into two overtimes, we trudged slowly out to the bus for the ride back to Minneapolis. I felt badly for my three-year roommate and best buddy, Rantala, because the goalies always seem to feel the worst but it wasn't his fault.

Our offense had missed the net on good or great chances on many occasions, let alone the other 64 times we got a puck on net for Long to save. We had six breakaways and didn't score on any of them. Unbelievable!

Looking back 40 years later, the only thing I remember after returning to the hotel was meeting my parents in the lobby and taking a walk with them, a really nice moment. I don't remember watching Bobby Krieger eventually scoring in the second overtime for Edina as they beat Warroad for the second year in a row. We got up early to play on Friday morning before a sparse gathering back at Met Center, playing against fellows we knew like Leo Marshall, Frank Krahn, and Dave Kvarnlov. In a game devoid of much emotion, Warroad beat us 4-2.

Within 12 hours, we had now lost to two games to teams we had beaten 8-2 and 8-4. One of the favorites and now we were out of the tourney and wouldn't be in a trophy game! One loss was a kick in the head and the other to the heart. Warroad coach Dick Roberts said after the game, "Greenway is the best team to ever lose two games in the state tournament." It made me feel worse and we felt we let our fans down.

The 1970 tournament would see six of the 11 games go into overtime and there would be a total of 15 overtime periods. Southwest beat Hibbing 3-1 in the first semifinal and Long was to continue with tremendous goaltending by making 52 saves in a 2-1 three-overtime loss to Edina in the other semifinal. While it was fun to see Bobby Krieger's jersey flying through the air, I'm not sure what it would been like trying to stop him. In the finals, another standout goalie stole the show. Southwest's Brad Shelstad, who would become a friend, made 22 stops as Dave Peterson's boys won a 1-0 thriller when Billy Shaw scored in overtime to win it for the Indians, who finished with a single tie (24-0-1) in their undefeated season.

It took several weeks to get over the state tournament disappointment of that senior season and the sting of the last two tourneys made it tough to watch the event the next few seasons. When tournament time comes around every year, it still reverberates a little. After playing for four years at St. Mary's in Winona, I started a 15-year coaching career at Shakopee and Farmington. I got the opportunity to coach some great kids and match strategy with a lot of outstanding gentle-men who served as opposing coaches. I have met some truly inspir-ing people through hockey and feel so privileged to have played and coached in the game for so long.

Though the game and the tournament have changed in so many ways, the main elements haven't. The drive and passion of the play-ers and fans is still the same, the pursuit of excellence and the simple love of playing the game and trying to win a championship for your school and community is intact. I was lucky to have participated in three state hockey tournaments and now I feel just as lucky to have had the chance to write this book.

Finally, I am indebted to all the former players, coaches, and oth-ers who have helped me with input for this book and who have con-tributed in making the tournament, indeed, something truly great. No doubt, there is a unique bond among the individuals who have made it so special. A heart-felt thanks to all the people over the last 67 years who have contributed in making the Minnesota State Boys' High School Hockey Tournament a real cultural institution and one of the top events in American high school sports. I am humbled and honored to have worked on such a project and hope that you find it both interesting and informative.

Top: The Roseau squad, 1946 state champions. (photo: MSHSL)

Bottom: St. Paul Johnson, 1947 state champions. (photo: MSHSL)

1 The 1940s

1) In what year was the first Minnesota state boys' high school hockey tournament conducted and what city and building hosted the inaugural event?

2) What were the roster sizes for the eight teams in the tournament for the first 11 years?

3) What St. Paul Schools city athletic director is given primary credit for establishing the state boys' hockey tourney?

4) What school earned the first state hockey crown, outscoring its three opponents 30-3?

5) What was the length of a period during state tourney competition in the 1940's?

6) Who scored the first goal in state boys' hockey tournament history on Feb. 15, 1945?

7) What high school team participated in the first tourney and hasn't been back since?

8) How many schools were competing at the varsity level in Minnesota during the first year of the state hockey tournament in 1945?

9) What player recorded the first hat trick in state tournament competition?

10) The most lopsided win in the entire history of the tournament took place in the first year. Who were the opponents and what was the score?

11) What St. Louis Park netminder, who later went on to star in goal for the Gophers, made 20 saves in the second period of a 1948 quarterfinal loss (10-8) to Warroad?

12) Which tiny northern Minnesota school played three times in the first years of the tourney with consecutive runner-up finishes in 1949 and 1950?

13) Who became the first team or school to win two straight titles?

14) What three schools played in each of the first four state tournaments from 1945 to 1948?

15) In the earliest years of the state tournament, the all-tournament teams were made up of just eight players. What two teams had seven of those picks among the first honorees?

16) Which player played every minute of his team's three games during the first tourney?

17) What school won the first-ever game in the Minnesota state boys' hockey tournament?

18) What legendary head coach led Eveleth to five state crowns in the first seven tourneys?

19) What team upset defending champion Eveleth in the semifinals in 1946?

20) What school had four players score hat tricks in a single game in the first-ever tournament?

21) In what year were all the quarterfinal games won by virtue of a shutout?

22) Which school became the first from the Twin Cities metropolitan area to win a state title?

23) What freshman forward scored a goal in each of his team's games in 1948?

24) Who became the first player to score four goals in a single game in tourney annals?

25) What team played in the 1947 tournament and has never returned?

26) Because few southern Minnesota schools had hockey teams at the time, the Minnesota State High School League determined in 1949 that the Region 3 participant would be the runner-up of two regions, alternating annually. Which regions alternated on this basis from 1949 to 1964?

27) In 1946, Roseau came to the tourney led by a high-scoring center. What was his name and what nickname was he given because of his unique eye-wear?

28) What school became the first team south of the Twin Cities metro area to play in a state championship game?

29) What Roseau player tied for the scoring lead in 1946 before embarking on a career with the Minnesota Gophers, a team his two sons would later compete for in the 1970's?

30) What Eveleth great scored nine goals and added five assists and was the leading scorer in the 1948 tournament with 14 points?

31) What future coaching legend was a major cog on the first team from Minneapolis Central to earn a trip to state in 1949?

32) What did Granite Falls goalie Gorman Velde wear for protective head-gear in the first tournament in 1945?

33) What was the total attendance for the inaugural tournament?

34) What referee had to actually inform the Granite Falls and Staples teams in the first tournament about various rules interpretations, including how to line up for face-offs and what the blue lines on the ice symbolized?

35) What was the cost of the first tournament program?

36) What St. Paul Johnson center played in the tourney in 1946 for the Governors (4th-place) and later coached White Bear Lake to three tourneys (1966, 1967, and 1970)?

37) What South St. Paul goalie was sterling for the Packers in 1948 with 105 saves?

Eveleth Golden Bears, 1945 state champs. (photo courtesy MSHSL)

38) In 1949, what two brothers played starring roles for St. Paul Murray?

39) In St. Paul Harding's first trip to state in 1948, what goalie (wearing uniform number 61) was the starter for his team, which finished as the consolation champion?

40) What Warroad brothers were standouts for the Warriors in the late 1940's, one earning all-tournament in 1948 and the other in 1949?

41) What number did Eveleth revelation John Mayasich wear in his freshman year playing for the Golden Bears in the 1948 state tournament?

42) Who is the first player to score a goal by converting on a penalty shot in tourney history?

43) In 1949, the format for selecting the Region 1 representative at state was changed. With southern Minnesota exhibiting minimal interest in hockey, it was decided to determine this region's champion by having the runner-up of both the St. Paul and Minneapolis Conferences vie in a playoff. Who was the first representative under this arrangement?

44) Which of the original teams to earn a state tourney berth in 1945 had to borrow uniforms from another metropolitan school for the first tournament?

45) What St. Paul Johnson player was all-tourney as a forward (1946) and defenseman (1947)?

46) What St. Paul Johnson player on the 1947 championship squad played both wing and goalie for the Governors that season?

47) Why did many players in the 1940s wear uniforms with numbers over 50?

48) When Eveleth won state titles in both 1948 and 1949, who was the starting netminder?

49) What two Eveleth stalwarts both scored hat tricks in an 8-2 thrashing of Warroad in the 1948 championship tilt?

50) In 1948, what Minneapolis Washburn player scored two goals in a 17-second span in a 6-1 consolation victory over Rochester?

51) Which entrant in the inaugural tournament in 1945 had just nine players on its roster?

52) In 1946, what was highly unusual about the way Region IV representative, Minneapolis West, made their way into the tournament?

53) What Williams skater scored in triple overtime in a 1949 semifinal as his team beat St. Paul Murray to gain the finals?

54) What South St. Paul skater was all-tourney in 1947 on the basis of his two goals and two assists as the Packers finished fourth?

55) What St. Paul Harding forward led his team with five goals and two assists in the 1948 tournament, including the overtime marker that gave the Knights the consolation title?

56) What Eveleth goalie recorded two shutouts in 1945 and another in 1946?

57) Which Rochester player competed in the first three tourneys and scored a point in each?

58) What two Thief River Falls skaters each scored five goals to lead the northwestern Minnesota school and Region 8 representative to the title game in 1945?

St. Paul Auditorium, 1945. (Photo: MSHSL)

59) What Minneapolis West player with an illustrious name in Minneapolis hockey circles scored two goals and added three assists in the 1947 tourney?

60) What Eveleth senior captain scored the tying and winning goals in the first-ever title game in 1945?

61) Which Rochester High competitor played in each of the first four tournaments?

62) Which St. Cloud player scored at least twice in the 1946, 1947, and 1948 tourneys?

63) What South St. Paul defender had two assists in the 1947 tournament, helping the Packers to a consolation title before returning to state eight times as coach for the same school?

64) What three linemates from the inaugural tournament, all honored on the first all-tourney team, became All-Americans in college hockey following their prep careers?

65) In the 1945 tourney, what two Thief River Falls players nearly led the Prowlers to a state title, losing 4-3 to Eveleth as each player had two points?

66) What St. Paul Harding skater tallied three goals and three assists in a 10-0 romp over St. Louis Park in a consolation game in 1948?

67) What Eveleth player scored a goal and three assists for the 1945 champs and then was all-tournament as a senior in 1946 when the Bears finished third?

68) Which St. Paul Washington player scored four goals as his team beat St. Cloud 7-1 in the first-ever third-place game in 1945?

69) Which Warroad competitor had seven points for second-place Warroad in 1948 and seven more for the third-place Warriors in 1949?

70) Who was the starting goaltender for White Bear Lake in the first two tournaments?

71) What Warroad player scored four goals in a 10-0 drubbing of St. Cloud in the final game of the quarterfinals in 1948?

72) On how many occasions did a player score consecutive goals in the first tournament?

◄ ANSWERS TO CHAPTER 1 - THE 1940's ►

1) 1945 at the St. Paul Auditorium in downtown St. Paul.

2) 12; from 1945 to 1956 rosters were set at that number. In 1957 the number was increased to 15.

3) Gene Aldrich, who was the Athletic Director for both the junior and senior high schools in St. Paul from 1936-59. In February of 1944, Aldrich began to work with the MSHSL and to get backing behind the scenes, primarily from Elmer Engelbert. However, the League didn't actually operate, control, or finance the tourney until 1946. Thus, the original tourney was state-sanctioned but not operated by the League.

4) Eveleth. The Golden Bears blasted Granite Falls 16-0 in the quarterfinals, St. Paul Washington 10-0 in the semifinals, and edged Thief River Falls 4-3 in the finals.

5) 12 minutes.

6) George Kieffer of White Bear Lake scored the historic goal in the first game on Feb. 15, 1945. In that first quarterfinal against Thief River Falls, Kieffer scored unassisted at 9:29 of the first period on Ralph Engelstad to give the Bears the lead before eventually losing 3-2. White Bear Lake had just four shots on goal the entire contest. Kieffer also scored a goal as the Bears won the consolation crown by virtue of a 4-0 victory over Granite Falls.

7) Staples, which lost both of its games. Granite Falls, another first-year participant, did return to the fold in 1946 but never made another tourney. Interestingly, neither team had matching uniforms in that first tourney. Staples' hockey program ended after 1947.

8) There were just 26 teams officially registered to play varsity ice hockey in 1944-45.

9) Julius Struntz. In the second game ever in 1945, the St. Paul Washington player scored all three goals in the first period of their 5-0 shutout of Rochester. Struntz finished with five goals and an assist as Washington finished third.

10) Eveleth beat Granite Falls 16-0. Four Bears players recorded hat tricks as the Granite Falls goalie, Gorman Velde, had just 15 saves in the onslaught.

11) Jim Mattson, whose total of 49 saves were a tournament record that stood for 22 years.

12) Williams, which was a town of just 375 people. The high school had an enrollment of just 90 students in grades 10-12 (grades counted for enrollment). Some students lived in nearby Roosevelt but most came from rural areas near Williams.

13) Eveleth won consecutive state titles in 1948 and 1949.

14) Eveleth, Rochester, and St. Cloud.

15) Champion Eveleth (Neil Celley, Clem Cossalter, Pat Finnegan, Wally Grant) and runner-up Thief River Falls (Robert Baker, James Doyle, Wes Hovie)

16) Jim Field of Granite Falls.

17) Thief River Falls, which nipped White Bear Lake 3-2.

18) Cliff Thompson, who coached the Golden Bears in each of the first 12 state tournaments (1945-56) and to a total of five championships and two runner-up finishes.

19) Rochester. The southern Minnesota upstart won 3-2 on the strength of two goals by Ray Purvis, both assisted by Alan Gilkinson. Goalie Clark Wilder made 25 stops as Eveleth outshot the winners 27-12.

20) Eveleth (Milan Begich, Neil Celley, Pat Finnegan, and Wally Grant). Not surprisingly, it is the only time in tourney history when this occurred.

21) 1947; Roseau 5-0 over St. Cloud, Eveleth 6-0 over Williams, St. Paul Johnson 4-0 over Rochester, and Minneapolis West 6-0 over South St. Paul.

22) St. Paul Johnson in 1947. The Governors beat Roseau 2-1 in the title match.

23) John Mayasich was a ninth-grader for Eveleth when he scored five goals in the three games as Eveleth won its second state title. Mayasich, of course, was on his way to establishing several major scoring records that still stand.

24) Wes Hovie of Thief River Falls. In the first-ever semifinal in 1945, Hovie scored twice in both the first and second periods as the Prowlers went on to hammer St. Cloud 12-0. Ironically, in the next semifinal game, Wally Grant of Eveleth scored four goals in a 10-0 win over St. Paul Washington.

25) Willmar, which lost 6-0 to Eveleth in the first round and 8-3 to St. Cloud before their ouster as Ken Johnson scored twice for the central Minnesota squad.

26) Regions 7 and 8, which covered northern Minnesota. This was tabbed as the Back Door. From 1965 to 1974, the two region runners-up conducted a playoff to determine the Region 3 representative. However, with the tradition of hockey in those areas and the strength of their teams, Region 3 participants often fared well at the tournament. On four occasions, they went on to win the state championship. The Back Door ended when the private schools began playing to earn the right to the state tourney in 1975.

27) Rube Bjorkman, The Masked Marvel. Bjorkman wore black goggles over his spectacles. He led the tourney in scoring in 1946

47

and later starred for the Gophers and U.S. Olympic teams in 1948 and 1952. He coached Greenway-Coleraine to the 1962 tourney.

28) Rochester, in 1946. They lost to Roseau 6-0 in the finals. The next team to make the finals from southern Minnesota was Rochester John Marshall, which won it all in 1977.

Roseau's Rube Bjorkman.

29) Bob Harris, whose sons John and Robbie would later play together at the U of M, winning a national title in 1974. Both sons were gifted golfers, with John winning both a Big Ten golf title and the U.S. Amateur title in 1996. John went on to play on the regular PGA tour and is presently on the Senior tour. Bob was a defenseman for Oscar Almquist at Roseau.

30) John Matchefts, who also tied for the tourney lead in 1947 with four others (all with six points). In both years, Matchefts's Golden Bears won the title. Matchefts scored 26 points (14 goals and 12 assists) in nine tourney games overall. Matchefts, later a two-time All-American at Michigan, won three NCAA titles with the Wolverines. He then coached two different schools to the state tourney before coaching collegiately at Colorado College and the Air Force Academy in Colorado Springs.

31) Bob Johnson, who continued his playing career with the Gophers before pursuing a career that would bring him three NCAA titles at Wisconsin and a Stanley Cup title as head coach with Pittsburgh in 1991.

32) His football helmet. Granite Falls was beaten 16-0 by Eveleth in the first round but beat Rochester 2-1 in consolation before losing 4-0 to White Bear Lake for fifth-place.

33) 8,434

34) John Gustafson, who was a regular as a referee in the first two decades of the tourney.

35) 10 cents

36) Carl Thorson, inducted into the Minnesota State Hockey Coaches Hall of Fame in 1992.

37) Rudy Lindbeck, who had 41 saves in an opening-round 2-1 win over St. Paul Harding and 37 more in a 5-3 semifinal loss to Warroad. South St. Paul was fourth, losing to St. Cloud 2-1 in the consolation final with Lindbeck making 27 stops.

38) Bill and Tom Wegleitner. Bill was a defenseman and Tom, who had two goals and four assists, was an all-tourney forward. Tom, later a scoring star for the Gophers, scored with under a minute left in regulation to tie Williams in the semifinals before Murray fell 5-4 in three overtimes.

39) Dave Peterson, who later went on to great fame as coach at Minneapolis Southwest and for the U.S. Nationals and Olympic teams. In 1948, Peterson had 17 saves in a 2-1 loss to South St. Paul before allowing no goals in two periods of a 10-0 whitewash of St. Louis Park. He then recorded 21 saves in a 2-1 overtime win over Mpls. Washburn in the fifth-place game.

40) Max Oshie was all-tourney in 1948 and Buster Oshie all-tourney in 1949. Max had five goals and four assists in 1948 while Buster had three goals and four assists as Warroad lost to Eveleth 8-2 in the final, with the Oshie boys tallying for the losers. The next year, Buster had five goals and two assists as Warroad finished third. Max holds the Minnesota record for goals in a game with 12 in a 16-2 thrashing of Thief River Falls on Jan. 6, 1948. The Oshie brothers were great-uncles to T. J., a Warroad star who led Warroad to Class A titles in both 2003 and 2005 and now plays for St. Louis.

41) Five (5). Mayasich wore his more well-known number eight (8) in his final three years of record-setting state tournament play. As a ninth-grader, Mayasich scored three goals and two assists but didn't make all-tourney. However, half of the all-tourney squad of eight players was made up of members of the champion Bears - Willard Ikola, Gene Klun, Dick Peterson, and John Matchefts.

42) John McKinnon of Williams, who scored a second-period goal on Eveleth's Willard Ikola in a 4-1 loss to the Golden Bears in the 1949 final. McKinnon was all-tourney in both 1949 and 1950, scoring two goals and an assist as a junior and two goals and three assists as a senior for the runner-up Wolves.

43) Minneapolis Central beat St. Paul Harding 8-4 in the playoff and finished sixth in the state tourney.

44) Both Granite Falls and Staples. Granite Falls coach Phil Minelli, a Hibbing native, was a teacher and counselor at the school who had to be pressured by students to head the team. Minelli contacted his college roommate at St. Thomas College, Frank Zucco, who was the coach at St. Paul Monroe. Zucco arranged to have Granite Falls wear their uniforms not just in 1945 but also in 1946. For Staples, the Cardinals borrowed uniforms from another St. Paul school, Mechanic Arts, for the first tourney in 1945.

45) Jim Renstrom, who had two goals and an assist in 1946 and a goal and two assists in 1947. Renstrom played on Johnson's top first line with Jim Sedin (three assists) and Dave Reipke (five goals and one assist). Reipke tied for the scoring lead that year with four others and was also an all-tourney pick. Sedin played on the 1952 U.S. Olympic team.

46) Lou Cotroneo, who later went on to even greater fame as an assistant coach, head coach, and referee in the tournament.

John Matchefts led Eveleth to consecutive titles in 1948 and 49. (photo: U.S. Hockey Hall of Fame Museum)

47) Many of the teams used football uniforms. St. Paul Johnson, incidentally, wore numbers 70-95 when they won the state crown in 1947.

48) Willard Ikola, who was all-tournament both as a sophomore and junior. As a freshman in 1947, he had a shutout against Williams in his first action at the tourney. He would go on to be all-tourney in 1950 when Eveleth won the third of four straight titles. Ikola had five shutouts in 12 tournament games; both records still stand.

49) John Matchefts and Tony Tassoni. Matchefts had a tourney-high nine goals along with five assists and Tassoni added six goals and an assist.

50) Bill Gettleman

51) Staples. The central Minnesota team lost both its games to St. Cloud (2-0) and White Bear Lake (5-1) and recorded just three shots on goal in each game. Wayne Stewart scored their lone tally.

52) Instead of earning state entrance by winning playoff games, the Minneapolis City Conference coaches simply decided to select West as their representative. West lost both games to Rochester (1-0) and St. Cloud (3-1).

53) Chet Lundsten, who beat Murray goalie Gordon Mallory. Lundsten had two goals and an assist in 1949 and four goals and an assist in 1950 and was all-tournament both years as his team lost to Eveleth in the finals in consecutive years.

54) Harley Woog, who scored three goals for the Packers in the 1947 tournament, including the game-winner in a 4-3 win over St. Cloud in the fifth-place contest. Woog's cousin, Doug, would later be a Packer star. Harley earned 13 letters at South St. Paul High, including ski-jumping, and also held the state pole vault record for many years.

55) Gene Lowe, who was all-tournament, also had Harding's lone goal in a 2-1 semifinal loss to South St. Paul. Teammate Leroy Tyler has three goals and four assists for the Knights.

56) Ron Drobnick. While his teammates were scoring 26 goals in defeating Granite Falls (16-0) and St. Paul Washington (10-0) in the first two rounds, Drobnick had to make just one save in the quarterfinals and only four in the semifinals to record his two shutouts in the inaugural tourney. However, he did make 11 saves in the 4-3 clinching win over Thief River Falls. In 1946, he had a 13-save shutout in a 1-0 third-place win over White Bear Lake.

57) Ray Purvis. He had an assist as Rochester bowed out in two games in 1945, scored twice when Rochester finished second to Roseau in 1946, and scored a goal in 1947 when the southern Minnesota school was gone after two losses.

58) Wes Hovie and Les Vigness.

59) Lloyd Lundeen, who led West to a third-place finish. The previous year, Lundeen had played in the tourney when they lost both of their games. Lloyd became a star pitcher for Dick Siebert at Minnesota and played in the Giants' minor-league system. He was also the

father of five sons who all played for stellar Minneapolis Southwest teams. Bob, the oldest, played in four tournaments (1968-71) and was all-tournament twice. Dave (1971-72), Tom (1972-73), Paul (1976), and Charlie (1980) also competed in the state tournament. The oldest four Lundeens all played collegiately for Wisconsin and the youngest, Charlie, skated for Northern Michigan.

60) Wally Grant, who later led Michigan to an NCAA title and was the Wolverines' first three-time All-American. Grant, nicknamed "Cedar Legs" for his bowed legs, scored the tying and winning goals in a 61-second span to spur Eveleth to the 4-3 victory and the first-ever Minnesota state boys' hockey title. Grant had a tourney-high nine goals and four assists for 13 points, tying linemate Pat Finnegan (eight goals, five assists). Another linemate, Neil Celley, finished with six goals and five assists. Thus, the first line for Eveleth accounted for 23 of the team's 30 goals in the tournament and 37 of their 50 total points.

61) Dale Gray, who tallied a goal and assist in 1948, his senior season.

62) Cliff Winter. Cliff scored two goals and an assist to help his team to a fifth-place finish as a sophomore, added three goals and two assists as a junior, and scored two goals and and assist as St. Cloud copped third-place his senior year.

63) Charles "Lefty" Smith, who made all of his appearances in an 11-year stretch from 1958 to 1968 and had an impressive record of 201-69-11 in his 15 years with the Packers.

64) Neil Celley, Pat Finnegan, and Wally Grant of Eveleth. Celley and Grant played at Michigan and Finnegan, believe it or not, at the University of California-Berkeley. All three players had starred for the Eveleth city senior team that won the Arrowhead League in 1944, playing in many cases against much older players.

65) Bob Baker had two assists in the championship game and Les Vigness scored twice. Baker finished with three goals and three assists while Vigness had five goals, including a hat trick in a 12-0 drubbing of St. Cloud in the semis.

66) LeRoy Tyler. Teammate Gene Lowe, who had five goals and two assists, scored in double-overtime to give the Knights a 2-1 win over Minneapolis Washburn for fifth-place.

67) Ron Martinson, a future Michigan star.

68) John Graham, who also tallied in Washington's 5-0 first-round win over Rochester.

69) Sam Gibbons. He had two goals and five assists his junior year, including two assists in the 8-2 finals loss to Eveleth. As a senior, he made all-tournament when he tallied six times with an assist. He scored four goals in a 7-5 third-place win over Murray.

70) Martin LaVasseur. He had 14 saves in the first-ever state tournament game, a 3-2 loss to Thief River Falls in 1945 and blanked St. Paul Washington 10-0 in the fifth-place game that first season. In 1946, LaVasseur gave up just four goals in three games as the Bears finished sixth. White Bear Lake lost 2-1 to Roseau in the quarterfinals and then 1-0 to St. Cloud in the consolation final.

71) George Gibault, who finished with five goals for the second-place Warriors.

72) 12. Two Eveleth players, Pat Finnegan and Wally Grant, did it twice.

2 The 1950s

1) What player once scored his team's first six goals in a game?

2) What player, who later went on to great fanfare as the goaltending coach for the 1980 USA Miracle on Ice gold-medal winners, was the goalie for St. Paul Johnson in 1951?

3) After winning their fourth straight Minnesota state title in 1951, Eveleth had their 78-game winning streak snapped by Hibbing in the 1952 Region 7 final. Yet those same two teams met in the state finals that year. How was that possible?

4) What all-tournament player scored all of his team's eight goals in the 1954 tournament?

5) What outstanding coach (and one of the game's pillars) led his team and school to the tournament eight times during the 1950's?

6) What team lost the 1958 title game 1-0 despite outshooting the winning team by a margin of 38-12?

7) What South St. Paul freshman led the Packers in scoring with four goals in 1959?

8) Who led St. Paul Johnson in goal-scoring in 1955 with three when the Governors won the championship by defeating Minneapolis Southwest 3-1?

9) One of the great hockey families in Minnesota lore is the Alm family, several of whom played for Minneapolis South during the 1950s. Which brothers played for the Tigers during their three appearances in the decade (1954, 1955, and 1957)?

10) Who was the scoring star for the Robbinsdale Robins when they made their only appearance at state in 1959, as he scored five goals, including four in one game?

11) In which year were all four semifinalists from the Twin Cities for the first time?

12) What player had the distinction of tying Eveleth junior John Mayasich as the leading scorer in the 1950 tournament?

13) Which International Falls star scored seven goals in the 1957 tourney, including two goals in the 3-1 final victory over Roseau, as the Broncos won their first state title under coach Larry Ross?

14) What tournament power helped build its tradition with consecutive state crowns in 1958 and 1959?

15) How many shutouts did Willard Ikola, the legendary Eveleth goaltender, total in his 12-game state tournament career from 1947 to 1950?

16) How many goals did tournament giant John Mayasich score in his four years of state tournament competition from 1948-51?

17) What St. Paul Johnson player was all-tournament in 1954 and 1955, scoring six goals in 1954 and two more in 1955 as the Governors won their second-ever title?

18) A member of an illustrious Minnesota hockey family led all scorers in the 1955 tourney with six points (five goals, one assist). What was the name of this Minneapolis Southwest stalwart?

19) What school, which would eventually establish itself as a powerhouse in the sport, played in its first three state tournaments representing Region 6 during the 1950's?

20) Who led the Thief River Falls club of 1954 to the first of two titles in the decade by scoring twice in the 4-1 finale versus Eveleth?

21) In 1950 and 1951, John Mayasich of Eveleth recorded a stunning total of 30 tournament points in leading his Iron Range club to two state titles as undefeated champs. How many *goals* did he score in the two tourneys overall?

Herb Brooks (top) celebrates the 1955 state title with St. Paul Johnson teammates. (MSHSL)

22) What brother duo for Roseau provided the scoring punch for the northern Minnesota juggernaut in their undefeated season (30-0) in 1959, beating Minneapolis Washburn 4-2 in the title match?

23) What were the nicknames of teammates Don Willer and Dick Lick, who played in the tourney for South St. Paul in 1953 and 1954 and later became a legendary refereeing tandem in high school hockey circles?

24) Who played for Eveleth on three tourney entrants from 1952 to 1954 and later coached Eveleth-Gilbert to the 1993 Tier II title?

25) On only five occasions has a championship game ended with a 1-0 score. Who scored the only goal in the first of those occasions in 1958 for champion Roseau?

26) What two future U.S. Olympians were key players on the Warroad High team that lost 4-1 to St. Paul Johnson in the 1953 finals?

27) Who was the primary scoring threat for St. Cloud in 1950, 1951, and 1952 and later coached Hastings to their first tournament appearance in 1971?

28) What two Eveleth players with the same last name were all-tournament for the Bears in 1951 and 1953?

29) What player scored a goal for St. Paul Humboldt in the 1953 tourney and later coached another team to seven tournaments?

30) Who scored two goals for Minneapolis Southwest in the 1953 tourney as the Indians finished sixth? (Hint: he is the uncle of a prominent Twin Cities newscaster.)

31) In 1952, this gentleman played on the Hibbing team that beat Eveleth 4-3 to break their conference rival's four-year stranglehold on the title. Later, as a coach, he was instrumental in changing the tournament from a single-class to a two-tier event and then a two-class arrangement in the 1990's. Can you name him?

32) What Thief River Falls player was all-tourney in both 1954 and 1955, helping his team to the 1954 title and scoring four goals in 1955 when they took fifth-place?

33) What two teams staged a remarkable and epic quarterfinal contest in 1955 that took 11 overtimes to determine the winner?

34) What all-tourney player for St. Louis Park in 1958 went on to become one of the state's top amateur golfers?

35) What tournament-leading scorer helped Hibbing to its first-ever state title in 1952?

36) What International Falls defenseman was all-tourney in 1950 for the third-place Broncos, and was an All-American wing for Minnesota's NCAA runner-up in 1954?

37) What long-time Virginia High school coach won a state title as a player with Eveleth in 1951, scoring three goals and four assists and added three goals and two assists the following year as the Bears finished second to Hibbing?

38) Who was the only Roseau player to earn all-tourney status both years as the Rams won two straight titles in 1958 and 1959?

39) When St. Paul Murray's Bill Wegleitner scored at 2:30 of over-time in a quarterfinal contest in 1950 against International Falls, why didn't the game end and how did his team end up losing?

40) What Minneapolis South product scored three of the Tigers' four goals in two straight losses in the 1950 tournament, but went on to be a stellar player for the Gophers and joined several Min-nesota teammates on the 1956 U.S. Olympic team?

41) In the historic 11-overtime quarterfinal game in 1955, who scored the winner?

42) For the first eight years of the tournament, the cost of a pro-gram was the same. It went up twice during the 1950's—in 1953 and in 1956. What was the price of the program in those years?

43) In a very unusual twist in the 1952 tournament, three players with the same first name scored all four goals for Winona in their only state appearance. Who were they?

44) After being a perennial entrant in the tourney since its incep-tion and a dominating presence nearly every time they participated, when was the first year that Eveleth did not earn a berth in the tourney?

45) What Duluth Central defenseman in the 1954 tourney went on to coach two colleges in Wisconsin to small-college national hockey titles?

46) What South St. Paul player was all-tourney in 1959 (one goal and three assists) and in 1960 (two goals and two assists) as one of the pivotal cogs on Packer teams that copped fourth-place both years?

47) In both 1951 and 1952, St. Cloud had three Saatzer brothers playing for the Stearns County club. What were their names?

48) What team won a four-overtime game over St. Louis Park in the first round, beat Eveleth by six goals in the semifinals, and beat Warroad by three in the finals in 1953?

The Roseau squad, 1959, undefeated state champs (30-0). (MSHSL)

49) What occurrence caused the delay in the start of the final 1955 quarterfinal between St. Paul Johnson and Roseau?

50) What St. Paul Washington player from 1956 is in the Minnesota Twins Hall of Fame?

51) Which school earned the distinction of becoming the first team to shut out perennial power Eveleth in state tournament play?

52) Entering the 1950 state tournament, Eveleth cruised to the Region 7 title by beating which three teams by a combined score of 46-1?

53) What International Falls junior winger set a tourney record that stood for 40 years when he assisted on five goals in a 10-0 thrashing of Hallock in a 1957 quarterfinal?

54) In which year were the players first identified in the tournament program by what grade they were in academically in school?

55) In 1959, what Minneapolis school finished runner-up?

56) What coach guided South St. Paul to four tournaments in the 1950's, worked 14 years as a tourney referee, and was also an award-winning cartoonist and illustrator?

57) Which Eveleth player was a three-year state champion with Cliff Thompson's charges and later played for Harvard?

58) What uniform number did St. Paul Johnson forward Herb Brooks wear for the proud east-side school in both 1954 and 1955?

59) Which Edina-Morningside goaltender was outstanding in the 1956 event as he stopped 54 Thief River Falls shots in a 3-2 three-overtime loss in the quarterfinals, 24 shots in a 3-2 win over White Bear Lake, and 31 more in a 1-0 loss in the fifth-place game with St. Paul Johnson?

60) What Roseau player came up big with a hat trick in the Rams' 4-2 title game win in 1959?

61) What little school from northwest Minnesota arrived in St. Paul for their first shot at a state title in 1957 but was quickly dispatched, getting blanked twice and outshot by 50 shots over two games?

62) What son played for his father's team in both the 1953 and 1955 tournaments?

63) In the three years prior to the arrival of Willard Ikola to Edina-Morningside in 1958, two other coaches led the school to the tourney. Who were they?

64) Who was the only player to be on the roster for Thief River Falls during both their 1954 and 1956 championship years?

65) What Minneapolis Roosevelt forward from 1956 had a goal and two assists as the Teddies finished fourth?

66) What future St. Paul Johnson coach played for St. Paul Murray in the 1951 event, when the team finished fifth by virtue of a 2-0 win over St. Cloud?

67) Which school, which took second, had three sets of brothers competing for them in 1955?

68) What Thief River Falls skater, who competed for the Prowlers in 1954 and 1955, became much more noteworthy for his dynamic and humorous work with engaged couples?

69) Which state champion in the 1950's landed five of the 12 all-tournament players that year?

70) Who scored the winning goal in the third overtime that gave eventual-champion Thief River Falls a 3-2 victory over Edina in the first round in 1956?

71) Who was the starting goaltender for South St. Paul in both 1957 and 1958, a long-time coach at Owatonna who was selected to the Minnesota Hockey Coaches Association Hall of Fame in 1993?

72) What Hibbing goalie was integral to ending Eveleth's run of four straight titles in 1952, as the Bluejackets prevailed over their Iron Range rival 4-3 in the championship game?

73) What rangy Eveleth center scored three goals and added an assist as the Bears took third place in 1956?

74) What forward scored seven goals in the 1952 tourney for state champion Hibbing, including a clutch two goals and an assist in the title game?

75) An all-tourney pick in 1958 for South St. Paul, what forward scored six of his team's nine goals as the Packers finished third?

76) Four players tied for the scoring lead in 1953 with five points, including Jack Stoskopf (Warroad), Mike Castellano (Eveleth) and Gerald Palkovich (Eveleth). The other was a major cog in St. Paul Johnson's drive to the state title. Can you name him?

77) A future Olympian, what International Falls forward possessed one of the best "backhand" shots in tournament history for the Broncos in both 1958 and 1959?

78) In what year during the decade did six of the 11 tournament games end in a shutout?

79) What Minneapolis school made their first-ever appearance in the 1956 tournament and finished fourth?

80) When St. Paul Johnson won the 1955 state title, their starting goalie gave up just two goals in their three victories. Who was he?

81) In the 1956 semifinals, which International Falls defenseman not only played the entire game but scored in the third overtime to give his team a 3-1 win over Minneapolis Roosevelt?

82) What St. Paul Johnson defenseman was all-tournament in both 1951 and 1952?

83) Which two goalies did not allow Eveleth's John Mayasich to score at least a hat trick against them in his last nine games as a tournament performer?

84) In the epic 11-overtime quarterfinal between Minneapolis South and Thief River Falls in 1955, how many penalties were called by referees John Neihart and Roland Vandell?

85) What St. Paul Johnson skater tied for second in scoring in the 1951 tourney for the second-place Governors with two goals and five assists?

86) After playing in the epic 11-overtime game and losing to Minneapolis South in the quarterfinals in 1955, how many overtimes did Thief River Falls play in their 1956 first-round match-up with Edina?

87) Which St. Paul Johnson netminder gave up just one goal in each game as he back-stopped the Governors to their second state title in 1953?

88) What do the following numbers represent from a tournament game played in 1955?

    A: 1 0 1 0 0 0 0 0 0 0 0 0 0 1
    B: 0 2 0 0 0 0 0 0 0 0 0 0 0 0
    C: 4 7 8 3 6 5 3 0 3 5 2 1 3 0
    D: 3 3 2 2 2 4 6 1 4 1 3 3 4 0

89) In the 1953 tourney, this Warroad goalie was outstanding for the second-place club from Region 8. He had 32 saves in a 5-0 shutout of Humboldt in the first game of the tournament, 24 in a 2-1 win over South St. Paul in the semis, and 39 more in the 4-1 loss to champion St. Paul Johnson in the climactic contest. Who was he?

90) What South St. Paul goalie was the starting netminder for three straight seasons (1953-55) for the Packers, making 202 total saves and recording two shutouts?

91) What two linemates switched jerseys prior to the third-place game in 1954, leading to a rather unique situation for South St. Paul in their 5-3 loss to St. Paul Johnson?

92) When was the first year that all three northern teams were beaten in the quarterfinals?

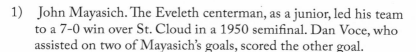

◀ ANSWERS TO CHAPTER 2 - THE 1950's ▶

1) John Mayasich. The Eveleth centerman, as a junior, led his team to a 7-0 win over St. Cloud in a 1950 semifinal. Dan Voce, who assisted on two of Mayasich's goals, scored the other goal.

2) Warren Strelow. The burly and wise goalie maven, who went on to be a goalie coach for three NHL teams, shut out White Bear Lake in the quarterfinals in 1951. After Johnson dispatched Thief River Falls 6-2 in the semis; Strelow made 19 saves in a 4-2 loss to Eveleth in the title game. Strelow coached at Mahtomedi for 14 years.

3) The "Back Door" scenario. Starting in 1949 and continuing until 1964, the Region 3 representative at state was the runner-up in Region 7 or 8, alternating annually. To Eveleth's benefit, the Region 7 runner-up received the bid in 1952. Eveleth defeated both Thief River Falls and St. Paul Humboldt to reach the finals. Hibbing, meanwhile, beat St. Cloud and Mpls. Southwest to earn the title game. In a classic final, Hibbing prevailed 4-3 to win their first title. From 1965-1974, the Region 3 participant resulted from the winner of a playoff between the losers of the Region 7 and 8 finals.

4) Dick Jinks of St. Paul Harding. Jinks scored twice in a 5-2 loss to Eveleth, five in the Knights' 5-1 win over Wayzata, and the only goal in a 1-0 victory over Minneapolis South in the consolation final. Bob Lundgren assisted on four of the goals and Dick Kinderman on three of them.

5) Rube Gustafson. The Governor mentor took teams from the St. Paul City Conference and Region IV to tourneys every year in the decade except 1950 and 1958. Gustafson's clubs won crowns in both 1953 and 1955.

6) St. Paul Harding. The Knights lost to Roseau because Rams' goaltender Dick Roth was spectacular in the nets for the champions, who won their second state title. Unfortunately for Harding, it was their only foray into the finals in eight total trips to state.

7) Doug Woog, who would go on to make three all-tourney teams and become one of the most significant persons in Minnesota hockey history. Woog totaled 19 points in his four tournament trips, including 12 goals.

8) Herb Brooks. Despite scoring twice in the title game, Herbie never made the all-tourney team. He had a goal and three assists as a junior in 1954 as Johnson claimed third-place.

9) Gary, Larry, Rick, and Tim all played in the tournament. Larry was all-tourney in 1955 and Rick in 1957. Brothers Tony and Mike also played for South High but never made it to state. Rick was the head coach and Larry his assistant as the Tigers made the 1993 Tier II tourney, their last berth in the tournament.

10) Len Lilyholm, who became a fine player for the Gophers and played on three U.S. National squads and the U.S. Olympic team in 1968. Lilyholm played one season for the Fighting Saints in 1972-73.

11) 1955; St. Paul Johnson (1st), Minneapolis Southwest (2nd), South St. Paul (3rd), and Minneapolis South (4th).

12) Ray Beauchamp of runner-up Williams, who had 12 points (five goals, seven assists) while Mayasich had 11 goals and one assist. He is tied for the second-most points in one game with seven as he tallied four goals and three assists in an 8-2 semifinal victory over Minneapolis South.

13) Oscar Mahle, who led all scorers with eight points. Mahle also scored both goals for his team as International Falls lost 3-2 in the 1956 finals to Thief River Falls. Teammate Dave Frank contributed six goals and an assist and joined Mahle, Jim Wherley, and Tom Neveaux as fellow Broncos on the all-tournament squad. Frank had four goals in a first-round throttling of Hallock.

14) Roseau

15) Five. Ikola had one in his freshman year, two in his junior year, and two his senior year. The future coaching great gave up a scant 13 goals in those 12 games.

16) 36; Mayasich scored three in 1948, seven in 1949, 11 in 1950, and 15 in 1951.

17) Stu Anderson, a future Gopher star.

18) Merv Meredith, who helped the Indians to the 1955 title game in which they lost to St. Paul Johnson 3-1. Brothers Bob (1951-52), Dick (1951), and Wayne (1955) also wore the Indian logo for Southwest at the St. Paul Auditorium and John played for Dave Peterson's club in both 1975 and 1976 at the Met Center and Civic Center, respectively. Dick was all-tourney in 1951 as the Indians took fourth-place as he had three goals and an assist. A left wing, Dick played four years at Minnesota and was on the silver-winning 1956 U.S. Olympic team and the gold-winning 1960 U.S. team.

19) Edina, which was then known as Edina-Morningside, played in the 1955, 1956, and 1957 tournaments. The Hornets lost their first seven games, getting outscored 21-4 in the process before getting their first win over Hallock (4-0) in a 1957 consolation game.

20) Marv Jorde, who was a Minnesota Gopher and later a long-time star in senior hockey. Jorde had three goals and three assists in 1954 as a co-captain and leading scorer. Jorde coached Park-Cottage Grove for 33 years and was a player/coach and general manager of the renowned St. Paul Parkers, which won 12 Minnesota state senior titles and seven national senior titles.

21) 26. Mayasich had 11 markers in 1950 and netted 15 more in 1951. He would go on to be a two-time All-American at Minnesota (1954, 1955), compete on five U.S. Nationals teams, and two Olympic teams (1956 and 1960).

22) Jim and Larry Stordahl. Jim tied for the tourney-high with seven points on the strength of four goals and three assists with International Falls' Dan Cullen while Larry scored three times. Both made the all-tournament team.

23) Whitey (Willer) and Beaver (Lick). Lick garnered six goals and two assists while Willer had two goals and four assists during those two tourneys. Willer also was at state seven times as an assistant coach with South St. Paul and on six occasions was a referee in the tournament in a 34-year career as an official.

24) Bob Kochevar, who had three goals and one assist in both 1953 and 1954.

25) Larry Anderson. The Roseau player scored in the first period and it stood up despite the fact that runner-up St. Paul Harding dominated most of the action. The other years that resulted in 1-0 finals were in 1961 (Roseau over So. St. Paul), 1970 (Mpls. Southwest over Edina, 1971 (Edina over Roseau), 1997 AA (Edina over Duluth East), and 2004 AA (Centennial over Moorhead).

26) Roger and Billy Christian, brothers who were also standouts on the American gold-medal winners at Squaw Valley in the 1960 Winter Olympics. Roger had two goals and two assists and Billy a goal and two assists for the Warriors in the 1953 title game.

27) Don Saatzer, who scored six of their 15 goals in those three tournaments.

28) Ron Castellano and Mike Castellano. Ron had two assists in 1950 and a goal and six assists in 1951. Mike had two goals and five assists in 1952 and three goals and two assists in 1953.

29) Gordy Genz, who led Alexander-Ramsey to six tournaments and what would then become Roseville Area to another after Ramsey and Kellogg consolidated. Genz won more than 500 games in a 35-year coaching career.

30) Pete Passolt, who also played collegiately with the Gophers. He was an uncle to Jeff, the news anchor for KMSP-Channel 9 and a former St. Cloud State standout himself.

31) Herb Sellars, who coached at neighboring Chisholm for many years. Sellars first proposed a two-pronged tournament plan to the hockey coaches association back in 1975.

32) Joe Poole. The Prowler had a goal and four assists as Thief River Falls won it all in 1954 and four goals and an assist in 1955 when his team won the consolation trophy.

33) Thief River Falls and Minneapolis South, with South finally prevailing 3-2 after 87 minutes and 50 seconds. The game took 4 hours and 53 minutes to complete and was attended by 7,575 fans. It was the longest game in tourney annals until being surpassed in 1996 when Apple Valley beat Duluth East 5-4 in five overtimes in a AA semifinal epic that lasted 93:12.

34) Bob Reith, Jr., who scored a team-high three goals as his team finished fourth. Reith was one of the best amateur golfers in Minnesota for decades and played briefly on the PGA tour.

35) Jack Petroske, who had three goals and eight assists. Petroske had a goal and three assists in the finals against Eveleth and five points in the first round versus St. Cloud.

36) Dick Dougherty, who also played on the 1956 U.S. Olympic team.

37) Dave "Boots" Hendrickson

38) Goalie Dick Roth, who had a 38-save shutout in Roseau's 1-0 win over St. Paul Harding in the 1958 final. He had another shutout of International Falls on their way to taking the 1959 championship, including a 4-2 victory over Minneapolis Washburn in the finals.

39) Because overtimes were not sudden-death (immediate win or loss) at that time. Overtimes would run their course of five minutes and if the game was tied, the game would advance into another overtime. This was the first occasion in history when each team scored in the first overtime. After Wegleitner's goal put Murray ahead, Int'l Falls tied it 30 seconds later with Bill Dougherty's tally on an assist from brother Dick. With just 13 seconds elapsed in the second extra session, Dick Dougherty beat Gordon Mallory on an assist from Bill. However, the Broncos didn't win until the overtime period was completed. It was the only time in tourney history that a team scored an overtime goal but lost the game.

40) Gene Campbell, who coached high school hockey for many years, most notably with Rochester Lourdes from 1982 to 1996.

41) Jim Westby of Minneapolis South, who beat Thief River Falls goalie Rod Collins with a slapshot at 1:50 from just outside the blue line. The goal was scored on the power-play, with the Prowler's Duane Glass in the penalty-box for tripping. It was the only penalty of the overtimes and just the third in the game. Collins finished with 36 stops while South goalie Rog Evenson had 50 saves. Westby played for the Gophers and for the 1964 U.S. Olympic team. His brother, Jerry, played on the 1954 and 1955 South clubs and for two U.S. Nationals teams.

42) In 1953, the cost of the program went up from 10 cents to 15 cents and in 1956, it went all the way up to 25 cents.

43) Roger Carrol (2), Roger Neitzke, and Roger Benson. Winona, the most-southerly school to play in the tourney for years, lost both games. However, the Winhawks' were very competitive, losing 2-1 to St. Paul Humboldt and 4-3 to Thief River Falls.

44) 1957. In the 12 previous years, Eveleth went 27-9 with five titles, two second-place finishes, and three third-place results. No shame for Eveleth in 1957 as International Falls beat them in the Region 7 final that year and went on to win the state title.

45) Wally Akervik, who led Wisconsin State-Superior to a NAIA title in 1976 and Wisconsin-Eau Claire to an NCAA Division III title in 1984.

46) Rich Brown

47) Twin brothers Don (right wing) and Ron (center), and Dick (defenseman). In 1951, St. Cloud finished sixth with Ron scoring twice. In 1952, St. Cloud was hammered 10-0 by Hibbing in the first round and downed 7-4 by St. Paul Johnson in consolation, as Don recorded a hat trick. Both Ron and Don went on to play minor league baseball in the Yankees' organization. Older brother, Leroy, played in the 1947 and 1948 events.

48) St. Paul Johnson. The Governors beat St. Louis Park 2-1 on Roger Bertelson's goal in the first round. Bertelson scored two goals in the 4-1 win over Warroad, too.

49) The evening's first game (7:30 start) between Minneapolis South and Thief River Falls was still tied 2-2 after nine overtimes, causing the two teams to wait it out while the epic match dragged on. However, tourney officials decided to start the Roseau-Johnson game at 11:33 p.m., originally slated to begin at 9:00 p.m. The Rams and Governors played their first period and Johnson led 1-0 on Ken Fanger's goal. South and Thief River Falls returned for a 10th overtime as South goalie Roger Evenson and Thief River Falls net-minder Rod Collins kept the opposition off the board. With the two separate games alternating every period, Roseau and Johnson played a scoreless second period. Back on the ice for an 11th extra-session, the game finally ended when South scored a minute and 50 seconds into yet another overtime. The game finally ended at 12:23 a.m. but Johnson and Roseau still had to complete their contest. Johnson's 1-0 lead held on to beat the Rams and later that night beat Mpls. South 3-1in the semifinals. The Governors then beat yet another Mill City school, Southwest, by the same margin in the tourney finals.

50) Jim Rantz, who was an All-American pitcher for the Minnesota Gophers and won the clinching game in the 1960 College World

Series. Rantz signed with Washington in 1960 and pitched in the minors for the Twins for five seasons before joining the club's front office. He has worked for the club for 52 years and has been the head of the farm system since 1986. He was inducted into the Twins' Hall of Fame in 2007.

51) Thief River Falls. The Prowlers blanked the Bears 3-0 in the 1956 semifinals with Rod Collins recording the shutout with 17 saves. Cliff Strand had a goal and assist.

52) Duluth Central (23-0), Grand Rapids (18-0), and International Falls (5-1).

53) Bob Miggins, who died in a plane crash in Reno, Nevada on Jan. 21, 1985 with 69 others.

54) 1958

55) Washburn, which lost 4-2 to Roseau. The Millers were led by Ken Hanson and John Simus, who each notched five points. Hanson had four goals, including a goal at 2:12 of the second overtime to give Washburn a 6-5 win over South St. Paul in the semis.

56) George Karn, who led the Packers in 1953, 1954, 1955, and 1957. Their best finish in those years was in 1955, when they were third.

57) Ed Mrkonich, who played on the 1949, 1950, and 1951 championship teams. Mrkonich, a tough defenseman, scored a goal in his junior season and two goals and two assists in his senior season and was named to the all-tournament squad.

58) Five.

59) Murray MacPherson, who deservedly made the all-tourney team after making 109 saves while allowing just six goals.

60) Don Ross, who finished with four goals and two assists. A year earlier, he had a goal and an assist as Roseau completed the decade with two successive crowns. Ross then played four years for North Dakota before stints on both the 1964 and 1968 Olympic teams. He also was a referee in three state hockey tournaments.

61) Hallock, located in extreme northwest Minnesota and the seat of Kittson County, was hammered 10-0 by International Falls in the first round and then obliterated 14-0 by Edina-Morningside in consolation. They were outshot 72-22 overall.

The Minneapolis South Tigers beat Thief River Falls 3-2 in the 1955 quarter-finals. The game went to a record 11 overtime periods. (Photo: Jim Westby)

62) John "Jack" Almquist, the son of Roseau head coach Oscar Almquist. The Rams lost both of their games those years. Jack, a goalie, didn't play in 1953 but started both games in 1955 when Roseau lost 1-0 to St. Paul Johnson and 4-3 to Thief River Falls.

63) Ted Greer (1955, 1956) and Ken Yackel (1957).

64) Rod Collins, a goalie who didn't play in 1954 but was the starter two years later and allowed just four goals in three games as the Prowlers took down Edina 3-2, Eveleth 3-0, and International Falls 3-2. Collins, a year earlier, was in the nets for the defending champs when Minneapolis South's Jim Westby beat him on the Tigers' first shot of the 11th overtime to win 3-2 in the marathon quarterfinal.

65) Bart Larson, who would later be a long-time assistant to Willard Ikola at Edina and would be head coach at both Edina-West and then Edina after Ikola's retirement.

66) Rod Magnuson, who led the Governors to the 1984 tournament. In the 1951 tourney, Murray was led by Dick Hedenstrom (four goals, one assist) and Fred Swenson (two goals, four assists)

67) Minneapolis Southwest, which lost 3-1 to St. Paul Johnson in the

finals. The brother duos included Dave and Roger Rovick, Ed and George Noble, and Merv and Wayne Meredith. Merv Meredith led the tourney in scoring with six points while the Rovick boys each tallied two assists as Roger, a senior center, was the only Indian to make the all-tournament team for the runner-up from Minneapolis. Roger and Dave Rovick both became instrumental in the growth of Edina Realty, with Roger becoming the Chairman after both played collegiately at Minnesota.

68) Jack Quesnell

69) Roseau, in 1959. Dale Olson, Jim Stordahl, Don Ross, Larry Stordahl, and Dick Roth all earned that status as the Rams won their second consecutive crown.

70) Cliff Strand, who had four goals and three assists as the top scorer that year.

71) Gene (Dudley) Otto. In 1958, Otto backstopped the Packers to the third-place trophy as South St. Paul edged St. Louis Park 3-2. He had 30 saves in a 3-2 overtime win over Minneapolis Roosevelt in the first round.

72) Don Vaia. The Bluejacket backstop had 27 saves in the finals over Eveleth, including 13 in the third period. Vaia had 30 stops in the 3-1 semifinal victory over Minneapolis Southwest and 16 saves in a 10-0 whipping of St. Cloud in the quarterfinals.

73) Gus Hendrickson, who would go on to coach Grand Rapids to their first state title in 1975 and then became the coach at UMD the next season. Hendrickson tallied twice as Eveleth beat Minneapolis Roosevelt 4-1 in the third-place game.

74) George Jetty, who had a hat trick in a quarterfinal hammering of St. Cloud and two goals in a 3-1 win over Minneapolis Southwest in the semifinals.

75) Ken Pedersen, who finished with eight points. Pedersen scored in overtime to give South St. Paul a win over Minneapolis Roosevelt in the first game of the tournament. He scored twice in each game, including a 6-3 loss to Roseau in the semis and the 3-2 win over St. Louis Park in the fifth-place game.

76) Roger Bertelson, who had four goals and an assist.

77) Dan Dilworth. The hard-skating Bronco had a goal and three

assists in 1959 as his team came away with the third-place trophy as he had two assists in the 3-2 win over South St. Paul. Dilworth scored six points in seven games in the 1964 Olympics.

78) 1957; three of the shutouts came in the quarterfinals as Mpls. South bested Edina 6-0, International Falls clobbered Hallock 10-0, and St. Paul Johnson downed South St. Paul 3-0. Edina beat Hallock 4-0 in consolation, International Falls handled Minneapolis South 4-0 in the semifinals, and South nipped Johnson 1-0 for third-place.

79) Minneapolis Roosevelt, which beat St. Paul Washington 4-0 but then lost to northern powers International Falls (3-2 in semis) and Eveleth (4-1 in third-place game). The Teddies played in nine state tournaments.

80) Tom Wahman. The Govies' goalie had a 24-save shutout in a 1-0 quarterfinal win over Roseau, 15 stops in a 3-1 win over Minneapolis South in the semis, and 21 saves in the 3-1 championship game victory over Minneapolis Southwest.

81) Elmer Walls, who beat Teddies' goalie Jerry Gangloff (42 saves).

82) Bob Schmidt, who also became a respected referee and was an official at state for several years. Schmidt scored the only goal for the Governors in the 1951 final, when Johnson lost 4-1 to Eveleth. He had a goal and two assists the next year.

83) Bob Gillie of Williams (one goal in 1949 finals) and Norm Elvig of Minneapolis Central (two goals in 1950 quarterfinals).

84) Three (one each in the second and third periods and one in the 11th overtime). That's right, there were no penalties in the first 10 overtime periods (5 minutes each)!

85) Warren Schaber. Teammates Bob Youngquist (four goals, assist) and Ray Youngberg (three goals, two assists) were also key contributors to the runner-up.

86) Three (3). Cliff Strand scored at 4:30 of the third overtime as the Prowlers beat the Hornets on their way to their second state title in three years. Strand beat Edina's Murray MacPherson, who was sensational between the pipes with 54 saves. He had 10 saves in the first overtime and 13 more in the second extra-session.

87) Gene Picha, who was all-tourney. He had 21 saves in a four-overtime win over St. Louis Park in the quarters, 17 in a six-

goal win over Eveleth in the semis, and 17 more in the 4-1 championship game win over Warroad.

88) A — The number of goals Minneapolis South scored by period in their first-round games versus Thief River Falls (total = 3)

B — The number of goals scored by Thief River Falls by period in their first-round game versus Minneapolis South (total = 2)

C — The number of saves by period made by South goalie Roger Evenson (total = 50)

D — The number of saves by period made by Thief River Falls goalie Rod Collins (Total = 38) Note: Mpls. South won 3-2 in 11 overtimes

89) Bob Lewis

90) Henry Metcalf, who shut out Duluth Central as a sophomore and Edina as a junior. In his final of nine games in the tourney, he made 31 saves as the Packers beat Minneapolis South 2-1 to take the third-place game after two straight years of losing it.

91) Don (Whitey) Willer and Dick (Beaver) Lick. Willer normally wore number 7 and switched to 8, while Lick switched to Willer's number 7. Why? Apparently, Willer was being hounded about not scoring more so they figured he would have a better chance by wearing Lick's jersey, who was known as more of a scorer. Sure enough, the Packer player wearing number 8 scored twice and Lick was credited with the goals but it was really Willer. Whitey's mother never did forgive Lick for the switch!

92) 1955; Minneapolis Southwest beat Eveleth 4-1, Minneapolis South edged Thief River Falls 3-2 (11 overtimes), and St. Paul Johnson nipped Roseau 1-0.

3 The 1960s

1) What school beat defending champ International Falls' 4-3 in 1963, in one of the most thrilling title games in tournament history?

2) What was the nickname for the Bloomington squad that represented Region VI in the 1965 tournament, finishing runner-up in its third appearance in five years?

3) In a scintillating semifinal game in 1966, what Roseau player scored in the third overtime to lead the Rams to a 5-4 triumph over St. Paul Johnson?

4) What St. Paul Murray skater scored a pure hat trick in less than nine minutes in a 5-1 win over Warroad in a 1963 quarterfinal contest?

5) What goalie was an all-tournament selection for first-time entrant Greenway-Coleraine in 1962 and later was a three-year starter for the Gophers under coach John Mariucci?

6) What strong-skating Roseau wing was all-tournament in 1962 and later played at North Dakota before winning two state titles in his first two years as an assistant coach at another northern Minnesota school?

7) After a record 12 consecutive trips to the state hockey tournament in St. Paul, the storied Eveleth Golden Bears sextet made its final appearance in the one-class tourney in what year?

8) Which of the celebrated Hoene boys from Duluth was an all-tournament player for Duluth East and scored the final goal

in the Greyhounds' 3-1 victory in the 1960 final over St. Paul Washington?

9) What flashy International Falls defenseman made the all-tournament team for three straight years and was noted for his wicked slapshot in 1963, 1964, and 1965?

10) Who was the winning goalie for St. Paul Johnson in the '63 tourney when the Govies earned the last of four state championships?

11) What twin brothers provided both scoring touch and a definite physical presence for top-rated Mounds View in 1968?

12) The 1966 state champion International Falls Broncos finished the season undefeated at 26-0. How many times did they trail in a game that season?

13) In 1969, what two teams squared off in a proverbial "David versus Goliath" match in the championship game that became legendary in tournament lore?

14) What coach led South St. Paul to third place in the 1969 tournament after taking over the reigns when "Lefty" Smith left the program to take over the Notre Dame coaching job?

15) What fiery and dynamic head coach brought his alma mater St. Paul Johnson to seven state tourneys, including five straight from 1964-68?

16) Who was the all-tournament netminder for International Falls in 1962 who later went on to star at UMD and for the U.S. Nationals and the 1972 U.S. Olympic hockey team?

17) What future Air Force Academy player scored in overtime to give Greenway-Coleraine a 4-3 win over top-ranked Mounds View in the opening game of the 1968 event?

18) What standout center for International Falls played in four tournaments in the 1960's and helped the powerful Broncos to three state titles in a row, and is considered one of the most accomplished players in tourney history?

19) Which Warroad standout became a force in Minnesota hockey after joining the varsity as an eighth-grader, but didn't get a chance

Mike Antonovich, Greenway-Coleraine center, led the Raiders to state titles in 1967 and 1968. (photo: United States Hockey Hall of Fame Museum)

to wow state tournament crowds at Met Center with his dazzling skating and stick skills until 1969, when he was a senior?

20) What St. Paul Johnson forward scored the overtime winner as his team took the 1963 crown from defending champion International Falls?

21) What forward for Bloomington in 1965 helped take his team to the finals, and later became an NAIA All-American at Bemidji State before coaching Bloomington Lincoln to its only state tourney appearance in 1975?

22) What North St. Paul luminary was the leading scorer in the 1967 tournament with 11 points, scoring six points (five assists) in a 7-6 quarterfinal win over Roseau?

23) Which two teammates tied as leading scorers for the champion Duluth East team in 1960, both earning all-tournament laurels?

24) What Bloomington goalie made 45 saves for his team as they lost 7-0 to a highly-favored International Falls powerhouse in the

1965 championship tilt?

25) What diminutive but creative center ice-man was the tournament's top scorer in both 1968 and 1969 and remains one of the tournament's all-time favorite characters?

26) What South St. Paul defenseman, a stout performer on both ends of the ice, made the all-tourney team in 1965, starred at North Dakota and later was a referee in the tourney and also a coach for Roseau in three tournaments in the 1970's?

27) What future Gopher star scored the overtime winner as St. Paul Johnson beat North St. Paul 5-4 in an exciting 1967 semifinal?

28) What St. Paul Washington star from the 1960 tournament led his team to the title game by scoring three goals and later coached for 31 years in the WCHA?

29) Who were the teams and what was the score in the final state tournament game contested at the St. Paul Auditorium in 1968?

30) What future Gopher coach and U.S. Hockey Hall of Fame inductee played in four state tournaments, earning all-tournament three times?

31) An all-tournament selection on both of Greenway-Coleraine's consecutive title teams in the late 1960's, what Raider defenseman later was a hero on the Itasca Community College squad that won the national junior college tournament in 1972?

32) What future Gopher and U.S. Nationals and Olympian competitor tied for the scoring lead in 1961 for St. Paul Johnson?

33) An imposing presence on the ice with his size, strength, and reach, what International Falls center was all-tourney in both 1962 and 1963 and was the leading scorer in each?

34) Playing four years in the tournament, what deft Roseau senior center scored all four goals in the Rams' 4-2 win over Greenway-Coleraine in a 1966 quarterfinal?

35) A future NFL linebacker for the Green Bay Packers, what high school defenseman was an all-tourney selection in 1966 for another Packer club?

36) What Edina Hornet player scored at 3:09 of sudden-death overtime to give Willard Ikola his first state title as Edina beat Warroad 5-4 in one of the most exciting final games in state history in 1969?

37) In one of the biggest upsets in the 67-year history of the tournament, what school dumped undefeated St. Paul Johnson 3-2 in a 1965 quarterfinal despite being outshot 38-10?

38) Not to be outdone by its school's impressive array of talent on the ice, what team was pumped up by a dynamic pep band that wowed every crowd it performed in front of?

39) What South St. Paul athlete ended up being the superintendent of schools at his alma-mater after playing in the tourney in 1959 and 1960?

40) Which Edina defenseman became the object of boos after heavily checking Warroad star Henry Boucha into the boards and knocking him out of the contest in the second period of the 1969 title game?

41) What Greenway-Coleraine center and future WCHA competitor led the tourney in scoring in 1966 with five goals and three assists as the Raiders copped the consolation prize?

42) In 1963, despite a roster with just three seniors, International Falls finished runner-up. Who were those senior Broncos?

43) Which Minneapolis Roosevelt forward tied for the scoring lead in 1961 as he assisted on five goals for the Teddies, who finished sixth?

44) Which dynamic first-line skaters helped International Falls to championships in 1965 and 1966.

45) Who was the coach for Roseau in the 1968 and 1969 tournaments following the retirement of coaching icon Oscar Almquist?

46) In 1961, what teammates joined Doug Woog from South St. Paul on the all-tourney team for the runner-up Packers?

47) What trio made up a stellar line for state champion Saint Paul Johnson in 1963?

48) What Greenway-Coleraine player scored a goal in each of his team's three games as the Raiders gained the semifinals in 1962? (In their loss, the Raiders were stymied by International Falls goalie Mike Curran, who had 31 saves in a 3-2 Bronco win.)

49) In 1968, what Roseau Ram and future NHLer was second in scoring with six goals and two assists as his team took fifth-place?

50) What talented center was all-tournament for International Falls in 1962, scoring twice and assisting on two others for the Broncos?

51) Which two key International Falls players were ruled ineligible for the 1962-63 season as they had already met their consecutive-semester limit at the school?

52) What team rallied from a 3-1 deficit with three third-period goals to end Greenway-Coleraine's attempt to win three straight titles in 1969?

53) What school made it to state in 1960 but wouldn't return for another 33 years?

54) What future Gopher football star was the starting goalie for St. Paul Harding in 1969?

55) What Roseau wing scored four goals and an assist in 1967 and became an NAIA All-American at Bemidji State?

56) What Minneapolis Washburn product was all-tournament in 1960 (four goals, one assist), a year after scoring three goals and an assist as the school finished with the consolation prize?

57) In 1967, what Hibbing line (all future Division I standouts) challenged opposing defenses mercilessly with their firepower?

58) What three South St. Paul skaters had hat tricks for the runner-up Packers in 1968?

59) In 1967, what Minneapolis Roosevelt standout scored three goals and added five assists for the fourth-place Teddies?

60) What man directed Duluth East to four tournaments, including three in the 1960's?

61) In a tremendous display of courage, what senior defenseman for

International Falls played throughout an overtime loss to St. Paul Johnson in the 1963 finals despite acute appendicitis?

62) Two of the most dynamic and colorful players in tourney history both played in the first-ever tourney at Met Center in 1969 —Mike Antonovich and Henry Boucha. Which schools did they represent and what uniform numbers did those standouts wear?

63) Who led the 1961 champion, Roseau, in goals with four and added a goal and two assists in 1962 when the Rams finished second to International Falls?

64) Who was the starting goaltender for top-rated Mounds View in the 1968 tourney, a guy who went on to be MVP of the MIAC in 1972 and a three-time all-conference player?

65) What future Minnesota legislator was a junior defenseman for South St. Paul in 1966?

66) What future Toronto Maple Leaf player scored a goal and had two assists for Roseau in the 1969 tournament with the Rams finishing fourth?

67) A smooth-skating centerman, what St. Paul Johnson star tallied five goals and two assists for the Governors in 1968, leading his team to a third-place finish?

68) What influential man in Minnesota hockey circles coached Minneapolis Patrick Henry to the state tournament in 1964?

69) One of the most important awards given out at the University of Minnesota hockey banquet each year is the one that goes to the Most Determined Player. What former St. Paul Johnson and Gopher player is it named in honor of?

70) A future head coach who would win a state title, what Roseau goalie was an easy all-tournament pick as he set a then-tournament record with 119 saves in 1966?

71) What Mounds View forward in 1968 donned a Space Age helmet and skated around the St. Paul Auditorium ice looking like a Martian?

72) What North St. Paul puckster (1967) became the Gopher captain and MVP (1971), played on the U.S. Olympic team in Japan (1972), and later became a revered minister in the metro area?

73) What star player and future tourney coach scored in his first eight games in tournament play before his team was shut out 1-0 in the championship game in 1961?

74) What Roseau goalie was the backstop for the Rams in both the 1961 and 1962 title games?

75) In the 1964 tournament, what St. Paul Johnson goalie racked up shutouts in both the quarterfinals and the semifinals?

76) Tied 1-1 after two periods in the 1968 final, what Greenway-Coleraine line erupted for five goals in a decisive 6-1 victory over South St. Paul?

77) What two players were the epitome of the term "defensive" defenseman for Edina in 1968, 1969, and 1970?

78) Who was the standout goaltender for South St. Paul in the 1966 tournament, allowing just four goals in the three games as the Packers copped third place?

79) What Mpls. Southwest senior center was all-tourney in 1969 after recording two goals and five assists and had a brother who played goalie for the Indians?

80) For 16 years (1949-64), the Region 3 representative at state was predetermined. The runner-up from Region 7 and 8 would fill the spot, alternating annually. Which region appeared at state in even-numbered years and which ones went in odd-numbered years?

81) In the 1966 consolation title game, what school took an 8-0 lead after two periods on just 21 shots, eventually claiming a 10-4 win over White Bear Lake?

82) What team won the state title in 1966 by scoring 186 goals and allowing just 28?

83) In 1965, what St. Paul Johnson goalie faced just four shots in his team's third-place 3-0 win over South St. Paul, a day after facing just 11 shots in a 3-2 semifinal loss to underdog Bloomington?

84) Who was the winning goalie for Edina in their storied 5-4 overtime win over Warroad in the 1969 championship game?

85) What Roseau forward scored three goals for the runner-up Rams in 1962 and three goals and an assist in 1963 as his team finished third?

86) Which Alexander Ramsey skater participated in three tournaments from 1963-65, totaling four goals and three assists in helping his team to consolation titles as both a sophomore and senior?

87) What man coached Bloomington to its first two state appearances in 1961 and 1964?

88) International Falls won three straight championships from 1964 to 1966. Which four Broncos played on all of those teams?

89) An all-tourney selection in 1961, 1962, and 1963, what Roseau skater scored six goals and two assists during those three tournaments as the Rams finished first, second, and third, respectively, during those seasons?

90) Mike Baumgartner and Mike Lundbohm each played in three state tournaments and were teammates for two seasons with which school?

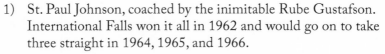

◄   ANSWERS TO CHAPTER 3 - THE 1960s   ►

1) St. Paul Johnson, coached by the inimitable Rube Gustafson. International Falls won it all in 1962 and would go on to take three straight in 1964, 1965, and 1966.

2) Bears. The Bloomington district renamed Bloomington High School, located on Penn Ave. as Bloomington Abraham Lincoln in the fall of 1965 when the second high school (John F. Kennedy) was opened up. Lincoln's final year as a school was 1981-82. Thomas Jefferson High School was started in 1970. Lincoln's colors, incidentally, were gold, green, and white, just like the original Bloomington high school.

3) Rocky Ammerman. His wrist shot at 7:06 of the third extra-session sent Roseau to the finals, where they were beaten 5-0 by two-time defending champ International Falls.

4) Jim Nyland, whose three tallies came within an 8:19-second span combining the first and second periods. It was the last of Murray's six trips to state; the others came in 1949, 1950, 1951, 1957, and 1958.

5) John Lothrop, whose Raiders were beaten 3-2 by Iron Range Conference rival International Falls in a tense semifinal. His son, Brent, was a goalie for Burnsville in the 1990 event.

6) Paul Rygh. The former Ram was a key assistant to Bob Gernander at Greenway-Coleraine when the Raiders won back-to-back crowns in 1967 and 1968.

7) 1960; Eveleth had gone three years without earning a berth in the tournament. They lost twice by a single goal to both Minneapolis Patrick Henry and Edina. Eveleth combined with neighboring Gilbert and won a Tier II title in 1993 and a Class A crown in 1998.

8) Mike, who had two goals and three assists overall. Mike's brother Bob was a teammate on the title team from the Twin Ports. In 1961, the Hoene boys were back in the tourney and finished third when Bill Sivertson scored in overtime to nip St. Paul Johnson. East lost 2-1 in the semifinals to South St. Paul, which got 36 saves from goalie Gary McAlpine. Peter Hoene, their younger brother, played for Henry Sibley in the 1976 tourney. Mike, Bob, and Peter were cousins to Phil (UMD), Kevin (Notre Dame), and Dick Hoene (North Dakota), who all played Division I hockey. Phil later played in the NHL with Los Angeles.

9) Gary Wood, who had three goals in 1963, one in 1964, and a goal and five assists in 1965.

10) Hank Remachel, who had 31 saves in the finals and 28 in the semifinals versus Roseau.

11) Brad and Bart Buetow, who were both 6'5" and over 200 pounds, considered to be giants at the time. Bart was all-tourney with four goals and an assist while Brad had an assist. Both were all-state in hockey, football, and track at Mounds View and, incredibly, both also played all three sports at Minnesota. Brad was the head coach

83

at Minnesota for seven seasons in the 1980's and logged a record of 175-100-20; he also coached at U.S. International and Colorado College. Bart played professional football in Canada and in the NFL with the Giants and Vikings.

12) Twice. One of those deficits came in the semifinals when they trailed South St. Paul but rallied to win 2-1 to advance and later beat Roseau 5-0 to earn their title.

13) Warroad and Edina. The Hornets won 5-4 in overtime in one of the most memorable games in prep hockey history.

14) Denny Tetu. He also brought teams to state in 1972 and 1977.

15) Lou Cotroneo. The buoyant Cotroneo finished runner-up twice, second to International Falls in his first season at the helm in 1964 and second to Greenway-Coleraine in 1967.

16) Mike "Lefty" Curran, who had a 29-save shutout in the 1962 final against Roseau.

17) Dave Stangl, with assists to Mike Meade and Mike Antonovich. Stangl was all-tourney.

18) Tim Sheehy. He would later star at Boston College, earning All-American status twice and played on the 1972 Olympic team and for teams in both the NHL and the World Hockey Association. Sheehy had three goals as a 10th-grader, three goals and an assist as an 11th-grader and three goals and an assist as a 12th-grader.

19) Henry Boucha. The lanky defenseman astounded the fans with his end-to-end rushes and his stamina as he rarely left the ice during his teams games. The Warriors lost 5-4 in overtime to Edina after Boucha was seriously hurt in the middle period. Boucha had two goals and three assists in his only tournament appearance. He was drafted by the Red Wings and played on the 1972 U.S. Olympic team. After starting his NHL career with Detroit, he played with the Colorado Rockies and the Kansas City Scouts before his career ended due to an eye injury while playing for the North Stars when Boston's Dave Forbes butt-ended him. Coincidentally, he was injured on the same ice surface where his high school career ended. Boucha scored 60 goals as a senior at Warroad.

20) Rob Shattuck. After scoring three times earlier in the tourney, Shattuck took a pass from linemate Mike Crupi and beat Falls'

netminder Larry Roche at 4:31 of overtime. Shattuck also scored both of Johnson's goals in a 2-1 semifinal victory over Roseau.

21) Terry Bergstrom, who had two assists.

22) Craig Sarner, who had the record for assists in a single tournament until it was broken in 1993. North St. Paul finished fourth, losing to Hibbing 6-4 in the third-place game as Sarner had three assists. Sarner played for Glen Sonmor at the "U" and for the 1976 U.S. Olympic team after playing seven games for the Boston Bruins. He was a star in Europe for many years.

23) Jim Ross (three goals, three assists) and Bill Sivertson (five goals, one assist). Ross, Sivertson, and Mike Hoene were all-tournament for the Port City champs.

24) Terry Smith. The record stood for the most saves in a title game until Edina-East's Gary Aulik had 48 saves in a 5-4 double-overtime win over Grand Rapids in 1978. Smith also had 36 saves in a 3-2 upset over St. Paul Johnson the night before.

25) Mike Antonovich. The Raider dynamo was the catalyst as Greenway won consecutive crowns in 1967 and 1968. Antonovich was the leading scorer in 1968 and 1969, when his team had to settle for the consolation prize. He had three goals and six assists his junior year and seven goals and an assist in his senior year. He finished with 22 points in nine games of tournament action.

26) Terry Abram. His 1971 Roseau team lost 1-0 to Edina in that year's final. Abram was an All-American at North Dakota in 1967-68.

27) Ron Peltier. He scored six points (four goals) in the tourney as his team succumbed to Greenway-Coleraine 4-2 in the 1967 final. Ron, who also played in both 1965 and 1966, was all-tourney with his brother Doug, who was all-tournament in both 1967 and 1968.

28) Jeff Sauer. Washington lost 3-1 to Duluth East in that 1960 final. Sauer won 655 games as a college coach at both Colorado College and Wisconsin, including two NCAA titles with the Badgers in 1982 and 1990.

29) Greenway beat South St. Paul 6-1 on February 24, 1968. The next year, the tourney moved to the Metropolitan Sports Center in Bloomington, the home of the North Stars.

30) Doug Woog. After scoring four goals as a freshman in 1959, Woog scored three goals and added three assists as sophomore in 1960. As a junior, he had three goals when the Packers lost a tense 1-0 final to Roseau. As a senior, he tallied two goals and four assists with South St. Paul claiming the third-place trophy.

31) Ken Lawson, whose brother Gary was a key performer on the 1967 team. His cousin, Bobby, was a regular on the 1968 team and a veteran on three tourney teams. Ken had three goals and an assist in 1967 and a goal and three assists in 1968 as team captain.

32) Craig Falkman, who tallied all his five points on goals to tie teammate Tom Brindley and Minneapolis Roosevelt forward Jon Hall for the honor. Hall would go on to be a teammate of Falkman at Minnesota. Falkman scored four consecutive goals in Johnson's fifth-place game with teammate Mike Gabriel adding four assists.

33) Jim Amidon, who tied Bronco teammate Glen Blumer with six points in leading them to the 1962 title. Amidon had eight points (four goals, four assists) in 1963 as his team fell 4-3 in overtime to St. Paul Johnson in one of the most memorable title games.

34) Bryan Grand, who would later become an All-American at Bemidji State and coached the Bemidji High Lumberjacks to two tournaments in the 1980's.

35) Jim Carter was a big hitter for the South St. Paul Packers in 1966 and also scored two goals as his team finished in third-place. South St. Paul lost a close 2-1 semifinal to champion International Falls. Carter played both football and hockey at Minnesota before a nine-year career at middle linebacker for Green Bay, including one Pro Bowl season.

36) Skip Thomas, who beat Warrior goalie Jeff Hallett with a slapshot from the right point.

37) Bloomington, which got two goals from Jack Nichols and 36 saves from Terry Smith.

38) International Falls ("The Dirty Dozen")

39) Dave Metzen, who captained the Gopher hockey squad in 1964. Metzen was also the head of the Board of Regents for the University of Minnesota from 2003-05.

40) Jim Knutson. After an end-to-end rush, Boucha's shot rebounded into the corner as both players tried to retrieve the puck. Knutson

elbowed Boucha and his head crashed into the glass. The hit ruptured his eardrum and forced him from the game and to the hospital. Warroad, down 4-2, rallied to force overtime on two Frank Krahn goals but Edina prevailed to win 5-4 in overtime.

41) Bobby Tok, who later played at UMD and was also a first-rate referee in the tournament.

42) Larry Roche, Les Eklund, and Kip Narbo.

43) Jon Hall, who also served as an on-ice official for three years.

44) Center Tim Sheehy, left wing Dan Mahle, and right wing Pete Hegg. Sheehy was all-tournament three times and all three were on three straight title winners. Mahle had a tournament-high five goals in 1965, including a hat trick in the finals.

45) Francis Macioh, who had played in the tourney in the first tournament for St. Paul Washington and scored a goal. Roseau won consolation honors in 1968.

46) Gary McAlpine and Vince Egan.

47) Mike Crupi, Greg Hughes, and Rob Shattuck. Shattuck had four goals, Hughes a goal and three assists, and Crupi a goal and two assists. As seniors in 1964, the trio all made all-tournament as the Governors lost 7-4 in yet another championship battle with their northern rivals. Hughes had four goals and two assists, Shattuck three goals and four assists, and Crupi three goals and two assists.

48) Jack Stebe

49) Earl Anderson, who played in the NHL for both Detroit and Boston, also scored two goals in the 1969 tourney as the Rams lost two one-goal games and were ousted. Earl had starred at North Dakota for three years and remains one of Don Cherry's most inspiring players. Anderson also has served as an on-ice official on nine occasions.

50) Keith "Huffer" Christiansen, who was an All-American at UMD and totaled 196 points in 102 career games for the Bulldogs and was elected to the U.S. Hockey Hall of Fame.

51) Bob O'Leary and Keith Christiansen. Both boys were from neighboring Fort Frances, Ontario, but were living with Christiansen's uncle in International Falls. The previous year each player had scored two goals for the title team.

52) South St. Paul. Ken Madden scored shorthanded from center ice with 19 seconds left in regulation as the Packers got revenge for their 6-1 loss in the 1968 title game.

53) Eveleth, which lost both games by one goal to Minneapolis Patrick Henry and Edina. In 1993, Eveleth finally returned to the tourney as a consolidated program. Eveleth-Gilbert won the second Tier II tourney with a 3-2 win over Lake of the Woods/Baudette.

54) Ollie Bakken, whose Knights were outscored 10-1 in losses to Roseau and Minneapolis Southwest. Bakken played linebacker on defense for Cal Stoll's clubs and was the team MVP in 1974. Bakken was drafted by the Vikings in 1975.

55) Bruce Falk, who played on the U.S. National team in 1970.

56) John Simus, who was also all-tourney in 1959, when the Millers finished second.

57) Bill Baldrica, Mark Barbato, and Bob Collyard, who helped the Bluejackets to the third place trophy with a 6-4 win over North St. Paul as Baldrica scored a hat trick. Collyard had two goals and six assists and Barbato tallied three times. Hibbing lost to champion Greenway-Coleraine 4-3 in a tense semifinal, the third time that they had lost to the Raiders by a single goal in the post-season as they also lost heartbreakers to their Iron Range Conference rivals in both district and region play. In all, the teams faced each other five times that season, with four one-goal Greenway wins and one tie.

58) Dale Abram, Joe Bonk, and Terry Madland.

59) Steve Hall, who played for Glen Sonmor at the U of M, also had an assist in the 1966 tourney when Roosevelt was eliminated after two losses. Hall's older brothers Tom (1958), and Jon (1961, 1962) also played for Roosevelt in tournament action.

60) Glenn Rolle. The Greyhounds won the 1960 title by beating St. Paul Washington 3-1. He also led East to the 1961 tourney when they finished third.

61) Dick Haugland, who had an appendectomy the next day. He played at Colorado College for Bob Johnson with fellow International Falls products Jim Amidon and Glen Blumer.

62) Antonovich wore "12" for Greenway-Coleraine and Boucha "16" for Warroad.

63) Dick Ulvin, a junior wing. Ulvin had a hat trick in a 4-3 semifinal triumph over North St. Paul and the game-winner at 5:25 of the third overtime on an assist to Bob Lillo.

64) Mike Schuett, whose Mustangs finished a disappointing sixth after losing 3-2 to Roseau in the fifth-place game when he made 26 saves. Schuett played collegiately for St. Mary's in Winona.

65) Tom Pugh, a Dartmouth grad who became the Minority Leader of the Minnesota House of Representatives for five years as a member of the DFL.

Larry Ross, the legendary coach of International Falls for 31 seasons, brought the Broncos to 14 state tournaments. Ross won six state titles, including three straight from 1964 to 1966. (Photo: United States Hockey Hall of Fame Museum)

66) Dale Smedsmo, who played briefly for the Maple Leafs but also played for three teams in the World Hockey Association. Smedsmo's step-son is Dustin Byfuglien, a defenseman for the Winnipeg Jets who was on a Stanley Cup winner with Chicago in 2010. Smedsmo officiated in six straight tourneys (1990-95), too.

67) Doug Peltier, who scored twice in the consolation title game over Southwest. He would be one of Glen Sonmor's top players with Minnesota, playing with older brother Ron.

68) Harry Brown, who guided the Patriots to third place as all-tourney pick Dick Subject totaled five points (three goals, two assists). Brown, who also coached Vocational and North, became instrumental in the growth of junior hockey in Minnesota.

69) Mike Crupi, who died in an auto accident in 1969. Crupi, who was injured in the 1963 title game, returned from a doctor's exam mid-game to get an assist on the game-winner.

70) Jim Nelson. He had 39 stops in the 1966 title game, a 5-0 loss to International Falls, 50 saves in a 5-4 three-overtime win over Johnson in the semis, and 30 stops in a 4-2 first-round win over Greenway-Coleraine. Nelson led Grand Rapids to the state title in 1976. Under his leadership, the Indians were also third in 1977 and second in 1978.

71) Don Hermes, who scored two goals and two assists for Tom Wegleitner's club. Hermes had suffered a concussion earlier in the season and was forced to wear a more protective head-gear, which had large holes in the outer shell.

72) Frank Sanders, who had a goal and an assist for the fourth-place Polars. Sanders, known for his toughness and fighting ability, played for the Fighting Saints in their first season in 1972-73 but quit the game to enter the religious life.

73) Doug Woog. The Packer center would go on to score in two of three games in 1962 when South St. Paul finished third. In 12 tournament games, Woog totaled 12 goals and seven assists.

74) Gary Johnson. He had a 14-save shutout of South St. Paul in 1961 but lost 4-0 to International Falls in 1962. In the first two games of that tourney, he gave up just two total goals.

75) Rich Peterson. The Govies' goalie had 12 saves in a 4-0 win over Alexander Ramsey and 18 more in a 9-0 whitewash of Minneapolis Henry in the semis. In the finals, however, he gave up seven goals and had just 17 saves in Johnson's 7-3 loss to International Falls.

76) Mike Antonovich (two goals, two assists), Tom Peluso (two goals, assist), and Jim Stephens (goal, assist).

77) Bill Nyrop and Steve Curry, who both were mainstays on the blue line as Edina won its first state title in 1969 and finished second in 1970. They both played at Notre Dame for four years and Nyrop would win a Stanley Cup in each of his three seasons with Montreal. Nyrop died tragically at age 43 of colon cancer.

78) Jim Quirk, who made 77 saves on 81 shots to earn all-tourney status.

79) Dixon Shelstad. His brother Brad was the starting goalie for Southwest from 1968 to 70 and his older brother Jeff coached Hastings to the tourney in 1971.

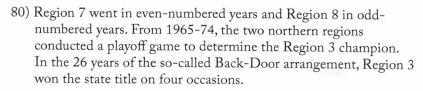

80) Region 7 went in even-numbered years and Region 8 in odd-numbered years. From 1965-74, the two northern regions conducted a playoff game to determine the Region 3 champion. In the 26 years of the so-called Back-Door arrangement, Region 3 won the state title on four occasions.

81) Greenway-Coleraine. The Raiders were led by Bob Tok's hat trick and Kent Nyberg's two goals and two assists.

82) International Falls, which beat Roseau 5-0 in the finals and is regarded by many as one of the top three or four teams in history.

83) Jim Resch

84) Jim Hastings, who had 30 saves for the Hornets. He also had 18 saves in a 7-1 semifinal win over South St. Paul and a 14-save shutout in a 5-0 victory over Mounds View.

85) Larry Skime, who was all-tourney as a senior.

86) Rick Wickre, an all-tourney performer as a junior for coach Gordy Genz.

87) Blake Jaskowiak. Unfortunately, the Bears lost both games in each tourney as they were outscored 23-5 overall in the four defeats.

88) Tim Sheehy, Peter Hegg, Steve Ross, and Ron Beck.

89) Bob Lillo, who is one of only 13 players to earn such status.

90) Roseau. Baumgartner was all-tourney in 1966 and 1967 (two goals and three assists) while Lundbohm was all-tourney in 1968 when he scored three goals and added five assists a year after notching five goals. The Rams earned a trip to state each year in the 1960's, except for 1960.

4 The 1970s

1) Only one team during the 1970s had a perfect season (undefeated and untied). Can you name it?

2) How many times did Willard Ikola's teams finish first or second during the decade?

3) What president and publisher of the periodic puck newspaper, *Let's Play Hockey*, played defense for Minneapolis Roosevelt in the 1974 tournament?

4) What eighth-grader played for Greenway-Coleraine in the 1970 tournament?

5) Which school became the first private school to play in the tournament in 1975, the first year that the MSHSL admitted private, Catholic, or independent schools into the post-season extravaganza?

6) When the tourney returned to St. Paul in 1976 after a seven-year hiatus in Bloomington, what was the most unique feature of the St. Paul Civic Center, according to many?

7) Which dynamite brother duo led Rochester John Marshall to the 1977 title with a heart-pounding 4-2 win over Edina-East in that year's final?

8) Which school scored four goals in a 3:19-minute span to break a 2-2 tie after two periods and went on to win the state title 6-3 over Alexander Ramsey in 1973?

9) What Henry Sibley star forward led the Warriors to the 1973 and 1974 state tournaments?

10) What immensely-talented Edina-East defenseman captained the Hornets to the 1974 title and later starred at Wisconsin?

11) What junior wing for Grand Rapids led the 1974 tourney in scoring (five goals and two assists) and later starred at UMD and was drafted by both the NHL and the WHA?

12) In Bloomington Lincoln's only tourney appearance in 1975, what future Gopher All-American was the team's scoring sensation?

13) One of the most-storied rallies in tourney history occurred in a 1974 semifinal, when what school stormed back from a 3-0 deficit to defeat Henry Sibley by tallying five times in the third period?

14) What Hibbing junior center was the catalyst on the 1970 Hibbing club and later earned All-American status with the Gophers in 1975 and eventually became a solid NHL defensive specialist and penalty-killer?

15) Three sons of a Minnesota Vikings' general manager played for Willard Ikola in the 1970's. What were their names?

16) What gangly forward, who led Hastings to the 1971 tournament, would later go on to play eight seasons in the NHL with Minnesota, New York, and Atlanta?

17) What future NHL blue-liner and All-Star scored twice for Bemidji in an 8-3 quarterfinal loss to International Falls in 1972?

18) A classic final in 1970 pitted two neighboring schools against one another. Who scored the overtime winner when a shot from the point deflected off his upper torso and into the net to give Minneapolis Southwest a 1-0 victory?

19) In what year were the players first required to wear facemasks?

20) In an eight-year span from 1974 to 1981, what school had one of the best runs in tourney history by winning three championships and claiming one second-place finish, two third-place finishes, and two consolation titles besides?

21) A future All-American at Bemidji State, what Alexander Ramsey center was stellar for coach Gordy Genz in both 1971 and 1972 with his crafty puck-handling and passing?

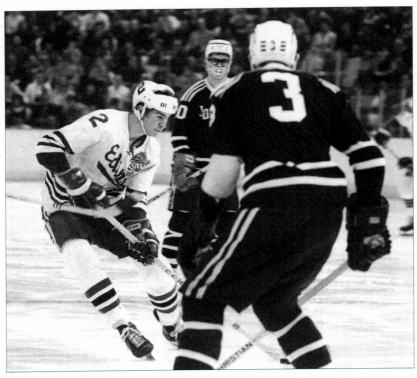

Bill Nyrop of Edina moved the puck up ice against St. Paul Johnson in a 1970 semifinal. (photo: Dave Johnson)

22) What school from the 1970's entered the tourney 23-0 and had scored at least 10 goals in 11 of their pre-state tournament contests?

23) Which two Iron Range Conference and Region 7 rivals vied for the 1972 state crown?

24) What school won a title in 1978 despite being outshot 52-23 in the title game?

25) What Minneapolis Roosevelt senior defenseman, a mainstay for the Teddies in the 1974 tourney, was noted for his blazing slapshot?

26) What Grand Rapids defenseman played twice in the tourney for the Indians in the mid-1970's and later was an All-American at the U of M and played an integral role on the 1980 U.S. Olympic gold-medal winning team?

27) Once the leading goal-scorer in the tourney, a decade later he coached Henry Sibley to four straight appearances from 1973 to 1976. Who was this player turned coach?

28) What St. Paul Johnson center scored the winning goal in the Governors' stunning 5-4 five-overtime triumph over Greenway-Coleraine in a 1970 quarterfinal?

29) What feature on the helmets of Grand Rapids players made the Indian skaters stand out as the school made seven tourney appearances in the 1970's?

30) Earlier overshadowed by teammate Henry Boucha, what Warroad defenseman (1969, 1970) was an all-stater for the Warriors and later played in the WHA and the NHL?

31) In what year did six of the eleven tournament games go into overtime—the most ever?

32) What Minneapolis Roosevelt player was a blue-line star for the Teddies in the 1978 tourney, when they lost 3-2 to eventual champ Edina-East in the opening round?

33) On a team loaded with offensive firepower, which Grand Rapids forward was the leading scorer with nine points as the Indians won their first state crown in 1975?

34) Who was the captain of the 1976 Hill-Murray team that copped third-place at the tournament? (He later played at Providence and coached his alma mater to a state title.)

35) What lanky Hibbing center, who later starred at defense for Herb Brooks at the U of M, led his team to the school's second-ever title in 1973 and also led the tourney in scoring with 11 points (seven goals and four assists)?

36) What rough-and-tumble winger was a force for St. Paul Harding in the mid-1970's and would later be a solid two-way player for nine years with the Philadelphia Flyers before ending his playing career with the North Stars?

37) Which of the Broten brothers who starred for Roseau in the late 1970s scored more tournament points, Neal or Aaron?

38) What White Bear Lake wing from 1970 became a key member of the 1971 Gopher team that lost to Boston University in the NCAA finals?

39) What Grand Rapids center played three years in the tourney for Grand Rapids and was a major force in the Indians' titles in both 1975 and 1976, and then became a prolific scorer at UMD, where he became the Bulldogs all-time leading scorer?

40) What versatile and shifty centerman was the key forward for Mounds View in the 1976 tournament, although his team lost two 4-3 decisions to finish sixth?

41) Before coaching Apple Valley (1992, 1993) and Hibbing (1994, 2003, 2004, 2011) to state tourney berths, what forward played in the tournament for the Grand Rapids Indians in the 1970s?

42) What Duluth East wing scored three goals for the Greyhounds in the 1975 tourney, and later was a strong player for Herb Brooks' Gopher teams in the late 1970's, eventually earning a roster spot on the 1980 U.S. Olympic team?

43) What two powerhouses met at the tournament two years in succession during the 1970s, with both games being decided in overtime?

44) What St. Paul Johnson defenseman did yeoman duty for Lou Cotroneo's 1970 and 1971 state entrants and later became an All-American at Minnesota in 1975?

45) What respected hockey writer gave the Grand Rapids Indians clubs of the 1970's the following nickname - "The Halloween Machine"?

46) What junior goaltender for St. Paul Johnson set a record that stood for 26 years when he made 61 saves, many of a spectacular nature, in an opening-round game in 1970?

47) A future Gopher defenseman, he played four years for his father at Hibbing as a tough and tenacious defender and later was head coach at St. Cloud State and Ferris State before engaging in a long career as an NHL scout? Who was he?

48) Which two South St. Paul teammates tied for the scoring lead in 1972 with six points, as each scored two goals and assisted on four others with the Packers finishing fourth?

49) Which talented Hill-Murray backstop was the first to play between the pipes at the tourney for coach Terry Skrypek, as Hill-Murray copped third-place in their first appearance in 1975?

50) What Edina wing (one of several swift Hornet forwards in that era) skated so fast that his jersey flew past him like the American flag in a tempest? (He played in the last of three tournaments in 1970 and played four collegiate seasons at Denver.)

51) He was a sturdy all-around defenseman for Grand Rapids on their title teams of 1975 and 1976 but missed out on a championship in his senior season in 1977, when Edina-East outlasted the Indians 6-5 in the semifinals. Who was this player who later went on to even greater fame in another capacity?

52) What was the main reason 21 more teams were eligible for the state boys' hockey tournament in 1975 than the previous season?

53) When International Falls won their sixth state crown in 1972, who was the acrobatic goalie for Larry Ross' Broncos?

54) In the first quarterfinal game of the 1970 tournament between Minneapolis Southwest and North St. Paul, what rare occurrence happened not just once but twice?

55) Which Edina goalie earned the shutout in the Hornets' 1-0 win over Roseau in the 1971 title game for their second state title in three years?

56) In a 1974 first-round match pitting Edina-East and St. Paul Harding, what two Edina-East skaters both scored hat tricks as the Hornets throttled the Knights 9-0?

57) Who were the goalie counterparts matched up in the 1977 final between Rochester John Marshall and Edina-East?

58) What two South St. Paul brothers from the 1972 Packer team were sons of a former Gopher All-American, a U.S. Olympian, a state tournament coach, and NHL player?

59) This Greenway-Coleraine wing (who later starred at Denver) possessed one of the best snapshots in tourney history and was an all-tournament selection in both 1969 and 1970. Who was this Raider, who also played on the 1968 title team?

60) In the thrilling 1970 championship game, Edina speedster Bobby Krieger was stopped on a breakaway deke by what Minneapolis Southwest goalie with 10 seconds remaining in regulation, forcing overtime?

61) In Hill-Murray's first-ever appearance in 1975, what senior center served as a solid two-way player? (Hint: his brother was a valued assistant coach.)

62) In what year during this decade was the all-tournament team selected for the final time before being reintroduced in the 1990s?

63) A future Gopher netminder, this Grand Rapids goalie was a fine puck-handler and backstop as the Indians won the 1976 title. Who was this three-time participant?

64) A future Gopher hero and Olympian immortalized with the 1980 U.S. Olympic team, what sharpshooting center led the tournament in scoring for Richfield in 1976?

65) Who served as the back-up goalie to starter Brad Shelstad on the 1969 Southwest team and later would be a co-head coach for Warroad when they copped the 2005 Class A title?

66) Who was the only freshman on the Roseau Ram state tourney team in 1975?

67) What school made its only appearance in the 22 years of its hockey program in 1974?

68) What school had 16 of the 18 players on its 1976 tournament roster play Division I hockey?

69) What Henry Sibley forward became a major factor in helping the Warriors get to the tourney in 1976 after transferring from Archbishop Brady, a Catholic school in West St. Paul?

70) What rugged Hopkins Lindbergh defenseman was a tough

presence all over the ice in 1975 for coach Dave Lund?

71) What classy, play-making center from Minneapolis Washburn recorded a hat trick in the second period of the Millers' 5-1 victory over St. Paul Harding in a 1979 consolation game?

72) What school won a title in the decade with just four seniors, a great accomplishment in an era with 18-man rosters?

73) What Roseau defenseman played on the 1976 U.S. Olympic team and was a sturdy blue-liner for the Rams in the 1971 tourney?

74) Who was the goaltender for the state champion Hibbing Bluejackets in 1973?

75) What future North Star defenseman played wing for Hill-Murray in 1978 and 1979?

76) A former assistant to Tom Wegleitner at Mounds View, who was the head coach at Irondale when they made the first of three consecutive tournament appearances in 1979?

77) Blessed with a bundle of talent, what Minneapolis Southwest defenseman played in four straight tournaments for Dave Peterson's Indians?

78) What Alexander Ramsey player from the 1971 and 1972 tournaments played six games in the NHL with Detroit and Los Angeles?

79) What gentleman served as the assistant to head coach Gene Sack with the Rochester John Marshall squads of 1977, 1978, and 1979?

80) What Edina-East Hornet player from 1977 was a senior center and the son of a former North Star and Fighting Saint forward?

81) Which Region 7 team was beaten by five goals (8-3) in the 1973 regional final but came back as the Region 3 representative at state to beat the same team 5-4 on their way to the title?

82) In the 1977 tournament, what school could boast that they not only held down the vaunted Roseau first-line of Broten, Broten, and Erickson but shut them out?

83) Possessor of one of the quickest and hardest wrist shots in high school annals, what future Gopher and North Star wing notched hat tricks in two games in the 1979 event?

84) In one of the most amazing offensive displays in tourney history, what school pumped a dozen goals into the Roseau net in a jaw-dropping semifinal win in 1979?

85) Which Edina-East forward scored the game-winner with 54 seconds remaining in a 4-3 victory over Minneapolis Roosevelt in a 1978 first-round contest?

86) What Rochester John Marshall standout and future Colorado College star had a goal and four assists in 1977 to help the Rockets win the state title?

87) A defenseman for Dave Peterson's Minneapolis Southwest teams from 1970 to 1972, who was this three-year regular who later played on an NCAA champion, in the Olympics, and in the NHL?

88) Which school was able to defeat the same undefeated team two years in succession in 1977 (quarterfinals) and 1978 (semifinals)?

89) What Hibbing senior scored a hat trick to give the Region 7 representative a 4-1 third-place win over St. Paul Johnson in 1970?

90) What four players made all-tourney for International Falls in 1972 as the Broncos won the last of Larry Ross's six state titles?

91) Which North St. Paul player scored game-winning goals in consecutive games in consolation play to help the Polars claim fifth-place in 1970?

92) What Minneapolis Southwest player followed his four older brothers by playing for the school in the state tournament in 1975 and 1976, and also became the fifth and final member of his family to compete for the Minnesota Gophers?

1) Edina-East (1974). They went 24-0, beating Bemidji 6-0 to cap a perfect season. Minneapolis Southwest was 24-0-1 in 1970.

2) Six. Ikola won state titles in 1971, 1974, 1978, and 1979 and was second in 1970 and 1977.

3) Doug Johnson, who later played collegiately at St. Thomas, has been the managing editor of "Let's Play Hockey" magazine since 1986.

4) Tim Lawson, a future UMD player. His brother, Bobby, was a senior captain for the Raiders and all-state defenseman that year and played under Rube Bjorkman at North Dakota. Their father, Bob "Beefy" Lawson was a referee in several tournaments.

5) Hill-Murray. The Pioneers, coached by Terry Skrypek, finished third in the first of many forays into the tournament. They were undefeated until losing to eventual-champion Grand Rapids in the semifinals.

6) The clear plexiglass boards that surrounded the rink.

7) Scott and Todd Lecy. Scott scored twice in the finals, including the go-ahead goal and Todd added an empty-netter for the Rockets. A senior, Scott tied for the scoring lead with Scott Kleinendorst of Grand Rapids with seven points and also scored the only goal in a 1-0 win over South St. Paul in the semifinals.

8) Hibbing. Two of the goals came off the stick of George Perpich, Jr., the son of head coach George Perpich, Sr. and the other two came from future NHL player Joe Micheletti.

9) Doug Spoden, who matriculated to UMD, had two goals and three assists for the Warriors. They finished fourth after losing a 3-0 third-period lead to Edina in the 1974 semifinals. Spoden had scored Sibley's only goal in two losses in 1973.

10) Craig Norwich, who controlled the flow of all three games. Norwich had five assists for the champion Hornets in 1974 and was a three-year state participant. Norwich is the first and only defenseman to lead his college team in scoring in a year in which it won the NCAA title (1977). He also played in over 100 games in the NHL.

11) John Rothstein, who also had three goals and five assists in 1975, when Rapids claimed their first state championship.

12) Tim Harrer, who went on to score 53 goals for the U of M in 1979-80 to earn All-American status. Harrer scored one goal as a junior in 1975 while his brother, Mike, who also competed for the Gophers, played as a sophomore.

13) Edina-East. The Hornets got two goals from Charlie Peterson and single tallies from Dick Pavek, Billy Thayer, and Bob Frawley and two assists each from Craig Norwich and Steve Polsfuss. The five goals came in a 6:09 span after Doug Spoden had given the upstart Warriors a three-goal cushion; Bob Baumgartner had scored two first-period goals for Sibley.

14) Mike Polich, who was the key forward for the third-place Bluejackets in his junior season. Polich had two goals and an assist in the 1970 tourney. So accomplished was he with his defensive skills, he was nicknamed "The Shadow" during his pro career with Montreal and the North Stars, where he was a three-year regular.

15) Jim, Dan, and Dave Finks, all sons of Jim Finks, Sr. The elder, a former NFL quarterback, was the Vikings' G.M. from 1964-74 and later was with the Bears when they won the Super Bowl in 1985 and with the Saints, too. Jim, Jr. played on the 1970 team that finished second, while Dan played on the 1971 title team and in 1972, also. Dave was on the 1974 team that went undefeated.

16) Dean Talafous, who had two goals and three assists as Hastings copped the consolation title. At 6'4", his great reach and expert stick-handling made him a real threat on offense. After being a Gopher assistant, Talafous took the coaching reigns at Wisconsin-River Falls and led the Falcons to the 1995 Division II title. In college, Talafous was the MVP of the NCAA tournament in 1973 when the Badgers won it all.

17) Gary Sargent. The powerful Sargent, a formidable physical force with tons of stamina, was an All-American at Bemidji State before playing for both the L.A. Kings and the North Stars. He played in over 400 NHL games but retired due to injuries. A cousin to Warroad's Henry Boucha, Sargent turned down a chance to sign a contract with the Twins for baseball and several football scholarships, as well.

18) Bill Shaw. The Indians' Bob Lundeen unloaded from the blue line after taking a pass from Jay Idzorek as Southwest edged Edina.

19) 1978

20) Grand Rapids. The Indians' went an impressive 19-5 in 24 games during that span.

21) Mark Eagles, whose team finished sixth both years.

22) Roseau. The Rams featured one of the state's most prolific lines ever, with the likes of Aaron and Neal Broten and Butsy Erickson, all future Gophers and NHL stalwarts. Roseau finished in third place, losing to Edina-East 5-3 in the semifinals.

23) International Falls and Grand Rapids. The Broncos prevailed 3-2 to give coach Larry Ross his sixth and final state championship.

24) Edina-East. Hornet goalie Gary Aulik was outstanding with 48 saves as his team outlasted Grand Rapids 5-4 in two overtimes. Aulik's total still stands as a record for most saves in a title game.

25) Reed Larson, who was a stud for the Gophers before a 14-year NHL career, mostly with the Detroit Red Wings. Larson played in 906 games and made three All-Star teams and became the first American to score 200 goals in the National Hockey League.

26) Bill Baker, a first-team All-American in 1979 when the Gophers won their third NCAA title. Baker was the steadying influence on defense for Gus Hendrickson's champs in 1975, his senior season.

27) Bob Boysen. Playing for Alexander Ramsey, Boysen scored six goals as his team won the consolation title in 1963.

28) Fran McClellan. The Governors were a big underdog after losing 8-2 to the Raiders in a regular-season contest played in Coleraine.

29) A wide black stripe down the middle of their orange protective headgear.

30) Alan Hangsleben. Similar to Phil Housley in style but a decade earlier, Hangsleben was skilled in all phases of the game and logged a ton of ice-time. Hangsleben was extremely valuable for coach Dick Roberts both years for Warroad, totaling three points in 1969 and four in 1970, when Warroad finished sixth. An All-American at North Dakota, the fleet Warroad skater played 185 NHL games, mostly with Washington.

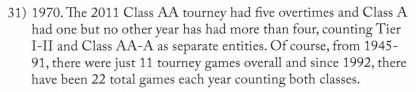

31) 1970. The 2011 Class AA tourney had five overtimes and Class A had one but no other year has had more than four, counting Tier I-II and Class AA-A as separate entities. Of course, from 1945-91, there were just 11 tourney games overall and since 1992, there have been 22 total games each year counting both classes.

32) Mike Ramsey, who assisted on both Roosevelt goals in their first game and scored two goals and added an assist in a 5-3 loss to Rochester John Marshall in consolation. He was a freshman on the 1979 Gopher sextet that won the NCAA title and a year later, was the youngest member of the U.S. Olympic team that shocked the world in 1980.

33) Erin Roth (three goals and seven assists) had a goal and three assists in the title game, a 6-1 win over Minneapolis Southwest. He scored both goals in a 2-0 semifinal win over Hill-Murray and four assists in an 8-3 quarterfinal triumph over Henry Sibley. ·

34) Jeff Whisler, who totaled seven points in the 1976 event, including four goals and an assist in a 7-4 triumph over Bemidji for third place. He had a goal and two assists as a junior, when Hill-Murray also finished third. Behind the bench, Whisler led the Pioneers to a title in 1991 (5-3 over Duluth East) and a runner-up finish in 1988. He later brought three Mahtomedi teams to the Class A state tournament.

35) Joe Micheletti. He played 158 games for St. Louis and Colorado in the NHL and 142 games in the WHA. Micheletti was a member of two NCAA champion Gopher clubs in 1974 and 1976 and was the MVP of the Final Four in 1976. He has established himself as one of the top hockey analysts in an impressive broadcasting career and presently works as a color analyst covering the NHL.

36) Paul Holmgren, who was the top forward for the Knights in 1972 and 1973, went on to play for the Gophers for a year when they won their first national title (1974). Paul then played briefly with the hometown Fighting Saints in the WHA before embarking on his NHL career with Philadelphia. Holmgren played eight seasons for the Flyers, scoring 144 goals and racking up 1,684 penalty minutes. He later was an assistant and head coach for Philadelphia and now serves as the team General Manager.

37) Aaron (Broten). A year younger than Neal, Aaron led the tournament in scoring in both his junior and senior years, 1978

and 1979, respectively. Aaron had seven points on four goals and three assists the first year and 12 points with six goals and assists each his second year. Neal, meanwhile, didn't score as a freshman and had two goals and an assist as a junior and a goal and six assists as a senior in '78. Aaron had 20 total points (10 goals, 10 assists) in nine games while Neal finished with nine points (three goals, six assists) in nine games. Another twist in Broten lore is that when Neal when the first Hobey Baker award in 1981, brother Aaron wasn't even an All-American selection despite scoring a national high and Gopher record of 106 points.

38) John Matschke, whose Bears were blanked by both Hibbing and North St. Paul.

39) Dan Lempe, who garnered 222 points in his collegiate career at Duluth. Lempe had two goals in the 6-1 championship game in his junior season and a goal and an assist in the 4-3 victory over Richfield in his senior year.

40) Rob McClanahan, who was one of the key players on the Minnesota Gopher NCAA champs in 1979 and then continued to play for Herb Brooks with the "Miracle On Ice" USA team that won the gold medal in the 1980 Winter Olympics. Rob had four goals and three assists for Tom Wegleitner's contingent in the state tournament.

41) Mark DeCenzo, who was a senior center and assistant captain for Rapids in 1974 before starring at Michigan State. His son, Nick, was all-tournament for Hibbing in 2011.

42) Phil Verchota, whose two goals were a big factor in East's 4-3 consolation-title game triumph over Hopkins Lindbergh.

43) Minneapolis Southwest and Edina. In 1970, Southwest won 1-0 to win the state title and in 1971, Edina won 4-3 in the opening round on their way to the championship.

44) Les Auge, who was a standout on the first-ever Gopher team to win the NCAA title in 1974 and was one of the last cuts before the final roster was completed for the 1980 U.S. Olympic team.

45) John Gilbert

46) Doug Long, who catapulted Johnson to a 5-4 (5 OT) win over Greenway-Coleraine. In the semifinals, he had 52 saves in a 2-1 overtime loss to Edina.

47) John Perpich, who played for his dad George at Hibbing, was with the Bluejackets in 1970, when they finished third. He was a four-year regular for Hibbing, as was teammate Dennis Fearing, another all-tournament defenseman bound for UMD.

48) John Shewchuk and Warren Miller; the latter played on both the 1974 and 1976 Gopher teams that won NCAA titles and later played 238 games in the WHA and 262 more in the NHL.

49) Steve Janaszak, who later would be the tournament MVP as he and his Minnesota Gophers won their third NCAA title in six years under the tutelage of Herb Brooks in 1979. Janaszak had 35 saves in the 4-3 win over North Dakota in the finals. The next season, he would serve as the understudy to Jim Craig for the "Miracle on Ice."

50) Bobby Krieger, who made the all-tournament team all three seasons. Krieger had two goals as a sophomore when Edina lost both games and had two goals and two assists as a junior when Edina won the state title. He had two goals and two assists as a senior, including a goal in the second overtime to beat Warroad 3-1 in the quarterfinals.

51) Don Lucia, who led his home-state University of Minnesota club to two-straight NCAA titles in 2002 and 2003. After playing at Notre Dame, Lucia became a head coach at both Alaska-Fairbanks and Colorado College before coming to the Gophers for the 1999-2000 season. Lucia has been a college coach for 28 years and became the winningest coach in Gopher history after notching his 391th victory in March 2015.

52) Prior to the 1974-75 regular season, the Minnesota State High School League had agreed to incorporate 21 schools that were either Catholic, private, or independent. Thus, 139 schools began sectional play that year, as opposed to 118 a year earlier.

53) Peter Waselovich. The Bronco netminder was all-tournament in 1972 by virtue of his outstanding play. Waselovich had 32 saves in a 3-2 final victory over Grand Rapids, 38 stops in a 2-1 overtime triumph over Minneapolis Southwest, and 27 in a first-round win over Bemidji (8-3). As a senior, he had a 24-save shutout to beat St. Paul Harding 4-0 for third-place after making 32 saves in upsetting Edina-East 2-1 in the quarterfinals. Waselovich was a four-year regular at North Dakota.

54) Two pure hat tricks were scored. North St. Paul's Dan Leigh gave the Polar a 3-0 lead with his tallies but Southwest's Paul Miller scored twice in the third period to tie and then won it in regulation to give the Indians a 4-3 triumph. Miller would tie Warroad teammates Frank Krahn and Lee Marshall with a tournament-high six points.

55) Dave Bremer, who had 18 saves in the shutout with Rick Wineberg scoring the only goal of the tense battle midway through the first period.

56) Tim Pavek and Steve Poltfuss.

57) Paul Butters helped John Marshall to the 4-2 win over Edina-East, which had Steve Carroll in the cage. Butters was the key in the finals as he was spectacular as Edina-East outshot the underdogs 39-14. Butters played for the Gophers the next four seasons while Carroll became a Division II All-American in 1980 and 1981 at Mankato State.

58) Chick and Ken Yackel, Jr., the offspring of Ken Yackel, Sr. Chick, just a freshman, had a goal in the 5-4 semifinal loss to Grand Rapids.

59) Tom Peluso. He had three goals and an assist in 1968, two goals and five assists in 1969, and two goals and two assists in 1970. Peluso scored 53 goals in two seasons at Denver and was drafted by the Chicago Blackhawks.

60) Brad Shelstad, who had 22 saves in the final as Southwest prevailed 1-0 in the extra session. Shelstad, an obvious all-tourney pick, later was the starting goalie on Minnesota's first NCAA champion in 1974 and was named the tournament's Most Outstanding Player.

61) Rod Romanchuk, who went to Wisconsin and played four years for the Badgers. His brother, Steve, was head coach Terry Skrypek's main assistant that year and for the next two state entries, and went on to be a head coach for over 30 years with Park-Cottage Grove, Woodbury, and Tartan.

62) 1972

63) Jim Jetland, started nine games over three years for Grand Rapids (1976-78). Jetland was on the 1979 Gopher national

championship team. A star left-handed pitcher in high school, he also played one year for the U of M baseball team.

64) Steve Christoff, whose Spartans were outshot 40-19 but lost just 4-3 to Grand Rapids as the state tournament returned to downtown St. Paul. Christoff totaled five goals and four assists, including two markers in the finale.

65) Denny Fermoyle, who along with Albert Hasbargen guided the Warriors (27-0-2) to their first undefeated season in the school's long and illustrious history. Fermoyle did play briefly as a goalie subbing for Brad Shelstad in both 1968 and 1969 for Southwest.

66) Neal Broten

67) Frank B. Kellogg. Coached by Whitey Aus, the Chargers finished sixth, losing to Hibbing 5-4 in the fifth-place game. Kellogg was a new school created in the Roseville area in 1965 and it closed in 1986 when Alexander Ramsey and Kellogg schools were melded into the present Roseville Area High School.

68) Grand Rapids; players on the roster to play Division I hockey includes: Jim Jetland (Minnesota), Don Lucia (Notre Dame), Bill Hoolihan (RPI), Dave Welliver (Providence), Dave Akre (Pennsylvania), Gary DeGrio (UMD), Tom Madson (Minnesota), Al Cleveland (UMD), Bill Rothstein (Notre Dame), Dan Lempe (UMD), Erin Roth (UMD), Doug Bymark (St. Lawrence), Mark Schroeder (Army), Scott Kleinendorst (Providence), Pete DeCenzo (RPI), and Dave Madson (UMD).

69) Pete Hoene, whose Warriors were ousted after defeats to Bemidji (4-3) and Mounds View (5-1). Pete played at Air Force and is now a Brigadier General in the U.S. Air Force. The rink in West St. Paul is named in honor of his father, George.

70) Jim Korn, who had three goals and an assist as Lindbergh finished sixth. Korn played in 596 NHL games for five teams (mostly with Toronto). He was a rugged player, booking 1,801 penalty minutes.

71) Rick Erdall, who also tallied two assists as Washburn finished sixth. Erdall was a fine playmaker for Brad Buetow's Gopher squads, often feeding Pat Micheletti for goals.

72) Rochester John Marshall. One of them, however, was Scott Lecy, who had two goals and two assists in the 1977 final. Lecy had 61 goals and 112 points that season.

Minneapolis Roosevelt's Brian Young checked Kellogg's Rich Pracht in the crease during a 1974 consolation game at the Met Center as Teddies' goalie Dick Bain looks on. Kellogg won 5-4. (MSHSL)

73) Gary Ross. Roseau lost 1-0 in overtime to Edina in the 1971 final. Ross played 12 games for the 1980 U.S. Olympic team but didn't make the final Winter Olympic roster at Lake Placid.

74) Tim Pogorels

75) Chris Pryor, whose team won consolation in 1978 but lost both games the next March. Pryor played 82 games in the NHL for the North Stars and Islanders and is presently the President of Hockey Operations for the Philadelphia Flyers.

76) Dave Manley. The Knights finished fourth in 1979 but came back to win consolation in 1980 and finish runner-up in 1981.

77) Bob Lundeen, who was all-tournament in 1970 and 1971. Lundeen, a swift skater with good size, had an assist on the overtime winner as Southwest nipped Edina 1-0 in the finale in 1970. In 1971, he scored twice but his team lost two 4-3 games to Edina and Alexander Ramsey. Lundeen controlled the flow at both ends of the ice and played collegiately at Wisconsin, where he was on the 1973 NCAA champion. He was drafted by the North Stars and played on the 1976 U.S.Olympic team. He is presently designing products to enhance stick-handling, shooting, and weight training for hockey players.

78) Steve Short, who was all-tourney in 1972, saw his teams finish sixth both years at state.

79) Les Neeb

80) Gordy Hampson, who played four games with Calgary after a collegiate career at Michigan. His father, Ted, played 17 years of professional hockey and was awarded the Bill Masterton Trophy in 1969 while competing for the Oakland Golden Seals.

81) Hibbing beat International Falls.

82) Edina-East. The Hornets won 2-0 behind Steve Carroll's 23 stops.

83) Scott Bjugstad. The left-handed sharpshooter scored three key goals in the third period of a 6-4 win over Washburn in the quarters and three more in a 9-7 loss to Roseau in the fifth-place game. Bjugstad scored 43 goals in the 1985-86 season for the Stars and played nine years in the NHL after a fine Gopher career.

84) Edina-East. The Hornets got hat tricks from Mike Lauen and Mark Gagnon and scored on five power-plays in a 12-4 thrashing. Lauen also scored at 3:37 of overtime with an assist to Gagnon to beat Rochester John Marshall 4-3 in the title game.

85) Steve Ikola, son of head coach Willard Ikola. The younger Ikola also scored the first goal in the finals, a 5-4 double-overtime win over Grand Rapids. The winner was scored unassisted by Tom Carroll at 1:06 of the second overtime off a goal-mouth scramble. Carroll hadn't played in the first two games and replaced an injured Mike Lauen in the first period of the first-ever championship game to go into double-overtime.

86) Bruce Aikens, who assisted on the winning goals in both the 1-0 semifinal win over So. St. Paul and the 4-2 championship triumph over Edina-East. Aikens scored 136 goals and 250 points in his high school career. He also had three goals and an assist in the 1978 tourney but John Marshall finished sixth. The former Rocket scored 100 goals and had 117 assists in his standout career with Colorado College.

87) John Taft, who was all-tourney in 1972 (goal and two assists) when the Indians were third after winning the title in his sophomore year. He was on Wisconsin's 1973 NCAA winner and the 1976 U.S. Olympic team and also played 15 NHL games for Detroit.

88) Edina-East. The Hornets beat Roseau 2-0 in 1977 and 5-3 in 1978. The 1978 Roseau club featured Neal Broten (120 points) and Aaron Broten (102 points). In 1979, Ikola's skaters beat the Rams again, blasting them 12-4 in the semifinals.

89) Richard Hocking, who finished with four goals and an assist.

90) Paul Brown, Craig Dahl, Jim Knapp, and Peter Waselovich. Brown scored the go-ahead goal in the 3-2 finale against Grand Rapids and the overtime goal in a 2-1 semifinal win over Minneapolis Southwest. Dahl had four goals and an assist, Knapp was a force in his own zone and Waselovich was brilliant in the nets.

91) Dan Leigh. After scoring a hat trick in a 4-3 overtime loss to Minneapolis Southwest, Leigh scored the only goal 1:35 into a third overtime to beat White Bear Lake and then tallied with just nine seconds left in regulation to give his team a 5-4 victory over Warroad.

92) John Meredith. The fleet-footed winger played for Dave Peterson's team in 1975 when they lost 6-1 to Grand Rapids in the finals. Meredith scored the only goal of that game for the Indians. He scored the tying goal in the third period of a 2-1 overtime win over Bloomington Lincoln in the semifinals and had three assists in a 5-3 quarterfinal win over Roseau. As a senior in 1976, Southwest lost both of their games in overtime by the score of 5-4, to Hill-Murray in the first round and to Bloomington Kennedy in consolation. Meredith had a goal and an assist. Meredith was 25 years younger than his brother Dick, who had played in the 1951 tournament for the Minneapolis school. John was a member of the 1979 NCAA champions with the Gophers.

5 The 1980s

1) What present Fox Sports Net hockey analyst was the starting goaltender for Burnsville when the Braves won the 1985 state hockey title?

2) What tournament dandy for Hill-Murray in 1985 and 1986 later became an infielder for the Minnesota Twins?

3) The Edina school district was split into two high schools, Edina-East and Edina-West, for nine years. In what year were they re-consolidated into one Edina team?

4) What team beat defending champion Grand Rapids in the opening game of the 1981 tourney 4-3 in overtime on their way to the first of five state titles?

5) What brother tandem led South St. Paul to a third-place finish in 1981?

6) What future Hobey Baker winner was the star netminder for Duluth Denfeld in 1986?

7) What behemoth Bemidji winger was a scoring and hitting sensation for Bryan Grand's club as the Lumberjacks took the consolation title in 1986?

8) What Burnsville mentor in 1986 became the first coach to win back-to-back titles since Willard Ikola's tandem wins with Edina-East in 1978 and 1979?

9) What Hill-Murray speedster was a stud for the Pioneers in the mid-1980's and later carved out a niche as a highly-regarded assistant coach in Division I hockey?

10) Cloquet earned its first trip to state with a Section 7 title in 1982 and the Lumberjacks copped the consolation prize. However, Cloquet fans rued the fact that the team played without what mighty-mite center, who broke his ankle in the sectionals?

11) What Edina star, who was a vital cog on the 1982 Edina Hornet championship club, later coached a Class A team to two state championships?

12) What Rochester John Marshall defenseman was sterling for the Rockets in the 1989 event, scoring four goals and playing outstanding defense as John Marshall finished second?

13) Who captained Greenway-Coleraine, coached by his father, to the third-place trophy in 1987 and later went on to a stellar career at the U of M and a long minor-league career with some NHL time with the Rangers?

14) What Grand Rapids two-way player in 1988 was on the inaugural Minnesota Wild roster in 1999-2000 after a standout career with the University of Minnesota?

15) What Hibbing rink rat led his Bluejackets to the 1982 tournament before starting a career that led to All-American status at the U of M and a brief career in the NHL with the North Stars?

16) Two sons of a four-time state participant played center for South St. Paul in the 1989 tournament, when the Packers finished sixth. Who were they?

17) What Bemidji High goalie was the starter for the 1986 Lumberjacks team that won the consolation title that year? (Hint: he is the son of a collegiate coach whose win total still ranks among the top ten all-time.)

18) Who was the high-flying forward who led Edina's Hornets to the state title in 1984?

19) Anoka had a superlative forward who was pivotal in the Tornadoes' third-place finish in the 1985 tourney who later played at Harvard and played professionally. Who was he?

20) What Hill-Murray skater scored one of the most noteworthy

goals in Pioneer hockey history when he scored the game-winner with 3:12 left to give his team a 4-3 win over Burnsville for its first-ever state title in 1983?

21) What three-sport star and future NFL player scored a goal for Cretin-Derham Hall in the 1988 tournament for the St. Paul Catholic school?

22) What Burnsville winger and future Gopher and NHL player was a headliner for the Braves in the 1983 tourney and was the son of a pro wrestling personality?

23) Three Hankinson brothers starred for the Edina Hornets and later for the University of Minnesota. Two played in the state tournament and two played in the NHL but who was the only one to do both?

24) What talented Grand Rapids skater was a force for the Indians in two tourneys (1980, 1981) and led the tourney in scoring his junior year?

25) In one of the biggest upsets in tourney history, what Columbia Heights netminder, with a truly magical name, shut out Edina 2-0 in a 1983 first-round crowd-pleaser?

26) What Grand Rapids goalie, a transfer from Greenway-Coleraine, stoned Hill-Murray in the 1980 finals with 31 saves as the northern Minnesota school beat the Pioneers 2-1?

27) What two dynamic scorers helped Bloomington Kennedy to the 1987 title and later had successful careers in the WCHA?

28) What Edina forward scored the winning goal for Edina as the Hornets beat Bloomington Kennedy 4-2 in the 1984 finals?

29) What Bloomington Jefferson defenseman and future Ivy League player was one of the Jaguar's top players in their unexpected title run in 1981?

30) For the first time since 1960, a penalty shot opportunity was successful when what Burnsville player scored the game-winner in a semifinal victory in 1983?

31) What future pro goalie played for Richfield during the 1986 tournament and is one of only nine goalies to ever be credited with a goal in NHL history?

32) A talented left-winger for Hastings in 1985, he had a goal and three assists in the tourney for the Raiders while featuring a full beard. Who was he?

33) In 1985, which two teams staged one of the most unforgettable games in boys' state tourney history when their quarterfinal game was not decided until after breakfast the following morning?

34) A terrific defensive defenseman, what Hill-Murray player from 1987 and 1988 has served as the assistant coach at his alma mater despite becoming a paraplegic after a tragic on-ice collision in a pro hockey game in Switzerland?

35) Though overshadowed by his two older brothers, what Roseau forward had a fine state tournament showing in 1983 and 1984 and did follow in both of their footsteps by carving out a nice career with the Gophers and as an NHL competitor?

36) Blessed with a powerful stride and a booming shot for a guy just 5'9", what Bloomington Jefferson player was clever with the puck and a smart defensive player for the Jaguars in both 1986 and 1988?

37) What Edina player had five assists in leading the Hornets to the 1989 consolation title before competing for Wisconsin and the New York Islanders?

38) Did former Minnesota Wild head coach Todd Richards ever play in the state boys' hockey tournament during his prep career in the western suburbs?

39) In 1985, what school set a record for the fastest four goals by one team?

40) Performing in his school's only appearance at state, what forward scored a hat trick in a 7-4 consolation semifinal loss to Irondale for Hopkins Lindbergh?

41) Perhaps one of the most talented passers in tourney history, what Warroad defenseman was a fan favorite in both 1987 and 1988 competing for the Warriors?

42) Before becoming an All-American and Hobey Baker award winner at UMD, what Bloomington Jefferson senior defenseman captained the Jaguars in the 1980 state tournament, coach Tom Saterdalen's first team to make it to state?

43) What lanky Grand Rapids forward had a goal and four assists for Grand Rapids' 1980 title team and now serves as an assistant to his brother at another Iron Range school?

44) What Bloomington Jefferson wing won the 1989 championship for the Jaguars when his shot beat Rochester John Marshall goalie Sam Pearson at 3:29 of overtime?

45) What St. Paul Johnson forwards led the Governors to the state tournament in 1984 when they finished fourth with Rod Magnuson at the helm?

46) This 6'2', 190-pound forward played for Edina-West in that school's only venture to the state tourney in 1981 and then played for the re-consolidated Edina Hornet team that won it all in 1982. Who was this player, who would go on to win both an NCAA crown and the Stanley Cup title within the decade?

47) Who was the Greenway-Coleraine netminder in 1987 who was a mainstay as the Raiders made their first tourney trip in 17 years worthwhile with a third-place finish?

48) Injured for nearly half of the season, what Bloomington Jefferson center returned in time to spur his Jaguar teammates to the 1981 state championship?

49) What Columbia Heights forward, (now the women's coach at St. Thomas University), was one of the stars on the upstart Hylanders club in 1983?

50) Which Burnsville center was a pivotal figure in the Braves' two straight titles in 1985 and 1986, scoring two goals in both finals and was the leading scorer with 10 points in the latter year?

51) An intelligent center for Bloomington Kennedy, who scored on a penalty shot for the Eagles' first goal in a 4-2 title-game loss to Edina in 1984?

52) What Edina forward in 1987 played collegiately for the Gophers in both hockey and baseball and played 13 years of minor-league baseball in the Houston Astros chain?

53) A long-time assistant under George Perpich, who took over for the veteran coach at Hibbing and brought the Range school to tournaments in three straight years in the mid-1980's?

54) An older brother to Dixon and Brad, what coach led Hastings to the 1985 tournament with stars named Stepan, Sagissor, Pauletti, and Williams?

55) What Hill-Murray netminder gave up just five goals in the entire tournament as his team was runner-up to Grand Rapids in 1980?

56) The 1986 event started with a bang. The fans were still racing to get to their seats when which Duluth Denfeld player scored just 10 seconds after the first puck was dropped?

57) What two schools combined for 14 penalties in a rough 1980 semifinal?

58) Who served as Tom Osiecki's assistant coach when Burnsville won back-to-back championships in 1985 and 1986?

59) A dynamic force on both offense and defense, who was Hibbing's standout defenseman in 1982, a major factor in the Bluejacket's third-place finish?

60) What Taconite resident won the Mr. Hockey award in 1987 as a defenseman for Greenway-Coleraine, which finished third?

61) What two Henry Sibley forwards catapulted the Warriors to its highest finish in school history by virtue of their 4-3 win over Columbia Heights in the third-place game in 1983?

62) In 1980, what two Irondale Knights tied Bloomington Jefferson's Jay North for the tournament scoring lead with seven points?

63) What brainy center for South St. Paul tied Bloomington Kennedy's Jason Miller with the scoring lead in 1987 with eight points?

64) What solid defenseman was a shot-blocking freak for Burns-ville High School in both 1985 and 1986 as the Braves swept to the title both years and later became the head coach at Ohio State?

65) Who was Duluth Denfeld's coach in three appearances in this decade (1986, 1988, 1989)?

66) What three-year tourney participant (1986, 1988, 1989) for Bloomington Jefferson scored just 16 seconds after the drop of the puck to open the 1988 tournament as the Jaguars beat Grand Rapids 5-4?

67) Playing for his father Bill, what junior center was a stalwart for Duluth Denfeld in 1986, scoring three goals in a span of 4:47 in the third period as the Hunters beat Hibbing 4-2 in the third-place game?

68) What senior center captained the 1988 Bloomington Jefferson team that took third place with a 5-4 win over Warroad?

69) What coach helped Apple Valley earn a first-ever tourney berth in 1981?

70) In 1983, what Burnsville player scored the final two goals of his team's victory by scoring each into an empty net?

71) A 6'3" center with great reach, what Hill-Murray player from the 1988 tournament was once the key player in a trade for Wayne Gretzky?

72) What 5'5" freshman for Columbia Heights was a sparkplug for his team as the Hylanders performed admirably in their first and only state tourney experience in 1983?

73) What amateur hockey giant served as one of two assistants for Grand Rapids as the Itasca County school won their third title in a six-year span in 1980?

74) In what year during this decade did the northern schools (two) not win a single trophy for the first time in tournament history?

75) What player scored overtime goals in both the 1988 and 1989 tournaments for his team?

76) Who was Warroad's starting goaltender in both 1987 and 1988, backstopping the Warriors' to fourth place and third place, respectively?

77) Overshadowed by team-mate Doug Zmolek, what heady Rochester John Marshall defenseman was outstanding for coach Bob Frerker in both 1988 and 1989?

78) What freshman forward played on Minnetonka's first state tournament team in 1985?

79) This Rochester Mayo star tied for the tourney scoring lead in 1982 with Jefferson wing Steve Bianchi with seven points. Who is this former Wisconsin collegiate player who now serves as the assistant executive director of USA Hockey?

Phil Housley as a South St. Paul sophomore (1979-80). That year the Packers fnished sixth at state. The next year they were third. (Photo courtesy Phil Housley)

80) A native of Illinois, what Burnsville goalie was in the nets for the Braves in the finals in both 1986 and 1987?

81) What school came out for warm-ups in the 1981 tournament and got quite a reaction from the crowd on account of their unusual uniforms?

82) Which two schools both won and lost games on the same day-March 8, 1985?

83) What team made it to the championship game in 1982 with the nickname of...Dolphins?

84) Which White Bear Mariner player tallied a pure hat trick in a 6:48 span of the third period in a 7-2 quarterfinal victory over Cloquet in the 1982 tournament?

85) What school in the 1988 tournament finished sixth despite having three players on the team who would play in the NHL?

86) What Hill-Murray defenseman played four years for Terry Skrypek (1977-80) and was a major reason why the Pioneers finished second in 1980 and copped consolation titles in both 1977 and 1978?

87) Which Edina-West players from a 1981 state tourney appearance helped a re-consolidated Edina team to the 1982 state title?

88) Only two defenseman have ever led the tourney in scoring and both did it in the 1980's. Who were these blue-liners, who both played collegiately for Minnesota?

89) A transfer from Blake, what Hill-Murray center was a go-to offensive spark for both Pioneer teams that lost to Burnsville in consecutive final-game losses in 1985 and 1986?

90) What two schools met in the finals in 1983, 1985, and 1986?

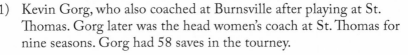

◀ ANSWERS TO CHAPTER 5 - THE 1980s ▶

1) Kevin Gorg, who also coached at Burnsville after playing at St. Thomas. Gorg later was the head women's coach at St. Thomas for nine seasons. Gorg had 58 saves in the tourney.

2) Tom Quinlan. The Pioneers finished second both years to Burnsville with Quinlan scoring a goal and an assist in 1985 and three goals and three assists in 1986. Recruited by the Gophers to play hockey, Quinlan spurned that offer to sign with the Toronto Blue Jays and later played parts of four years in the big leagues. He was drafted by Calgary of the NHL.

3) 1982. The Hornets won it all that year, too, by whipping White Bear Mariner 6-0 in the finals and allowing just seven shots on goal. A year earlier, Edina-West won the Section 6 title. The two Edina schools had separate teams from 1973-81.

4) Bloomington Jefferson

5) Phil and Larry Housley. Phil had two goals and three assists and Larry had two goals and an assist. Phil, of course, would go on to be the #1 draft pick of the Buffalo Sabres and go on to a 22-year NHL career and still ranks as the second-leading scorer in league history among American-born players with 1,232 points. Phil played for eight NHL teams and played 1,495 games. He was named to the U.S. Hockey Hall of Fame in 2004 and the Hockey Hall of Fame in Toronto in 2015.

6) Robb Stauber. The future Gopher standout helped the Hunters to the third-place trophy after losing to eventual-champion Burnsville 3-1 in the semifinals. Stauber won the Hobey Baker award in 1988, when he was an All-American for Doug Woog and the MVP of the WCHA. Stauber played 62 games in the NHL and now operates Stauber's Goal-Crease, one of the premier goaltending training centers in the nation in both Edina and Blaine.

7) George Pelawa, who was 6'4" and 240 pounds. Pelawa had three goals and four assists. He had a scholarship at North Dakota but was killed in an car accident months after his impressive performance in St. Paul. Pelawa was the Mr. Hockey award winner in 1986 and was a first-round draft choice (16th overall) by Calgary.

8) Tom Osiecki, who brought five teams to state from Burnsville and served as head coach there from 1966-99 after starting his career at St. Agnes.

9) Steve Rohlik, who had a goal and an assist as a sophomore and junior, and a goal and two assists as a senior captain. Rohlik served many years as an assistant to Scott Sandelin at UMD and is now the head coach at Ohio State University.

10) Corey Millen. The explosive Millen, remindful of Doug Woog as a skater and player, became one of the U of M's top scorers, notching 95 goals in 128 games. Though just 5'7", Millen was a true scoring threat at every level. He scored 46 goals in just 18 games as a senior at Cloquet and had 90 goals in his NHL career for five teams. He scored 20 goals three times, twice for Los Angeles and once for New Jersey. Millen also was one of the top forwards on the 1984 and 1988 U.S. Olympic teams. Ironically, the person who replaced him on Cloquet's roster was his brother Scott, a tenth-grade wing.

11) Wally Chapman. He scored the overtime winner in a semifinal win over Jefferson for Willard Ikola as Edina went on to a 6-0 win in

the finale. Chapman led the Breck School to the Class A title in both 2000 and 2004 as their head coach.

12) Doug Zmolek, who was the North Stars' top draft pick that year. John Marshall lost 5-4 to Bloomington Jefferson in a thrilling final contest in 1989.

13) Kenny Gernander. His dad, Bob, coached five Raider teams to state. In 1987, the Raiders lost 4-2 to eventual champion Bloomington Kennedy in the semifinals after giving the Eagles their only loss of the season in a regular-season match in Bloomington. Gernander had a long minor-league career and played sparingly in the NHL for the Rangers.

14) Jeff Nielsen. He had two assists in the tourney for Grand Rapids, which was making its first appearance in seven years and finished sixth. Nielsen also played for Anaheim and New York in the NHL.

15) Pat Micheletti, had a goal and three assists as Hibbing copped third place. He was a 1985 Gopher All-American and was the youngest of seven Micheletti brothers to play for Hibbing. He remains the second-leading scorer in Gopher history with 269 points and is second in goals (120) and third in assists (149). Pat scored 48 goals in 44 games in 1985 for Minnesota and played 12 games for the North Stars in 1987-88.

16) Steve and Dan Woog, the offspring of former Packer player and coach Doug Woog. Steve played for Northern Michigan and Dan for his dad at Minnesota.

17) Steve Peters, whose father Bob was the legendary head coach at Bemidji State for 35 years where he won 702 games. He won 744 games overall as a college mentor.

18) Paul Ranheim, who was also a standout at Wisconsin before a 15-year career in the National Hockey League, mostly with Calgary. A Missouri native, Ranheim played in more than 1,000 NHL games and scored 161 goals. He had four goals and three assists for seven points to lead all scorers in 1984 and was noted for his aggressive forechecking and penalty-killing abilities.

19) Tod Hartje, who tied Hibbing's Pat Marolt for the scoring title that year with six points as he had three goals and three assists. Hartje won an NCAA title at the Civic Center with the Crimson in 1989 and even played a year of pro hockey in Russia.

20) Jim Jirelle, a junior center who had assists in both the 6-5 first-round win over Kennedy and the 3-1 semifinal triumph over Henry Sibley. He would play college hockey for the Air Force Academy.

21) Chris Weinke. The Raider wing was also a baseball and hockey star for the St. Paul Catholic school. Weinke played six years of minor-league baseball for Toronto as a third-baseman and at age 26 matriculated to Florida State to play quarterback for the Seminoles. In 1999, he led Bobby Bowden's club to the national title and the next year, at age 28, became the oldest player to win the Heisman Trophy. His NFL career was undistinguished, serving mainly as a backup for seven years.

22) Todd Okerlund scored two goals and had six assists for Burnsville and was the leading scorer in the tournament as the Braves lost 4-3 to Hill-Murray in the final with Okerlund recording two assists. A bull up front for the Gophers, he then played in the Calgary Olympics in 1988 for the U.S. and played four games for the Islanders that year. He is the son of "Mean Gene" Okerlund, a cult hero among pro wrestling aficionados.

23) Ben, who had a goal and two assists in the 1987 tournament, when Edina was ousted in two games. Ben scored three goals playing for New Jersey and Tampa Bay from 1993-95 and is now a certified NFL agent. Younger brother Casey played 18 games for Chicago and Anaheim but never played in the tournament. Older brother Peter was on the 1984 Edina title team, scoring a goal and adding three assists but never reached the NHL.

24) Tony Kellin, who had three goals and six assists in his senior season. As a 10th-grade regular on defense, his Indian team copped the state crown. Kellin starred for the Gophers, too, and played for the Washington Capitals in the pros.

25) Reggie Miracle. The Hylanders, in their only trip to state, got 29 saves from the acrobatic Miracle to the delight of the sellout crowd. Columbia Heights was tied 2-2 with eventual-champ Burnsville with less than five minutes to go but lost 5-2 in the semifinals and finished fourth.

26) Jon Casey, who would lead North Dakota to a NCAA title in 1982 and was a first-team All-American in 1984. As a pro, he nearly catapulted the North Stars to a Stanley Cup title in 1991. Casey

played 12 years in the NHL and won 170 games with Minnesota, Boston, and St. Louis.

27) Jason Miller and Joe Decker; Miller was a Golden Gopher and Decker was a regular for Wisconsin's Badgers.

28) Marty Nanne, who scored at 5:07 of the final stanza. Nanne's father, Lou, did the color commentary of the goal on television. Marty, a Chicago draft-pick, played with the Gophers for three seasons.

29) Rob Ohno, who played at Harvard and graduated in 1986. Ohno scored a goal when Jefferson claimed third place in 1980. In 1981, he had an assist in the Jaguars' exciting 3-2 victory over Irondale in the title game. As a senior, he helped secure Jefferson's third-place win (5-3) over Hibbing with a goal and an assist.

30) Dave MacNulty, whose goal broke a 2-2 tie with Columbia Heights as Burnsville eventually won 5-2. Twenty-three years earlier, Edina's Paul Rosendahl was the last player to score on a penalty shot against Mpls. Washburn.

31) Damian Rhodes, who had 22 saves in a first-round loss to Hill-Murray. He was an all-WCHA goalie at Michigan Tech and went on to play 10 years in the NHL. In 1999, he was credited with scoring a goal in a 6-0 win over New Jersey while with Ottawa. He also played with Toronto and Atlanta.

32) Brad Stepan, who son Derek is now performing for the New York Rangers after playing collegiately at Wisconsin.

33) Minnetonka and Bloomington Jefferson. The game, tied at 3-3 after the third overtime, was suspended to allow the final quarterfinal between Bemidji and Burnsville to be played. (Burnsville won 5-3.) The Minnetonka-Jefferson game was resumed at 9:00 a.m. the next morning and Jefferson finally prevailed when Brock Rendall scored at 2:21 of the fourth overtime. It ranks as the fifth-longest game in tourney history at 78 minutes and 21 seconds. A rule was passed in 1977, directing that any of the first three quarterfinals that weren't decided after three overtimes must be played the following morning out of concern for the teams waiting to play the last quarterfinal.

34) Pat Shafhauser. The Pioneer defender had a goal and assist in 1987 as Hill-Murray finished sixth. As a senior, his team lost 5-3

to Edina in the finals as he had an assist. Drafted by Pittsburgh, he played two years at Boston College. Playing in Europe in December of 1995, he had a collision with another player and suffered a compression fracture of the C-6 and C-7 vertebrae.

35) Paul Broten, who had two goals and two assists in Roseau's wild 9-8 win for the fifth-place trophy in 1984. Broten played four years at the "U" and then surprised many naysayers by playing seven years in the NHL for the Rangers, Stars, and Blues. His older brothers, Neal and Aaron, are both in the U.S. Hockey Hall of Fame.

36) Tom Pederson, who scored two goals and two assists in 1988 as Jefferson copped third. After a stout career with Minnesota, he played 240 games in the NHL with San Jose and Toronto. He is the creator of the "Green Biscuit", an off-ice stick-handling and passing aid which stays flat on just about any surface.

37) Dan Plante. Now a player agent, Plante played 159 games in the NHL.

38) No. Todd, who grew up in Crystal and played at Robbinsdale Armstrong, never made it to the tournament, losing once to Edina in the sectional finals. Despite some strong squads, Armstrong never made it to state as a school. Richards played four years as a stout defenseman at Minnesota and 12 years in the minors. His NHL playing career consisted of eight games with the Hartford Whalers. His brother Travis, another Gopher defenseman, played three NHL games with the Dallas Stars.

39) Anoka, with four goals in a 2:02 span in the second period of an 11-5 first-round win over Hastings. Bill Carlson scored two of the goals for the Tornadoes.

40) Bo Snuggerud, who later was a Division III All-American at St. Thomas University.

41) Larry Olimb. The deadly-accurate passer and crisp playmaker was a major contributor as his team was fourth in 1987 and third in 1988. Olimb had two goals and an assist as a junior and two goals and four assists as a senior. Olimb is the Gopher's all-time leading assist leader with 159 and scored 218 points, one of only nine players with 200 points.

42) Tom Kurvers, who was adept on the power-play with his strong shot and his pinpoint passing. He scored 76 points in 43 games

at UMD in 1983-84 when he was All-American and the Hobey Baker winner. He won a Stanley Cup with the Montreal Canadiens in 1986 and played 12 years in the NHL.

43) John DeCenzo, who had a goal in the Indians' 2-1 championship game win over Hill-Murray. John is the assistant at Hibbing, where his older brother Mark is the head coach.

44) Chris Tucker, who scored his third goal of the game as Jefferson won 5-4. He had also assisted on the tying marker with 3:59 left in regulation.

45) Jim Hau and Dewey Wahlin, who each scored three goals for Johnson, which was playing in its first state tourney in 13 years. Wahlin (54) and Hau (37) combined for 91 goals for the proud school that was making its first tourney showing since 1971.

46) Dave Maley, who played at Wisconsin when they won the NCAA title in 1983. He was also a member of the Stanley Cup champion Montreal Canadians in 1986. He now does color commentary for the San Jose Sharks broadcasts.

47) Jeff Stolp, who had 25 stops in a 4-2 loss to eventual champion Bloomington Kennedy and 24 more in the 4-3 victory over Warroad for third place. Stolp would become the regular goaltender for the Gophers.

48) Steve Bianchi, who had 30 goals in just 14 games prior to the state tournament. In 1981, Bianchi scored the tying goal in a 4-3 overtime win over Grand Rapids in the first round and an assist in the 3-2 victory over Irondale in the finals.

49) Tom Palkowski

50) Scott Bloom, who had five goals and five assists in his senior season to lead all tourney scorers. Burnsville won the final in 1986 over Hill-Murray 4-1 with Bloom scoring twice and assisting on another. In his junior year, he scored on a 40-foot wrist shot with 27 seconds left to beat Hill-Murray 4-3 in the 1985 championship. Bloom tallied the go-ahead goal in a 4-1 semifinal win over Bloomington Jefferson.

51) Dallas Miller beat Edina's Chris Schwartzbauer for his fourth tourney goal.

52) Tommy Nevers. Talented enough to play as a freshman for Edina

in the 1987 tourney, Nevers scored twice as a junior as Edina claimed the consolation title. Nevers was the top pick of the Houston Astros in 1990 and reached AAA but not the majors.

53) Bill Olson and the Bluejackets came to St. Paul in 1984, 1985, and 1986. Hibbing was third in 1984 and fifth in 1985. Olson served under Perpich for 18 years.

54) Jeff Shelstad. His Raiders, however, were shelled 11-5 by Anoka and 6-1 by Hibbing.

55) Jeff Poeschl, who had 14 saves in the 2-1 loss to Grand Rapids. Poeschl played in eight games in the tourney for the Pioneers and has brought Mahtomedi to five Class A tournaments since 1998.

56) Bill Stauber, with an assist to Mike Vukonich. Stauber's brother, Robb, had 27 saves for Denfeld as they beat Jefferson 4-2. Bill also had a goal and assist in the Hunters' 4-2 win over Hibbing for third place.

57) Hill-Murray downed Minneapolis Southwest 7-2 with Mark Kissner and Tom Xavier each scoring twice.

58) Bruce Anderson

59) Scott Sandelin. A big contributor at North Dakota, he was an assistant in Grand Forks for several seasons before taking on the head coaching job at UMD in 2000. He played 25 NHL games for three teams, including one with the North Stars.

60) Kris Miller, who had a goal and four assists as his club beat Warroad 4-3 for third. Miller competed collegiately at UMD.

61) Tom Genz and Steve Fleming. Genz had three goals and an assist while Fleming had three goals and three assists, including the game-winner over Columbia Heights. Henry Sibley had won just one game in their past five trips to state prior to 1983.

62) Scott Richart and John Bader. Richart had six goals and an assist and Bader had two goals and five assists as Irondale took fifth place, beating South St. Paul 4-3. The year previous, Bader had three goals and six assists as the high-octane Knights claimed third place with a rousing 9-7 win over Roseau in one of the fastest-paced games in tourney history.

63) John Young, who had two goals and six assists as the Packers finished fifth. A slick passer, he was a standout at Michigan Tech

and with the minor-league Minnesota Moose despite his small stature.

64) Mark Osiecki. Playing for his father, Tom, Osiecki was a machine clearing opposing players away from his net and denying the opposition scoring chances. He was on an NCAA winner at Wisconsin in 1990 and played for five teams in a three-year NHL career.

65) Bill Vukonich. The Hunters' claimed third place in 1986 by downing Hibbing 4-2 after losing to Burnsville 3-1 in the semifinals. Robb Stauber had 40 saves in the semis and 30 more in the third-place game while Vukonich's son, Mike, totaled three goals and an assist. After taking the consolation crown in 1988, Denfeld took third the next year with Troy Skorich scoring twice and assisting on five others.

66) Tony Bianchi, who was on Jefferson's title team in 1989. He scored the tying goal late in the third period against Rochester John Marshall. The Jaguars prevailed 5-4 in overtime.

67) Mike Vukonich, a future Harvard star who scored 74 goals for the Crimson.

68) Jeff Saterdalen. Son of coach Tom Saterdalen, he had three goals and two assists. In 1986, Jeff had two goals and two assists as the Jaguars finished sixth. At St. Cloud State, he scored 179 points from 1988-92 and was the school's leading scorer for 18 years.

69) Larry Hendrickson, who later would return to the Eagles and lead them to a state crown in 1996. In 1981, Apple Valley finished fourth, losing to eventual-champion Bloomington Jefferson 4-1 in the semis.

70) Todd Skime, who scored with 34 seconds left and again with 13 seconds remaining to secure the Braves' semifinal win over Columbia Heights. Skime also had a goal and an assist for Burnsville in their 4-3 loss in the finals to Hill-Murray.

71) Craig Johnson, who helped the Pioneers to a runner-up finish after losing 5-3 to Edina. Johnson, a fine Gopher player for three years, was traded by St. Louis to Los Angeles for Gretzky and two other players and two draft picks in February of 1996. Johnson played seven season for the Kings and scored 75 NHL goals. He also played in the 1994 Olympics in Lillehammer, Norway.

72) Bill Peterson, who had two goals and an assist. His junior brother, Tom, had two goals.

73) Ted Brill, who aided Buzz Christiansen. Brill worked tirelessly for the Minnesota State Hockey Association (now Minnesota Hockey), serving in many capacities for over 40 years and also with USA Hockey.

74) 1983; International Falls lost twice and Roseau lost 6-1 to Edina for fifth place.

75) Chris Tucker. The Jaguar winger beat Grand Rapids (5-4) in the opening quarterfinal in 1988 and then scored an even bigger game-winner with a goal in the first extra session in another 5-4 victory in the 1989 finals against Rochester John Marshall.

76) Chad Erickson was an All-American at UMD in 1990 and also played two games in the NHL with New Jersey. Erickson's best game his junior season came with a 24-save effort in a 5-1 quarterfinal win over Hill-Murray. As a senior, he blocked 23 shots in a 3-1 quarterfinal victory over Duluth Denfeld and had 22 saves in a 2-1, two-overtime loss to Edina in the semis.

77) Eric Means. John Marshall was second in 1989 as Means had two goals and an assist and he had a goal in 1988 as the Rockets were ousted after two losses. Means was an assistant for 14 years at Minnesota-Mankato and was head womens' coach there for six seasons.

78) Tim Hanus, a Quebec Nordiques draft selection and St. Cloud State competitor.

79) Jim Johannson, who had five goals and two assists for the Spartans, who were making their first tournament appearance. Johannson played for Wisconsin, which won the NCAA title in 1983, and with the U.S. Olympic team in both 1988 and 1992.

80) Tom Dennis. In 1986, he had 22 saves as Burnsville defeated Hill-Murray 4-1 in the finale after he made 17 saves in a 3-1 semifinal triumph over Duluth Denfeld and goalie Robb Stauber (40 saves). In 1987, he had 18 saves in a 4-1 finals loss to Bloomington Kennedy.

81) South St. Paul, which was wearing "Cooperalls."

82) Minnetonka and Jefferson. After having their quarterfinal game

suspended from the night before after three overtimes, the Skippers lost 4-3 after just 2:12 of the fourth overtime the next morning. Jefferson's Brock Rendall scored on a 40-foot slapshot past Tonka goalie Dale Rohel at 2:12 of the fourth overtime in front of approximately 6,000 spectators who were attending at no charge. Minnetonka then beat Bemidji 3-0 in consolation play shortly thereafter. Jefferson then played in the second semifinal that night, losing to Burnsville 4-1 to become the second team in a matter of hours to celebrate a victory and mourn a loss on the same day for the first time. On Saturday, both teams lost as Anoka beat Jefferson 6-1 for third and Hibbing beat Minnetonka 5-4 for fifth.

83) White Bear Lake Mariners, who lost to Edina 6-0.

84) Scott Brydges, who also added an assist in that game.

85) Grand Rapids (Chris Marinucci, Jeff Nielsen, and Jon Rohloff). The Indians lost 5-4 to Bloomington Jefferson in the opening game and then lost in the final minute of regulation to Duluth Denfeld (4-3) in the consolation game. Marinucci played 13 games with the Islanders and one with the Kings. Rohloff played 150 games for Boston. Nielsen played 252 NHL games, mostly with Anaheim.

86) Ben Belde

87) Forwards Wally Chapman, Dave Maley, John DeVoe, defensemen Tom Rzeszut and Mike Roberts, and goalie Jim Lozinski.

88) Tony Kellin had three goals and six assists for nine points for Grand Rapids in 1981. Larry Olimb had two goals and four assists for six points for Warroad in 1987, tying Keven Degel of Jefferson and Chris Marinucci of Grand Rapids.

89) Tray Tuomie, who had a hat trick in a 4-1 win over Anoka in the semifinals as a junior and had two goals and five assists as a senior.

90) Hill-Murray and Burnsville. The Pioneers won 4-3 to cap an undefeated season (28-0) in 1983. Burnsville beat Hill-Murray 4-3 in 1985 and 4-1 in 1986 to win consecutive titles.

6 The 1990s

1) What school was a powerhouse team in the decade by virtue of their three state titles and their 59-game unbeaten string?

2) Only one girl ever scored a point in a state boys' hockey tournament game. Can you name her?

3) What Duluth East tandem were "Batman" and "Robin" for the Port City school as the Greyhounds won the 1995 Class AA title?

4) The Tier I and II format that started in 1992 was based on placing teams in one of the two levels based on what particular criteria?

5) In the 1990 final, what two northern teams matched up in the championship game for the first time in 18 years for the tradition-laden schools from "up north"?

6) What Richfield High skater was the catalyst for his club in 1991 as the Spartans went on to take the consolation title and is presently an NHL assistant coach?

7) What school scored a whopping 23 goals in winning the final one-class tourney in 1991?

8) What former Minnesota Wild forward led Moorhead to the 1995 AA finals where the Spuds lost 5-3 to Duluth East?

9) What lanky goaltender was a huge factor in Eveleth-Gilbert's Class A title in 1998?

10) What school won its fifth-ever state title in 1990, their first since 1961 and their first without legendary mentor Oscar Almquist at the helm?

11) In 1992, the third son of Bloomington Jefferson assistant John Bianchi joined his two older brothers as a member of a state championship club. What was his name?

12) Who scored the winning goal in the longest game in tournament history?

13) What future NHLer was the dominant force when his team won the 1997 Class A crown, beating the same team that beat his squad by seven goals in the previous year's final?

14) What mercurial and high-flying wing scored nine goals in consecutive Class AA tourneys in 1995 and 1996?

15) Has a team that is small enough to play in the Class A tournament by enrollment ever won the Class AA title by choosing to "opt-up" with the larger schools?

16) What Bloomington Jefferson player was a star among stars on Jaguar teams that won three straight titles in the 1990's and was the state's Mr. Hockey in 1994?

17) In 1990, who captained Grand Rapids to a second-place finish (3-1 loss to Roseau) and later was an All-American playing in the WCHA?

18) What identical twins helped Hill-Murray catapult their team to the 1991 title?

19) What trio of players led Hastings to the tourney in 1999 when they finished second, losing to Roseau 4-0 in the Class AA final?

20) What two Cloquet linemates each scored 13 points in the 1993 Tier I tourney, the highest total for any player since John Mayasich scored 18 in 1951?

21) In all, among the 16 teams that qualified for the 1992 state tournament (Tier I and Tier II), how many schools were making their first tourney appearance?

22) What Moorhead luminary scored eight goals and led the AA tourney in scoring in 1994 as the Spuds finished in second place behind Bloomington Jefferson?

23) What 5'8", 160-pound goaltender for Apple Valley set the all-time mark for saves in a game with 65 in the epic 1996 Class AA semi between Apple Valley and Duluth East?

24) What two Red Wing teammates were all-tournament for three straight years from 1996-98 as the Wingers finished second, first, and third, respectively?

25) Who was the stellar two-way Moorhead center who had a goal and three assists for coach Terry Cullen in the 1992 Tier I tournament?

26) Which Roseau sniper scored two goals in the finals to lead the Rams' to the 1990 state title and tied Minnetonka winger Justin McHugh with the tourney scoring lead as each scored four goals and two assists?

27) In 1994, Bloomington Jefferson had four defense-man who all would go on to play Division I hockey. Who were they?

28) Despite a storied past, what school finally won their first state title by claiming the Class A crown in 1994 with a 24-4 record?

Farmington's Amber Hegland moves the puck up the ice in a 1994 Class A quarterfinal game against Mahtomedi at the St. Paul Civic Center. Hegland was the only girl ever to play in the boys' state tourney. (Photo: Doug Heikkila)

29) What gritty Apple Valley center was the heart and soul for the Eagles' championship in Class AA in 1996, the son of a former tourney player and Gopher defenseman?

30) What Greenway-Coleraine forward was an all-tournament selection in Tier II play in 1992, following in the footsteps of his famous father who also played there?

31) What Bloomington Jefferson forward showed future promise at higher levels with his play for the Jaguars from 1993-95, a major component in state titles in 1993 and 1994?

32) In the 1999 Class A tournament, this red-clad flash was the tourney scoring leader with nine points, including seven goals, as his Benilde-St. Margaret's club won their first of two titles (the other coming in 2001). Who was this future Gopher?

33) Besides Bloomington Jefferson (28-0) in 1993, which was the only other school to complete an undefeated season in the 1990's?

34) What Irish center scored four goals as Rosemount beat Cambridge 7-1 in a Tier II semifinal in 1992?

35) In the 1998 Class AA tourney, what two brothers were big threats for Duluth East as Mike Randolph's charges copped the title with a 3-1 win over Anoka?

36) The leading scorer in the 1997 AA tournament, what Moorhead Spud scored four goals in a 7-1 win over Anoka in an opening quarterfinal game?

37) What Duluth East dynamo tied John Mayasich's 1951 record by recording a hat trick in each of his team's three games in 1995?

38) In terms of actual playing time, what was the duration it took to complete the historic five-overtime battle between Apple Valley and Duluth East in a 1996 AA semifinal?

39) A long-time coach in the MIAC, what Minnetonka wing helped the Skippers' to the third-place trophy in 1990 and is the son of a former North Star hero?

40) What three Bloomington Jefferson skaters were on all three of Bloomington Jefferson's title teams from 1992-94?

41) Jim Pohl served as hockey coach and athletic director at Red Wing for many years and was able to witness all four of his boys play in the state tournament for the team he formerly coached. What were their names?

42) Which school, representing Section 8 in the Class AA tournament, surprised many by claiming the consolation title in 1996?

Bloomington Jefferson, 1993 Tier I state champions (Photo courtesy Tom Saterdalen)

43) What sophomore center recorded five assists for White Bear Lake in the 1990 tourney as the Bears claimed the consolation title?

44) What Elk River defenseman, all-state in both football and hockey, led the Elks to a third-place finish in 1999, scoring a goal and four assists?

45) In the 1995-96 season, what team won the Class A title and gave up just 38 goals in 28 games?

46) What Bloomington Kennedy player had three goals and two assists in a 5-3 win over South St. Paul in the 1990 consolation final?

47) All-tourney in 1999 playing for his father, what Hastings forward scored the tying goal with 51 seconds remaining and then the game-winner with less than a second left on the clock in the Raiders' thrilling 7-6 quarterfinal win over Blaine?

48) A veteran of more than 10 NHL seasons, what Bloomington Jefferson star was an integral part of three Jaguars teams playing in Class AA in the 1990's?

49) Which Duluth East forward was the main offensive threat for Duluth East in 1991 as the Greyhounds finished second to Hill-Murray that year?

50) With five consecutive appearances in the 1990's, what school brought some pride to southern Minnesota hockey by winning one Class A title and finishing second and third in two others?

51) What school entered the Tier II tournament with one regular-season win in 1992?

52) What Alexandria skater made all-tournament in the 1992 Class AA tournament on the basis of his one goal, five assist effort?

53) What brother duo (freshman defenseman and sophomore forward) were mainstays for Hill-Murray in 1991 as they cruised to their second state title?

54) A present WCHA head coach was the coach at Henry Sibley when the Warriors took third place in the Tier II tourney in 1993. What was his name?

55) A son of a former state participant for Minneapolis Roosevelt, who was the starting goalie for Edina when they won the AA title in 1997?

56) What Duluth East goalie gave up just three goals in three games in the 1997 Class AA tournament in earning all-tourney honors?

57) A future NFL tight end, who tended goal for Hastings in the 1998 tournament when the Raiders took the consolation title?

58) What International Falls player scored the game-winning goal in both the semifinals and finals as the Broncos won the 1995 Class A title?

59) Which defenseman for 1998-99 Class A winner Benilde-St. Margaret's scored the tying goal in the Knights' 4-2 championship game win over East Grand Forks and was a two-time All-American at Boston College?

60) A native of Thief River Falls, what Warroad center was a star for the Warriors in the 1994 Class A tournament with his brilliant play in pressure situations?

61) What future Gopher forward played in the 1990 and 1991 tournaments with two different suburban schools?

62) In the Class A tourney in 1996, what two Warroad teammates tied Red Wing's Johnny Pohl for the scoring lead?

63) A future Notre Dame forward, what Minnetonka skater led the Skippers in scoring in the 1994 season and coached his former high school to the AA tourney in 2010?

64) What Blaine player scored on a penalty shot against Alexandria in the 1996 AA tourney?

65) What Roseau goalie was the starter for the Rams during their Class AA title run in 1999?

66) What Breck center made his dad, a former NHL star, proud with his play in both 1996 and 1997 for the Mustangs, who took third and fifth, respectively, in Class A?

67) What team, playing in the first Class A tourney in 1994, had two players from Cannon Falls on its roster?

68) What Bloomington Jefferson wing tied for the scoring lead in the first Tier I tourney in 1992 and also scored the overtime goal in a 5-4 semifinal win over Cloquet?

69) What former Hill-Murray star coached rival White Bear Lake to the tourney in 1998?

70) What versatile Duluth East defenseman was all-tournament in AA for Mike Randolph's club in both 1997 and 1998?

71) When Eveleth-Gilbert won the second Tier II hockey crown in 1993, what player scored the game-winner at 2:05 of the second overtime against Lake of the Woods/Baudette?

72) A darting forward for Edina, what Hornet forward had two goals and two assists as his team finished in third place in the 1995 AA tourney?

73) Which Roseau player joined three other teammates on the Class AA all-tourney team in 1999, totaling nine points with seven goals and two assists?

74) In the 1999 Class AA tourney, what Elk River player scored on a penalty shot with just 22 seconds left to give the Elks' a 3-2 third-place triumph over Holy Angels?

Bloomington Jefferson goalie Randy Koeppl covers the puck before an on-rushing Moorhead forward can get to it in the 1992 Tier I championship game. Jefferson beat Moorhead 6-3 on their way to the first of three straight state titles. (Photo: MSHSL)

75) What former Pioneer star coached his alma mater Hill-Murray to the Tier I tournament in 1993 and the Class AA tournament in 1997?

76) What Apple Valley forward provided yeoman service with his all-round play and earned all-tournament as the Eagles won the Class AA event in 1996 and now serves as an assistant coach at his alma mater?

77) Which Mahtomedi brothers were all-tourney in the 1994 Class A tournament as the Zephyrs copped third place?

78) What Duluth East defenseman played on four consecutive Greyhound teams to earn berths in the Class AA tourney from 1994-97?

79) What former Minneapolis South star coached the Tigers in the 1993 Tier II tourney, its first tourney appearance since 1957?

80) What two Totino-Grace brothers were all-tourney players for

coach Mark Loahr as the Eagles lost a 3-2 thriller to International Falls in the 1995 Class A finals?

81) Perhaps a decade later, this Duluth East player might have been awarded a goal in the classic 1996 Class AA semifinal against Apple Valley in the second overtime but video replays were not yet in use. Who was this frustrated Greyhound?

82) What coach led Eveleth-Gilbert to the Class A title in 1998, becoming one of just nine coaches to win a state title in their first-ever trip to the state tourney?

83) What Roseau goalie was superb in the 1990 title game, blocking 28 Grand Rapids shots as the Rams beat the Indians 3-1 in the all-northern final?

84) What Bloomington Jefferson defenseman and future NHL player played on the 1994 AA title team and played on a Stanley Cup winner with Tampa Bay in 2004?

85) What Minneapolis Roosevelt center led the Tier II tourney with nine points in 1992?

86) What stylish center led Lake of the Woods to the brink of a Tier II title in 1993 before Eveleth-Gilbert finally prevailed 3-2 in one of the most exciting finals ever?

87) What goaltender was outstanding, allowing just two goals to lead Bloomington Jefferson to the first Class AA state title in 1994?

88) In the 1990 tourney, Chad and Don Palodichuk played for South St. Paul. How many members of the Palodichuk family have made a tourney appearance for the Packers?

89) What East Grand Forks player had four goals and three assists in the Class A tourney in 1998 as the Green Wave claimed the consolation title?

90) What Hill-Murray all-tourney forward had two goals and three assists in the 1997 AA event?

1) Bloomington Jefferson. Coach Tom Saterdalen's dynasty won consecutive crowns in 1992 (Tier I), 1993 (Tier II), and 1994 (Class AA). The Jaguars record over that three-year span was 75-1-2, including a 49-game winning streak.

2) Amber Hegland. Playing for Farmington in the 1994 Class A tournament as a third-line center, she assisted on Troy Pilger's goal in a consolation game against Hermantown at Mariucci Arena. Hegland became the first girl to play in the boys' tourney as the Tigers lost to Mahtomedi 5-3 in the quarterfinals at the Civic Center. Hegland later went on to become a first-team All-American in softball at the University of Minnesota and also was captain of the 1998-99 Gopher women's hockey team that was third in the NCAA.

3) Dave Spehar and Derek Locker. Spehar scored a hat trick in each contest and led AA in scoring and scored the final two goals in a 5-3 win over Moorhead in the final game. Locker added a goal and seven assists. A year later, Locker would score 11 points,

Duluth East coach Mike Randolph pours water on star wing Dave Spehar as teammate Chris Locker looks on between the fourth and fifth overtimes of a 1996 Class AA semifinal eventually won by Apple Valley. (Photo:

including five assists in a 9-2 thumping over South St. Paul in the fifth-place game.

4) Performance during the regular-season. At the end of the regular-season, coaches in each of the eight sections rated the teams in order of their excellence. The top eight schools were placed in the top tier (Tier I) and the remainder of the teams were placed in the lower tier (Tier II). Thus, the ninth-ranked team in a given section was placed in Tier II. The size of the school or hockey program was not a factor. As a result, schools with large enrollments and lackluster records were relegated to Tier II. After two seasons of this experiment, it was decided that a two-class tournament would be established in 1994 based on enrollment.

5) Roseau beat Grand Rapids 3-1. In 1972, International Falls had beaten Grand Rapids 3-2 in an all-northern final.

6) Darby Hendrickson. Darby scored six points (four goals) in the tourney. A versatile player at the "U" for two years, he then played for the U.S. Olympic team in Norway in 1994. He played for five teams in the NHL, including four with the Wild. He scored the first goal for the Wild at the Xcel Energy Center. Hendrickson became a Wild assistant in 2010 after previously doing television work with Fox Sports Net.

7) Hill-Murray. Jeff Whisler's charges beat St. Paul Johnson 7-1 in the opener, hammered Grand Rapids 11-3 in the semis, and downed Duluth East 5-3 in the final.

8) Matt Cullen, who had seven points in the tourney. Cullen had two goals and an assist in the finals and scored a goal in double-overtime to give Moorhead a 5-4 win over Rochester Mayo in the semifinals. The son of head coach Terry Cullen, he later played two seasons at St. Cloud State before embarking on his NHL career. He won a Stanley Cup in 2006 with Carolina and is noted for his fine all-around play and his superior skating ability.

9) Pete Samargia, who surrendered just three goals in the three games.

10) Roseau. The Rams beat Grand Rapids 3-1 in the final with International Falls native Dean Blais as the head coach. Blais, a Gopher star and a two-time NCAA champ as coach at North Dakota, is now coach at Nebraska-Omaha.

11) Joey, who scored six goals to lead all scorers that year. Steve, who

played collegiately at Notre Dame and Providence, was the first to win it all in 1981. Tony, who was a Gopher player for three seasons, was on the 1989 Jaguar championship team.

12) Aaron Dwyer. In the famous 1996 semifinal contest, the junior defenseman from Apple Valley ripped a 40-foot shot past goalie Kyle Kolquist to give the Eagles a 5-4 win at 2:12 of the 5th overtime. The game lasted a record 93 minutes and 12 seconds, outdistancing the 1955 quarterfinal game between Minneapolis South and Thief River Falls (South won 3-2 in 11 overtimes) which lasted 87:50.

13) Johnny Pohl of Red Wing. The Wingers beat Warroad 4-3, a year after losing 10-3 to the Warriors. Pohl, a future Gopher All-American and NHL player, totaled six points in 1997. Pohl was the state's career scoring leader for 11 years after finishing his sterling high school career with 378 points (144 goals and a state-record 234 assists).

14) Dave Spehar. As a junior in 2005, Spehar had a hat trick in each game, including the AA title game when East downed Moorhead 5-3 to win its first state crown since 1960. As a senior, he scored nine goals and four assists to lead AA in scoring, tied for the third-highest one-tournament total. However, his team was ousted in the semifinals when Apple Valley beat them 5-4 in the semifinals in the longest game in tourney history. Spehar is just one of seven players to lead the tourney in scoring two years in a row. As a tenth-grader in 1994, Spehar had two goals and five assists as the Greyhounds took third place. In nine tourney games, Spehar had 20 goals and nine assists for 29 total points, second-best all-time.

15) Yes. Schools that qualify by enrollment for Class A (smaller schools) may opt up to play in Class AA and Roseau has done it twice (1999 and 2007).

16) Mike Crowley. The offensive-minded Crowley, perhaps the most creative defenseman since Phil Housley, was a regular as a sophomore when Jefferson won the first Tier I title in 1992. He was all-tourney in 1993 as Jefferson won the second and last Tier I crown, whipping Hill-Murray 4-1 as Crowley had a goal and assist in the finale. In the first Class AA championship game in 1994, Crowley also had a goal and assist in a 3-1 win over Moorhead. Crowley became an All-American at Minnesota in 1996 and 1997 and had 120 assists in just three seasons as a Gopher. He played 67 games for the Anaheim Mighty Ducks over parts of two seasons.

17) Chris Marinucci, who won the Hobey Baker award at UMD in 1994. As a 10th-grader at Grand Rapids in 1988, Marinucci tied Kevin Degel of Bloomington Jefferson and Larry Olimb of Warroad for the tourney scoring lead with six points with a goal and five assists.

18) Mark and Mike Strobel. Mark led the tourney in scoring with seven points (four goals and three assists) while Mike had four goals and two assists. The brother duo then played together at Wisconsin.

19) Dan Welch, Ben Tharp, and Jeff Taffe, all who earned scholarships to Minnesota. Taffe, the 1999 Minnesota Mr. Hockey award winner, later played in the NHL for six teams, including the Wild.

20) Jamie Langenbrunner and Sergei Petrov. Langenbrunner also broke the single tourney assist mark with 10 as Cloquet won the consolation title. Petrov had six goals.

21) Nine. Three teams in Tier I (Blaine, Eden Prairie, Moorhead) and six in Tier II with Alexandria, Cambridge, Mahtomedi, New Ulm/New Ulm Cathedral, Orono, and Rosemount all making their initial showing.

22) Ryan Kraft, who scored Moorhead's only goal in a 3-1 loss to champion Jefferson. Kraft had a hat trick in a 4-3 semifinal win over South St. Paul and four goals and an assist in a 7-3 first-round triumph over White Bear Lake. In 1993, he scored the overtime winner in the second extra-session of a 4-3 victory over Elk River in the third-place game. As a sophomore in the first Tier I tourney a year earlier, Kraft had two goals and three assists as Moorhead was second again, losing 6-3 to Jefferson. As a Gopher, Kraft scored 62 goals and eventually played seven games in the NHL for the San Jose Sharks.

23) Karl Goehring, who had 37 saves alone in the overtimes. Goehring would backstop the Eagles to the title with 21 more saves in the 3-2 final win over Edina. Goehring won an NCAA title at North Dakota in 2000 and twice was Academic All-American.

24) Tom Moore and Johnny Pohl. Moore totaled 12 goals and six assists over that span and had six goals and three assists in his senior season. Pohl, meanwhile, is tied for third all-time with 28 points in career scoring at the state tournament.

25) Jason Blake. The tough 5'10" speedster was All-American at North Dakota in 1998-99 and played in the Turin Olympics in 2006 and play 14 NHL seasons for four clubs. He won the Bill Masterton Award in 2007-08.

26) Chris Gotziamann, a New Jersey draft pick who played four years at North Dakota.

27) Mike Crowley (Minnesota); Ben Clymer (Minnesota), Ryan Trebil (Minnesota) and Josh DeWolf (St. Cloud).

28) Warroad (24-4), which beat Hibbing 5-3 in the finals.

29) Erik Westrum, whose father Pat played for Minneapolis Roosevelt in the 1966 event and later captained Minnesota. Erik tallied a hat trick in the unforgettable 1996 win over Duluth East and five points overall in that tournament. Erik went to the U of M where he was twice an MVP. He also played 27 games in the NHL with three teams, including 10 with the Wild.

30) Jeff Antonovich, whose father Mike was one of the tourney's most dynamic performers in the late 1960's. Jeff had three goals and three assists in the tourney, joining teammates Jason Koski, Jason Alto, and Mike Vekich on the Tier II all-tourney squad.

31) Mark Parrish, an offensive-zone dynamo. Parrish scored a goal in the 1994 AA final, a 3-1 win over Moorhead and a goal and three assists as the Jaguars claimed fifth place. He was a great player at St. Cloud State for two seasons before embarking on a pro career that saw him play for several NHL teams, including the Wild for two seasons. He played on the U.S. Olympic team in 2006 in Turin, Italy.

32) Troy Riddle, yet another tourney star who went to the University of Minnesota on scholarship. Riddle had a pure hat trick in a first-round win over Hermantown and two goals in the 4-2 win over East Grand Forks in the finals.

33) Red Wing (28-0 in 1997 in Class A).

34) Chris Hvinden, whose team ended up runner-up to Greenway-Coleraine (6-1 loss) in the first of two Tier II championship games. Rosemount, a large school by enrollment, was relegated to Tier II status due to their 1-20-1 regular-season record. However, the Irish won five straight to reach the finals at Target Center.

35) Ross and Rheese Carlson. Rheese had two goals and two assists and Ross had a goal and two assists.

36) Brian Nelson, who finished with five goals as Moorhead took third place.

37) Dave Spehar. The Greyhound sharpshooter tied John Mayasich's record performed in 1951. Spehar had three goals each against Jefferson in the first round, Edina in the semis, and Moorhead in the finals. His nine points led AA in scoring. Spehar scored 171 career goals at East, a state record until broken by Ben Hanowski of Little Falls in 2009. Spehar is second in state tourney hat tricks with five.

38) 93 minutes and 12 seconds. Three regulations periods totaled 45 minutes so the teams played 48:12 of sudden-death overtime, more than the equivalent of two games. The Minneapolis South-Thief River Falls 11-overtime quarterfinal in 1955 took 87:50 and the Minnetonka-Hill Murray semifinal in 2010 took 86:31 while the 2011 AA final between Eden Prairie and Duluth East culminated in 80:43.

39) Sean Goldsworthy, the offspring of North Star wing Bill Goldsworthy, who scored 267 goals for Minnesota over 11 seasons and had his number 8 retired by the team before they moved to Dallas. Sean has been the head coach at St. Olaf since 1997.

40) Mike Crowley, Joe Bianchi, and Ian Peterson.

41) Johnny (1995-98), Mark (1996-99), Mike (2002), and Tom (2002). All four of them earned all-tournament status, too.

42) Alexandria, which beat White Bear Lake 7-2 in a decisive fifth-place game triumph. They had played eventual champ Apple Valley tough in the first round, losing 3-1 in an evenly-fought contest that was tied with 12 minutes remaining.

43) Brian Bonin. The Bear center had an assist on Matt Henderson's goal in the second overtime as White Bear Lake bested Bloomington Kennedy 5-4 for fifth place. Bonin was Mr. Hockey as a senior (1992) and became a two-time All-American at Minnesota in 1995 and 1996, winning the Hobey Baker award in the latter year. Bonin played in 12 games with the Wild and Penguins.

44) Paul Martin, who was apparently talented enough to have been an all-state player on the basketball court, too. He was Mr. Hockey

his senior year and then was an integral part of two NCAA championships with Minnesota for Don Lucia and has played in the NHL with New Jersey and Pittsburgh for the past 11 years.

45) Warroad, which capped a 24-4 season by beating Red Wing in the finals. The Warriors shut out Detroit Lakes 6-0 and Breck 5-0 before allowing three goals in their final game.

46) Chris Markstrom

47) Dan Welch, whose team lost 4-0 to Roseau in the finals. Welch's father Russ was the Hastings mentor who brought four teams from the river city to the tourney after five trips as the coach at South St. Paul.

48) Toby Peterson. A standout for Colorado College for four years, Peterson played for Pittsburgh, Edmonton, and Dallas in ten NHL seasons as a two-way wing.

49) Derek Locker, who had two goals in the championship game and another in a 2-1 semifinal triumph over Burnsville.

50) Red Wing, which won Class A in 1997, was runner-up in 1996, and third in 1998.

51) Rosemount was 1-20-1 entering sectional play in the first year of the Tier I and II experiment. A larger school playing in the Lake Conference, the Irish were relegated to Tier II based on their performance. They won all three sectional games, defeating Farmington in overtime in the finals. They then beat Mpls. Roosevelt 2-1 in overtime on Matt Hansen's goal and then downed Cambridge 7-1 before being handled 6-1 by Greenway-Coleraine/Nashwauk-Keewatin in the Tier II finals. The Raiders entered the post-season with a lowly 10-12 mark before winning six straight to finish 16-10.

52) Jay Kopischke

53) Jason and Brent Godbout. Jason had a goal and an assist and Brent three assists. In 1992, Hill-Murray was fourth in Tier I, with Brent scoring four goals and two assists and Jason adding a goal and three assists. In 1993, the Pioneers lost 4-0 to Jefferson in the title game in Class AA as both Godbout's were all-tournament. Jason scored three goals and added three assists and Brent contributed two goals and two assists.

54) Tom Serratore, who has been in charge at Bemidji State since 2001. Sibley's George Awada had a goal and five assists in the 1993 Tier II tourney.

55) Jeff Hall, the son of Jon Hall, who was one of three leading scorers in 1961. Jeff had a 20-save shutout as the Hornets edged Duluth East 1-0. It was his second shutout as he had nine saves in a 3-0 first-round win over Henry Sibley.

56) Kyle Kolquist, who allowed only a first-period goal in a 1-0 loss to Edina in the finals and finished with 16 saves. In the semis, he blanked Moorhead 3-0 with 12 saves.

57) Ben Utecht. The 6'6" goalie, whose grandfather Bob was the public-address announcer for the North Stars, had 28 saves in the 6-4 win over Edina for fifth-place. Utecht also started in the quarterfinals when Duluth East, the eventual champs, beat them 5-4. He was the backup in 1989 when Hastings lost 4-0 in the finals but made four saves in mop-up duty. A Gopher star, Utecht played for the Colts when they won the Super Bowl in 2006.

58) Jon Austin. The diminutive center scored with just 18 seconds left as International Falls nipped Totino-Grace 3-2 in the championship game. A day earlier, he tallied with 5:02 left to down Warroad 3-2. Austin scored twice in a 5-1 win over Detroit Lakes, too.

59) Andrew Alberts, a sound defensive defenseman who played ten NHL seasons with Boston, Philadelphia, Carolina, and Vancouver.

60) Wyatt Smith. All-tournament both years, he led Warroad to the 1994 A title and scored the tying and winning markers in the 5-3 finale against Hibbing. In the semis his overtime tally beat Mahtomedi 3-2. Smith assisted on Zach Hallett's game-winner in a 4-3 victory over Hermantown. In 1995, he had three goals and two assists as Warroad finished third. Smith played for 5 NHL teams, including a year with the Wild in 2006-07.

61) Brandon Steege. In 1990, Steege had two assists for Burnsville as the Braves bowed out with two consecutive losses. The next year, playing for Richfield, Brandon scored five points as the Spartans took fifth place. Steege had three goals and two assists and tallied in overtime to give his team a 4-3 win over Roseau in a consolation semifinal.

62) Kaine Martell (two goals, five assists) and Josh Heppner (one goal, six assists).

63) Brian Urick, who had a goal as Minnetonka lost to Duluth East (3-1) and Osseo (4-3).

64) Jason Miskowic. The Bengal player scored against Blair Hovel of Alexandria in a 3-2 consolation-round loss after scoring his team's only goal in a 7-1 first-round defeat to Duluth East.

65) Jake Brandt, who had a 19-save shutout in the 4-0 win over Hastings. Brandt also had 19 saves in a 6-2 semifinal defeat of Holy Angels and 14 in a 4-2 win over Rochester Mayo in the first round.

66) Jon Maruk, the son of Denis Maruk, who played for seven years with the North Stars and totaled 356 goals in his long NHL career. Jon had two goals and three assists in 1996 and two goals and five assists in 1997 as he was all-tourney his senior year.

67) Farmington. Justan Duden and Geron Schramske, both scored a goal for the Tigers, who were coached by Shawn Anderson and were appearing in their first state tourney.

68) Tim McDonald, who had a hat trick in the semis, finished with four goals and three assists.

69) Steve Hurt, who played in the 1984 tourney.

70) Nick Angell. In both seasons, the Greyhounds made it to the championship game, losing 1-0 to Edina in 1997 and winning 3-1 over Anoka in 1998. Angell, who was a regular for the Gophers when they won the 2002 NCAA title, had a goal and two assists in 1997.

71) Zach Young, who also had an assist on Josh Studier's overtime goal in a 5-4 first-round win over Orono. Young finished the tourney with three goals and four assists.

72) Dan Carlson, who would captain Notre Dame prior to a long minor-league career.

73) Mike Klema, who led the tourney in scoring, had two goals in the finals, a hat trick in the semis and two in the first-round.

74) John Brummer, his second goal of the game.

75) Steve Rohlik, who was a standout for Hill-Murray in the mid-1980's. The Pioneers were second in 1993 and fourth in 1997.

76) Chris Sikich. The stocky center had a goal in the 3-2 final win over Edina and two assists in the unforgettable 5-4 five-overtime triumph over Duluth East the night before.

77) Jesse and Brandon Sampair. In a 7-2 win over St. Cloud Cathedral in the third-place game, Brandon had four goals and an assist and Jesse assisted on five goals, including each of Brandon's markers. Jesse finished with two goals and seven assists while Brandon had five goals and three assists overall.

78) Dylan Mills, who was a four-year regular for Don Lucia's Gophers and assisted Mike Randolph in the tourneys from 2011 to 2015.

79) Rick Alm. The Tigers lost 4-2 to St. Cloud Cathedral and 3-0 to Orono.

80) Aaron and Ryan Radfield. Aaron, a goalie, allowed just five goals in the tourney and Ryan had two goals and an assist.

81) Matt LaTour, who appeared to tip in Dylan Mills's point-shot but the whistle never blew and play continued. During a television time-out, replays were rather convincing in indicating that LaTour did, indeed, score.

82) Craig Homola, the Eastern Collegiate Hockey Association MVP in 1979-80 for the Vermont Catamounts. Eveleth-Gilbert downed Hermantown 4-2 in the finals with Tony Dolinsek scoring twice.

83) Jerome Butler, who gave up just four goals in the entire tourney.

84) Ben Clymer, who was a first-round choice of the Boston Bruins but played all of his 483 NHL games with either Tampa Bay or Washington. He's now an analyst on *Fox Sports North*.

85) Scott Lynch, who had four goals and five assists as the Teddies finished fifth. He had two goals and three assists in the 5-4 fifth-place game, including the winning goal in overtime, assisted by his brother Sean, who had a goal and three assists.

86) Mark Amundsen, who ended up as the leading scorer in the second and last Tier II tourney. Amundsen, whose father John coached the team, finished with six goals and four assists. He had six points alone in a 7-4 first round win over Totino-Grace, which included a natural hat trick in a 4:17 span later in the final stanza.

Amundsen and four of his teammates were from Rainy River, Ontario, which is in a cooperative with Lake of the Woods?

87) Jeff Heil, an all-tourney pick for his brilliant play in the nets for the Jaguars. Heil had 29 saves in the 3-1 championship victory over Moorhead, 21 saves in a 2-1 nail-biter over Duluth East in the semis, and 18 saves in a 1-0 blanking of Osseo in the first round as Jefferson wrapped up their third straight title.

88) All told, eight members of the Palodichuk family with the proud last name have performed in the state tournament for the Packers. Tony (1961-62), Larry (1962, 1965), Al (1965), John (1966), Roger (1968), Jeff (1978), Don (1989-90), and Chad (1990).

89) Tyler Palmiscno, who had two goals and two assists in the 6-2 fifth-place win over Jeff Poeschl's Mahtomedi's Zephyrs. In 2014 and 2015, he coached his alma mater to state titles in Class A, with both victories over Hermantown.

90) Brandon Sampair, who also appeared in the 1994 tourney with Mahtomedi.

Apple Valley players swarm Aaron Dwyer, who scored the winning goal to defeat Duluth East in an epic five-overtime semifinal, 1996. (photo: Rick Orndorf/Dakota Co. Tribune.)

7 The 2000s

1) Who is the only school to win a state title without being scored on?

2) In the 2001 AA tourney, what two future Gopher teammates were the go-to players for Greenway-Coleraine as the Raiders took third place?

3) What cowboy-boot-wearing coach led his team to the AA title in 2001 by hammering Moorhead 8-1 in the championship game?

4) What Eden Prairie defenseman led the Eagles to the 2009 AA title with his superlative all-around game and later was drafted in the first round by his hometown Minnesota Wild?

5) The number of teams in Class AA currently totals 72. How many teams played in Class A as of the 2014-15 season?

6) Both the champions in 2000 were first-time state titlists and each school's name started with the letter "B". Who were these Class AA and A schools, respectively?

7) What Edina senior led Class AA in scoring in 2009 with nine points (one goal and eight assists) after transferring from St. Thomas Academy for the 2007-08 season?

8) All-State in both hockey and football his senior season, what Virginia/Mt. Iron-Buhl defenseman and present NHL regular led his 2005 team to a tourney berth?

9) What Little Falls standout became Minnesota's all-time leading scorer in 2009 and led the way for the Flyers in the state tourney, where they finished third in Class A?

10) Grand Rapids finished second in consecutive years (2006, 2007) in Class AA and was outscored 12-1 overall in those two finals. What player scored the only goal for the Thunderhawks in those two finals?

11) What rugged Holy Angels winger scored four goals in a semifinal win over Roseville in the 2002 Class AA semis and was critical in helping the Stars to the title?

12) What future Gopher forward scored a hat trick for Red Wing in their 5-2 semifinal win over Rochester Lourdes in the 2002 Class A tourney?

13) Two Wayzata multi-sport stars in the 2004 Class AA tournament later made it in the National Football League. Who were those players?

14) What present NHL player scored two hat tricks in Breck School's 2004 "A" title drive?

15) Who was the 8th-grade prodigy who starred for St. Thomas Academy at forward in the 2005 Class A state tourney and even made the all-tourney team?

16) The length of periods in state tourney play was extended from 15 minutes to how many minutes for the 2004 tournament?

17) In the 2011 Class A title game, what St. Thomas Academy forward was clutch in bringing the Cadets back from a 3-0 deficit and an eventual 5-4 overtime triumph with a shorthanded goal to make it 3-1 and the tying marker in the third period?

18) A former state tourney player with White Bear Lake in 1967, what tough-as-nails defenseman for the Gophers and Fighting Saints, led his alma mater as coach to the 2001 tourney where they finished sixth?

19) In 2005, what dynamic forward led Holy Angels Academy to the AA crown with four goals and two assists as the Stars won their second title in four years?

20) What Duluth East goalie set a then-tourney record for saves in a single period with 22 in the second period in a AA semifinal loss (4-1) versus Moorhead in 2005?

21) Class AA champion in 2007, Roseau had two standout sophomores who went on to play in the WCHA? Who were they?

22) In the 2001 Class A championship, what two brothers each tallied to give Benilde-St. Margaret's a 2-1 win over Rochester Lourdes?

23) What Little Falls scoring line combined to score an incredible 313 points prior to the 2007 Class A tournament?

24) During the 2002 Class AA tourney, which school's fans held up signs that read,"WE GAVE UP LOSING FOR LENT"?

25) Who was the offensive catalyst that catapulted Grand Rapids to two straight title games in Class AA in 2006 and 2007?

26) What Lakeville High goalie made 111 saves in his three starts as the Panthers finished sixth in the 2004 Class AA tourney and later won a Division III title as a collegian?

27) What Holy Angels defenseman was a standout for the Stars in the 2003 Class AA event, starred at Colorado College and then competed in the NHL?

28) In 2007, Burnsville's head coach was a fellow named Janne Kivihalme. What European nation does he hail from?

29) Minnetonka, a talent-laden club playing in the 2010 Class AA event, possessed three Division I defenseman. Who were they?

30) Teammates Quinn Ellingson and Cory Ellertson tied for the Class A scoring lead in 2005 with seven points each. What school did they play for?

31) What NHL forward first made his mark as a dynamite all-around player for Warroad, helping them win Class A titles in 2003 and 2005?

32) What Eden Prairie sophomore goaltender had a .939 save percentage, including a 28-save blanking of Moorhead in the finals, as the Eagles claimed the AA title in 2009? (As a senior, backstopped his team to a second AA crown in 2011 with 63 saves and a .955 save percentage.)

33) In 2002, what muscular wing scored a goal and three assists for Roseville in leading the Raiders to a third-place finish in AA?

34) A power forward for Blaine in 2000, who helped lead the Bengals to the AA title that season by scoring three goals and four assists for a tourney-high seven points?

35) What South St. Paul goaltender wowed the crowds with his puck-handling abilities in the 2004 Class A tournament?

36) What Warroad stud led Class A in scoring in 2010 with 11 points on the strength of six goals and five assists?

37) Which school upset top-seeded Roseau in the 2008 AA tournament semifinals by the score of 6-2, breaking the Rams' 42-game undefeated streak?

38) What Hibbing tenth-grade forward led Class A in scoring in 2003 with three goals and six assists as the Mark DeCenzo-coached Bluejackets finished fifth?

39) A freshman for Apple Valley was all-tournament in 2010 after recording a goal and assist as the Eagles finished fourth with a youthful roster? Who was he?

40) What two teams played in the longest-ever championship game in Class A in 2005?

41) What St. Thomas Academy players both scored twice in a 5-1 win over Duluth Marshall in the Class A title tilt in 2008?

42) What St. Thomas Academy goaltender was all-tournament all three seasons as the Cadets won three straight Class A titles in 2011, 2012, and 2013.

43) Who was Mr. Hockey in Minnesota in 2004 and capped off his high school career by being an integral part of the Centennial Chiefs' state championship run that season?

44) The leading scorer in AA in 2006, what Cretin-Derham Hall player had three goals and six assists for the Raiders?

45) What feisty defenseman was all-tournament for Totino-Grace in 2005 when the Eagles lost 4-3 in double-overtime to Warroad?

46) What Cretin-Derham Hall center scored a AA-high six goals in the 2006 tourney, balancing his offense with two tallies in Raider victories over Eagan, Blaine, and Grand Rapids?

47) What Hermantown junior forward led Class A in scoring in 2007 as the Hawks copped their first title by going unbeaten (29-0-1)?

48) In 2002, what Totino-Grace player scored two goals to spark his team to its only Class A state championship as the Eagles edged Red Wing 3-2?

49) What Cretin-Derham Hall defenseman from the 2009 Class AA tourney was all-state in both football and hockey and turned down an offer to play quarterback at Iowa?

50) What two Blaine forwards each scored twice to lead the Bengals to a 6-0 triumph over Duluth East in the 2000 Class AA championship game?

51) Possessing a famous name in Warroad hockey, what sophomore forward scored the goal in the second overtime that gave the Warriors the 2005 Class A crown?

52) Who was the colorful Burnsville player who tied for the scoring lead in Class AA in 2007 with four goals and three assists and scored tying goals to send two games into overtime?

53) Who was the leading scorer in the AA tourney in 2001 for the first-place Elk River Elks?

54) What Rochester Lourdes defenseman played in the 1999-2000 tournament and has played the past ten NHL seasons with Boston, Atlanta, and Winnipeg?

55) What Elk River player had a hat trick in the Elks' 8-1 romp over Moorhead in the Class AA final in 2001?

56) Who was the Breck eighth-grader who helped Breck to fifth place in the 2011 A tourney?

57) Anoka's starting goaltender on the 2003 Class AA champion gave up just one goal in both the semis and finals that year. Who was this all-tournament netminder?

58) He recorded 21 saves in a 6-0 shutout over Duluth East in the 2000 Class AA final. What was the name of this Blaine goalie?

59) What Breck goalie was all-tournament two years in succession as his Mustang club, coached by Les Larson, won consecutive Class A crowns in 2009 and 2010?

60) What Edina forward scored four goals in the consolation title game in AA in 2009 and three in the consolation semifinals on his way to all-tournament status?

61) What junior Cretin-Derham Hall defenseman was all-tourney in the AA tourney in 2006 with his strong all-around skills, scoring twice in the 7-0 thumping of Grand Rapids in the championship game?

62) What school scored three goals in the final 2:47 to tie Grand Rapids in the 2007 Class AA semifinals before losing in overtime?

63) In the 2006 Class A event, what St. Thomas Academy forward scored the winning goal for the Cadets not only in the semifinals but also in the finals?

64) What Moorhead defenseman was voted Mr. Hockey in 2005 and was all-tournament for the second-place Spuds?

65) Adept at both providing scoring chances and diffusing them, what Centennial defenseman was a huge factor in keeping all three opponents scoreless in the 2004 Class AA tourney?

66) Who led AA tourney scoring in 2003, a Moorhead player who had four goals and an assist?

67) Champion of Class AA in 2002, which two Holy Angels forwards shared the scoring lead that year with seven points?

68) What Duluth Marshall forward scored four goals in a 9-2 first-round pounding of Little Falls in Class A in 2005 and scored two more in a 3-1 third-place triumph over St. Thomas Academy?

69) A sophomore for Minnetonka, he scored his only point of the 2010 AA tourney when he scored at 2:31 of the fourth overtime as the Skippers beat Hill-Murray 2-1 in a semifinal that ended well past midnight. Who was this player?

70) An all-tourney forward for Blaine's AA champions in 2000, what player scored three goals and two assists for the Bengals that year, and has played for Colorado, Edmonton, Nashville, and Washington in the NHL after four seasons at St. Cloud State?

71) A defenseman for Holy Angels in both 2003 and 2004, which Stars player later became the first Minnesotan ever to become the top pick in the NHL draft in 2006?

72) An all-tourney pick in 2004 in AA, what Centennial forward scored twice and assisted on another in a 3-0 win over Wayzata?

73) When A.J. Reid of champion St. Thomas Academy was awarded the Class A Herb Brooks Award following the 2011 state title game, what former St. Thomas Academy defenseman presented it to him?

74) What White Bear Lake forward, who scored a goal in the 2001 AA tourney, had his name engraved on the Stanley Cup when he was called up to play four games for the Anaheim Mighty Ducks in the 2007 finals against Ottawa?

75) Which Roseau skater led the AA tourney in scoring in 2010 with a goal and five assists and as a freshman in 2007 totaled four assists for the champion Rams?

76) What Fergus Falls forward was all-tourney in Class A in both 2001 and 2002 and tied Hermantown's B.J. Radovich for the 2001 scoring lead with nine points (seven goals)?

77) What Anoka forward was all-tournament for the champion Tornadoes in the Class AA tourney, scoring the winner in a 4-3 quarterfinal win over Duluth East with 18 ticks left?

78) Blessed with great reach and leverage, what lanky Moorhead center was magic with the puck in leading the Spuds to the AA championship game in 2005?

79) A future star for the hometown UMD Bulldogs, what superb Duluth Marshall puck-handler was a key performer on Hilltopper squads that were second in Class A in 2006 and 2007?

80) What Eden Prairie forward was all-tourney in both 2009 and 2011 as the Eagles claimed Class AA titles both years?

81) What team scored the second-most goals ever in a tournament game with 13 in a Class A first-round game in 2011?

82) What Duluth East junior trio formed the first forward line for the Greyhounds that lost a 3-2 heartbreaker to Eden Prairie in three overtimes in the Class AA final in 2011?

83) What Hermantown linemates combined for nine goals and 20 points in leading the Hawks to a runner-up finish in the 2011 Class A event?

84) What two sets of twins played vital roles in Eden Prairie's 3-2 three-overtime win over Duluth East in the 2011 Class AA championship game?

85) What dynamic Hibbing sophomore forward recorded a natural hat trick in a span of 3:29 in a 6-4 semifinal loss to Hermantown in Class A in 2011?

86) Who was the Benilde-St. Margaret's goaltender who played a vital role on both of the Red Knights' Class A championship teams in 1999 and 2001?

87) What school made just their second state tourney appearance in 46 years in 2011 and claimed third place with a 3-0 win over Hibbing/Chisholm after going to state eight times from 1951-65?

88) Which two Duluth East defenseman were all-tournament for Mike Randolph's young team in 2011 with their solid defensive-zone play and rugged body checks?

89) Sauk Rapids-Rice made its lone appearance in Class A in 2000 and finished fourth and was led by what sophomore skater who eventually played in the NHL?

90) Which two St. Thomas Academy forwards were all-tournament for the 2011 Class A champions and tied for the scoring lead with seven points and also were freshmen on the 2008 Cadet team that won the A crown?

91) What Red Wing defenseman displayed a well-rounded game to earn all-tourney as the Wingers finished runner-up to Totino-Grace (3-2 loss) in Class A in 2002?

92) Which Anoka all-tourney player became one of the few players to win a state title with his father coaching the team in the Class AA tournament in 2003?

93) Which Duluth East forward recorded a hat trick and two assists in a 7-4 win in the third-place game of the 2004 AA tourney and was the overall scoring leader with five goals and three assists?

94) Who is the only team in state history to win 30 games and not win a state championship?

95) He was all-tourney player in AA in both 2006 and 2007 and a major reason why the Grand Rapids Thunderhawks made it into the championship game those years. What was this defenseman's name who played collegiately at Dartmouth?

96) Always a steadying influence on his team, what Duluth Marshall defenseman was all-tourney in 2007 and 2008 as the Hilltoppers were runner-up both years in Class A?

97) He won the Herb Brooks award for Class AA in 2008 but he also posted a .977 save percentage and recorded two shutouts in a dominating performance. Who was this Hill-Murray goalie who had 83 saves and allowed just two goals as the Pioneers won their third state crown?

98) What Breck forward capped off his career by scoring a goal and three assists as the Mustangs defeated Warroad 7-3 in the Class A title game in 2009?

99) What Edina freshman wing had an assist in Edina's 4-2 title-clinching win over Minnetonka in AA in 2010, bringing fond memories of 1984 for his namesake?

100) Who was the highest-scoring defenseman in the 2011 AA tournament, scoring two goals and four assists in helping Eden Prairie to their second title in three years?

101) In what year did the Class AA semifinals draw the largest crowd to ever witness an indoor hockey game in Minnesota history?

102) In 2015, what AA team finished as the runners-up despite fielding a roster with one 8th-grader and three freshmen?

103) In one of the most electrifying efforts in the history of state championship games, what Benilde-St. Margaret's forward scored all five of his team's goals in a 5-1 triumph over Hill-Murray in the AA final in 2012?

104) What stalwart Moorhead goalie was outstanding for the Spuds in both 2011 and 2012 and now is a star netminder for Bemidji State University?

105) What two Rochester Lourdes forwards were outstanding players for the Eagles in four tourneys from 2010-13, finishing among the top ten among all scorers in career points?

106) What school became the first team from southwest Minnesota to earn a state tourney berth in 2013?

107) What school from northwestern Minnesota won consecutive Class A crowns under the auspices of a former "Green Wave" player in 2014 and 2015?

108) In what year did each of the top four seeds in Class AA lose in the quarterfinals?

109) What three stalwarts made for a potent first line for East Grand Forks in 2014 and 2015, leading the skaters from the Red River Valley to Class A titles both years?

110) What two teams played the longest scoreless game in tourney lore on March 4, 2015, a game that didn't see a goal scored until more than 56 minutes had elapsed?

111) What St. Thomas Academy sophomore scored a power-play goal with just six seconds left to give his team a 5-4 win over Hermantown in the Class A title game in 2013?

112) What two Hermantown forwards made Class A all-tournament in both 2014 and 2015 as top-liners for the Hawks?

113) The Mr. Hockey Award winner in 2012, what Lakeville South center and future Gopher paved the way to a third-place finish in AA for the Cougars?

114) What Duluth East player was a standout on defense for Mike Randolph on Greyhound teams for four seasons (2011-14), earning

all-tournament his final two seasons?

115) What defenseman for St. Thomas Academy scored four goals for the Cadets in a 11-0 semifinal win over East Grand Forks in Class A in 2013?

116) What talented winger helped lead Edina to Class AA titles in both 2013 and 2014?

117) What Hermantown defenseman was exceptional on both offense and defense for the Eagles from 2010-12, as he was named all-tournament in Class A each of those seasons?

118) Unseeded Benilde-St. Margaret's won the 2012 Class AA title by virtue of beating Hill-Murray 5-1 in the title game. It was a storybook ending for a team that had to deal with a tragic injury to one its players on December 30, 2011 that season. What was the name of the Red Knight player who was paralyzed after a check in a game at St. Louis Park?

119) What three brothers, all bound for St. Cloud State, led Lakeville North to the 2015 AA title in 2015 and a runners-up finish in 2014?

120) In what year were eight of the 16 head coaches in their first year coaching in the state tournament?

121) What Hill-Murray 8th-grade forward played a regular shift as the Pioneers' took second in the 2013 AA tournament?

122) Which six players were members of the St. Thomas Academy team that won three-straight Class A titles in 2011, 2012, and 2013?

1) Centennial won the AA crown in 2004 by not allowing a single goal. The Cougars beat Holy Angels 2-0 in the first round, blanked Wayzata 3- 0 in the semis and then edged Moorhead 1-0 in the final. Greg Stutz recorded all three shutouts.

2) Gino Guyer and Andy Sertich, whose team played overtime in each of its three games. Guyer (three goals, three assists) and Sertich (two goals, four assists) each scored six points with each getting a game-winner. Guyer was Mr. Hockey in 2001 and both the former Raiders were on the national champion Gopher team in 2003. Sertich (249) and Guyer (282) combined to score 531 points for Greenway in their joint career there.

3) Tony Sarsland, who led the Elks (29-1-1) to their first-ever title in their third trip to state, outshooting Moorhead 31-17 in the finals.

4) Nick Leddy, who was also named Mr. Hockey following his senior season before playing one season with the Gophers. Leddy scored 5 points in 2009. He made his debut in the NHL for Chicago in 2010 and is currently playing for the Islanders.

5) Eighty-seven schools play in Class A; 41 teams are cooperatively sponsored. The team with the most high schools joined together playing hockey presently is Minneapolis with eight different schools joining forces. At present, 153 teams participate in boys' ice hockey.

6) Blaine was the AA champ by virtue of their 6-0 blanking of Duluth East while Breck School was crowned with the A title by besting Warroad 3-2.

7) Anders Lee, who played in three tourneys for St. Thomas, totaling six points in those years for the Cadets. He scored 16 total points in his 15 state tournament contests. Lee is currently playing for the Islanders.

8) Matt Niskanen, who played at nearby UMD before performing admirably for the Dallas Stars for eight years. He signed a long-term deal with the Washington Capitals prior to the 2014 season.

9) Ben Hanowski, who led Class A in scoring in both 2008 (10 points) and 2009 (9 points). He scored 7 goals to lead both classes those years and finished his four-year stint in the state tournament

with 19 goals and nine assists for 28 points, tied for third all-time. Hanowski played for St. Cloud State after setting the all-time Minnesota high school boys' hockey mark for most points with 405. He holds the state record for career goals (196) and also totaled 209 assists in his 4 years with the Flyers. He also holds the state single-season mark for both goals (73) and points (135), both set in 2009. He made his NHL debut with Calgary in 2013.

10) Corey Kosak. The junior defenseman, whose father Jim played for Greenway-Coleraine in 1969 and 1970, scored the only goal in a 5-1 loss to Roseau in 2007. Cretin-Derham Hall shut out Grand Rapids 7-0 the previous season in the championship match.

11) Dan Kronick, who later played collegiately at UMD.

12) Tom Pohl. The Wingers lost to Totino-Grace 3-2 in the title game. Pohl finished with seven points, just a point behind Class A leading scorer Brandon Harrington of Rochester Lourdes, a sophomore who had three goals and five assists. Mike Pohl, a brother to Tom, John and Mark, tallied six points.

13) James Laurinaitis and Dominique Barber. An All-American linebacker at Ohio State, Laurinaitis had three assists for the Trojans, who lost 1-0 to eventual-champ Centennial in the semifinals. Laurinaitis is now starring for the St. Louis Rams. Barber, who has played with the Houston Texans as a defensive back, had an assist.

14) Blake Wheeler, who had three goals in the opener versus Albert Lea and three more in the final against Orono. At 6'5", Wheeler exhibited deceptive speed and exceptional hands. Now with Winnipeg after tours with Atlanta and Boston in the NHL, Wheeler totaled 11 points in that tourney and later played three seasons with the Gophers and was the MVP of the 2007 WCHA Final Five after scoring the overtime winner against North Dakota.

15) Jordan Schroeder, who had two goals and three assists as STA finished fourth. Schroeder had a goal in the 2006 Class final to help St. Thomas to a 4-3 win over Duluth Marshall to earn all-tourney again. He played two years with the Gophers. He was drafted in the first round by Vancouver in 2009, and after playing sparingly for the Canucks, was acquired by the Wild prior to the 2014-15 season. Another eighth-grader, Anders Lee, also competed for the Cadets but did not score.

16) 17 minutes

17) Andrew Commers. In 2012, Commers led the Cadets in scoring with 2 goals and 4 assists as they dumped Hermantown again (5-1) for the Class A title.

18) Bill Butters, who played mostly with the Minnesota Fighting Saints in 217 games in the WHA. He also was in 72 NHL games, all with the North Stars. Butters was a college assistant for several years and has been actively involved in Christian Athletes Hockey Camps.

19) Jay Bariball, who captained the Gophers in 2010-11.

20) Chris Sall, who had 48 saves overall. Interestingly enough, Rochester Mayo's Alex Kangas had broken the old record of 20 with 21 of his own in the second period of a 2-1 consolation semifinal loss to White Bear Lake earlier that same day. In 2013, Mason Campion of Marshall made 28 stops in one period to set a new standard.

21) Aaron Ness, a play-making defenseman who competed at Minnesota, and Mike Lee, a goalie backstopping for the St. Cloud Huskies. Ness displayed expert passing and ice awareness while Lee had 28 saves in the championship game and allowed just five goals while facing 81 shots. Both underclassmen were all-tourney in AA. Aaron's father, Jay, played with Roseau in the 1982 event and played defense at North Dakota.

22) Rickey and Ryan Hopkins, with Ryan getting the go-ahead marker.

23) Jared Festler, Beau Hanowski, and Ben Hanowski. The trio scored 132 goals prior to the tourney but the team was limited to just five goals as they lost both games. Festler and Ben Hanowski each tallied twice.

24) Academy of the Holy Angels, a Catholic school in Richfield.

25) Patrick White, who totaled five points (all goals) as a junior and four as a senior before playing for Don Lucia at the U of M for four seasons. White's best game was a four-goal effort in a 7-4 first-round win over Roseau in 2006. He was selected to the AA all-tournament team both years.

26) B. J. O'Brien, who gave up just five goals on 116 shots, was

A helmetless Kyle Rau is chased down by his Eden Prairie teammates after scoring the winning goal in the third overtime of the Eagles' 3-2 win over Duluth East in the 2011 Class AA championship. (Kyle Oen)

justifiably included on that year's all-tourney team along with Centennial goalie Greg Stutz. In 2011, he was the star when St. Norbert's won the Division III title at Ridder Arena in Minneapolis and was named the tourney's Most Outstanding Player.

27) Jack Hillen, who played 8 NHL seasons with the Islanders, the Predators, and Capitals.

28) Finland. His Blaze team beat Blaine but then lost overtime games to Grand Rapids and Rochester Century to finish fourth.

29) Justin Holl (Minnesota); Troy Hesketh (Wisconsin), and Andrew Prochno (St. Cloud). The favored Skippers lost 4-2 to Edina in the finals in 2010.

30) Albert Lea, which went to three tourney's in the decade (2004, 2005, 2007). Each of the entrants were coached by Roy Nystrom. Ellingson had four goals in the 9-1 rout of Little Falls in the consolation final.

31) T. J. Oshie, who scored eight points in 2003 (three goals, five assists), including two assists in the 3-1 final over Simley. In 2005, Oshie had an assist on Warroad's overtime goal that gave them a

4-3 win over Totino-Grace in the climactic game. Oshie led the state in scoring with 100 points in 2005 and was a first-round pick of St. Louis and is now playing for Washington. In an epic performance at the 2014 Olympics at Sochi, Oshie scored on four of six shoot-out attempts to lead the U.S. to a 3-2 win over Russia. He is a first cousin of former Bemidji star Gary Sargent and a second cousin to Warroad legend Henry Boucha.

32) Andrew Ford, who gave up just seven goals in six tournament games and became one of the few goalies to be the starting netminder for two state champions.

33) Mark Van Guilder, who at 6'2" and 205 pounds, was an imposing player in front of the net and in the corners. He played his college hockey at Notre Dame. He made his NHL debut as a 30-year-old wing with Nashville in 2014.

34) Brandon Bochenski, who had a goal and assist in the 6-0 title-game win over Duluth East. Bochenski was North Dakota's leading scorer for two seasons and played 156 games in the NHL for seven teams.

35) Alex Stalock, who went on to be a star at UMD, winning the MVP award at the WCHA Final Five and earning All-American status in 2008-09. The Packers finished fourth, losing the consolation game 4-3 to Hibbing in overtime. Stalock had 41 saves in a 3-2 loss to Breck in the semifinals. Stalock plays in the NHL with the San Jose Sharks.

36) Brock Nelson, who later played at North Dakota. As a junior, Nelson had four goals and three assists as Warroad lost 7-3 in the finals to Breck. As a tenth-grader, he had a goal and an assist as Warroad was third. Nelson played his first full NHL season with the Islanders in 2013-14.

37) Hill-Murray, which went on to win the state title with a 3-0 shutout of Edina with Ryan Furne scoring two goals. In the Roseau game, goalie Joe Phillippi had 34 saves and Isaac Kohls had two goals.

38) Shea Walters. His junior brother, Drew, totaled eight points and scored four goals in the 8-4 win over Fergus Falls for the consolation title.

39) Hudson Fasching

40) Warroad beat Totino-Grace 4-3 in double-overtime for the Class A crown. The game lasted 70 minutes and 36 seconds.

41) James Saintey and Christian Isackson. Saintey had 4 goals and 3 assists overall while Isackson had three goals and three assists.

42) David Zevnik, who made 140 saves in 9 total games of state tourney action. Zevnik had one shutout as a sophmore, two as a junior, and then shared two with backup goalie Conor Murphy as a senior.

43) Tom Gorowsky, who had a goal and four assists, including three assists in a 3-0 win against Wayzata in the semis. Gorowsky played collegiately at Wisconsin.

44) Ben Kinne, who had two goals and three assists alone in a 5-2 win over Eagan in the quarterfinals and a goal and assist in the 7-0 thrashing of Grand Rapids in the finals.

45) Brian Schack, a future Gopher. Schack had two goals and an assist in a first-round win over Shakopee and an assist on Erik Bredesen's goal 32 seconds into overtime as the Eagles nipped Duluth Marshall 2-1 in the semis.

46) Chris Hickey, who interestingly enough, scored the first goal in each game as Cretin-Derham Hall closed out the year with its superb performance in the 2006 event.

47) Drew LeBlanc, who had four goals and four assists. Hermantown beat rival Duluth Marshall 4-1 in the title game. LeBlanc had a hat trick and two assists in a 6-3 first-round win over Little Falls. LeBlanc won the Hobey Baker Award with St. Cloud State in 2013 and played two games in the NHL for Chicago that spring.

48) Trevor Graham, who also scored the only goals for the Eagles in their 2-1 semifinal win over Fergus Falls.

49) Mark Alt, whose father John was an All-Pro lineman for the Kansas City Chiefs. Alt had three assists in 2009 as the Raiders finished in fourth-place. Alt won a state football title for Mike Scanlan's team as a junior. He was drafted by Carolina but played his first NHL game for Philadelphia in March 2015.

50) Trevor Frischmon and Matt Moore. Frischmon also added two assists in a semifinal win over Hastings while Moore had a goal and an assist in a 4-1 victory over Rochester Mayo in the opener.

Edina head coach Curt Giles congratulates one of his players, Charlie Taft, after the Hornets take the AA title in 2010 with a 4-2 win over Minnetonka. (Kyle Oen)

51) Aaron Marvin, the grandson of the legendary Cal Marvin, who was elected to the U.S. Hockey Hall of Fame in 1982.

52) Tyler Barnes. The Blaze center scored with 42 seconds left in the semis to tie Grand Rapids and with 26 seconds remaining to tie Rochester Century in the third-place game. Unfortunately, Burnsville lost both games in overtime.

53) Trevor Stewart, who had four goals and five assists. Stewart had a goal and four assists alone in the title game, an 8-1 whipping of Moorhead and he also recorded a hat trick in Elk River's 4-3 semifinal nail-biter over Hastings.

54) Mark Stuart, who had two goals and two assists as a Class A all-tourney pick for the Eagles, who finished sixth. Stuart played college hockey at Colorado College and has had a 10-year NHL career with Boston, Atlanta, and Winnipeg.

55) Kelly Plude, who was an all-tourney pick. Plude also had two assists in a 4-3 win over Hastings in the semis.

56) Keegan Iverson, who had a goal and assist. His older brother Wesley had two goals. In 2012, Breck finished third with Keegan

scoring once. Iverson left school early to play 4 years with the Portland Winterhawks in the Western Hockey League.

57) Kyle Olstad, who had 15 saves in the 3-1 championship game win over Roseville.

58) Steve Witkowski. He also had 24 saves in a 4-3 semifinal win over Hastings and 16 saves in a 4-1 victory over Rochester Mayo in the first round.

59) John Russell. As a junior, he had 33 saves in the title game as Breck beat Warroad 7-3. He followed that up with 30 saves in 2010 as Breck outlasted Hermantown 2-1 in the finale. Russell's save percentage was .950 and .951 in those two seasons, respectively.

60) Marshall Everson. Edina claimed the fifth-place trophy with a 5-2 win over Hill-Murray after dismissing Duluth East 6-4.

61) Ryan McDonagh, who also added three assists. A Wisconsin standout, McDonagh was drafted by Montreal and is now playing with the New York Rangers. McDonagh won the Mr. Hockey award as a senior in 2007.

62) Burnsville. Jake Hendrickson scored and then Tyler Barnes added two more to tie the Thunderhawks but sophomore Sam Rendle scored at 1:09 of overtime to sink the Blaze.

63) Jack Baer. He scored unassisted in the late stages of the 4-3 win over Duluth Marshall a day after scoring in double-overtime to down Hermantown 6-5 in the semis. Baer was all-tourney after totaling three goals and three assists.

64) Brian Lee. The smooth-skating Lee had a goal and two assists. Lee played at North Dakota before playing for Ottawa and Tampa Bay in the NHL.

65) R. J. Anderson, who had three assists and was flawless in his defensive zone.

66) Josh Frider, who had two goals in a 4-3 fifth-place game loss to White Bear Lake.

67) Jimmy Kilpatrick and Kevin Rollwagen. Kilpatrick had a goal and a tourney-high six assists and Rollwagen had three goals and four assists. The Stars beat Hill-Murray 4-2 in the finals.

68) Scott Kozlak, who was an obvious all-tourney pick.

69) Eric Baskin, with assists to Sam Rothstein and Troy Hesketh. It ended the fourth-longest game in state history. Baskins' goal ended an incredible scoring drought for both teams as there was no scoring for 71 minutes and 59 seconds, including 35:31 of sudden-death action. After Andrew Prochno had scored for Minnetonka, Chris Casto of Hill-Murray tied it with 28 seconds left in the first period.

70) Matt Hendricks

71) Erik Johnson, whose team finished third and fifth, respectively, those seasons. Johnson was selected first overall by St. Louis and now plays with Colorado. He was on the 2010 and 2014 U.S. Olympic teams.

72) Tim Ornell

73) Dan Brooks, Herb's son. After graduating from STA, Brooks played at Denver.

74) Ryan Carter, who has played for 5 NHL teams: Anaheim, Carolina, Florida, New Jersey, and Minnesota. He played collegiately at Mankato State.

75) Adam Knochenmus, who had also had two goals in 2008 as Roseau was fourth.

76) Ryan Miller, who had a hat trick in a 6-3 quarterfinal win over Mound-Westonka in 2001 and another in a 5-4 loss to Hermantown in the third-place game. In 2002, he tallied six points (four goals) as the Otters were fourth both years.

77) Ben Hendrick, who also had an assist in the 3-1 win over Roseville in the title match.

78) Chris VandeVelde, who had a goal and two assists in the 6-4 loss to Holy Angels, was all-tourney. He also competed in the previous tourneys for Moorhead and was a standout for North Dakota in college before making his NHL debut in 2011 with Edmonton. He now competes for Philadelphia.

79) Jack Connolly. Small but shifty, Connolly had two assists in a 4-3 title-game loss to St. Thomas Academy and four points overall in 2006. The next year, he had Marshall's only goal in a 4-1 loss to Hermantown in the A championship and six points total.

Connolly was an All-American in 2011 when the Bulldogs won the NCAA title, and he was the WCHA MVP in 2012.

80) Kyle Rau. The Mr. Hockey Award winner for 2011, Rau scored the winning goal in the AA three-overtime saga against Duluth East with a full-length dive for the puck in his senior season to give the Eagles a thrilling 3-2 win. Rau also tied White Bear Lake's Brandon Wahlin for the AA scoring high with seven points as each player scored five goals and two assists. As a sophomore, Rau scored the tying and winning goals in a 4-2 semifinal win over Blaine. He later became a captain and All-American at Minnesota.

81) St. Thomas Academy. The Cadets hammered New Ulm 13-2 and tied a tourney record for most goals in a period with seven in the first period.

82) Jake Randolph, Dom Toninato, and Trevor Olson, who each scored four points. Both Randolph and Toninato were all-tourney; however, Olson scored both of East's goals in the title game. In 2012, the threesome totals 16 points as the Greyhounds took the consolation crown with Toninato earning all-tourney.

83) Jared Thomas (7), Andrew Mattson (7), and Garrett Skrbich (6). Each scored three goals and Thomas and Skrbich were both all-tournament.

84) Curt and Kyle Rau and David and Mark Rath. Kyle Rau scored the game-winner with 3:17 remaining in the third overtime, knocking in a rebound of his brother's shot from the point. The Rath boys scored third-period goals in regulation and each scored four points in the tournament.

85) Adam Johnson, who was all-tourney after scoring four goals and an assist as the Bluejackets finished fourth. His linemate Nick DeCenzo, was also all-tourney on the strength of two goals and four assists.

86) Jake Schuman. As a sophomore, he recorded a shutout in a 6-0 semifinal win over Fergus Falls. His senior season, he allowed just four goals in playing all three games as his team won its second title in three seasons. Schuman had 20 saves in the 2-1 finale against Rochester Lourdes and made the all-tournament team.

87) Thief River Falls, whose only other trips to state since 1965 came in 2006 and 2012.

88) Hunter Bergerson and Nate Repensky. Bergerson was all-tourney in 2011 and Repensky in 2011 and 2012.

89) Nathan Raduns, who had two goals and three assists for the Storm. Raduns competed at St. Cloud for three years and appeared in one game for the Flyers in 2008-09.

90) A. J. Reid and Zach Schroeder, who tied Rochester Lourdes' Jason Samuelson and Hermantown's Jared Thomas and Andrew Mattson for the Class A scoring lead. Both Reid and Schroeder had three goals and four assists.

91) Reid Cashman, who logged plenty of ice time and recorded four assists.

92) Tim Manthey was an all-tournament defenseman for his father, head coach Todd. The younger Manthey had an assist on the go-ahead goal as the Tornadoes beat Roseville 3-1 in the finale.

93) Rob W. Johnson, who led the Greyhounds to third-place finishes in both his junior and senior seasons. In 2005, Duluth East actually had two players named Rob Johnson; Rob W., then a senior and Rob A., a freshman forward. Both players scored a goal in East's 5-3 win over Tartan for third place that year.

94) Little Falls. The Flyers were 29-0 entering the 2009 Class A semifinals but Breck downed them 6-1. Ben Hanowski scored with 22 seconds left in the third-place game to give his team a 4-3 win over St. Cloud Cathedral as the Flyers finished 30-1.

95) Joe Stejskal, who had a goal and three assists in 2006 and two assists in 2007. A Montreal draft pick, Joe won the Herb Brooks award for Class AA in his senior season and played 4 years for the Big Green of Dartmouth.

96) Dano Jacques, who scored his third goal of the game in double-overtime to beat St. Thomas Academy 3-2 in a thrilling 2007 semifinal.

97) Joe Phillippi, who who also started a game in 2007 for the Pioneers.

98) Joe Rehkamp, who had three goals and five assists total in his all-tourney performance.

99) Lou Nanne, the grandson of broadcaster Lou Nanne and son of Marty, who scored in the finals for state champ Edina in 1984.

In 2012, brothers Lou and Tyler played in front of grandpa for the Hornets. In 2013, Tyler scored the game-winner in a 3-2 win over Duluth East in the semis and celebrated the title the next night when the Hornets beat Hill-Murray 4-2 for the AA crown. In 2014, Tyler won another title with Edina after being switched back to defense. Lou was drafted by the Wild and Tyler by the Rangers.

100) Nick Seeler, who was equally solid defensively for Lee Smith's team.

101) 2015. Attendance was 21,609 to see Edina vs. Duluth East and Eden Prairie vs. Lakeville North. The following night for the AA finals also set a record with 19,495 at the Xcel Energy Center. Six of the eight sessions set attendance records that year for a record of 136,618.

102) Duluth East. The Greyhounds had 8th-grader Ryder Donovan on defense and freshmen Gilbert Worth, Ian Mageau, and Luke LeMaster at forward. The unseeded Greyhounds lost 4-1 to champion Lakeville North in the finals.

103) Grant Besse, who led AA in scoring with 11 points (eights goals, three assists). Three of Besse's goals were shorthanded goals, including two on breakaways. The sniper now plays for Wisconsin.

104) Michael Bitzer, who won the Frankie Brimsek award as the state's top senior goalie in 2012. Bitzer was all-tourney as a senior; he had a 34-save shutout in a 4-0 win over Eagan in the opening quarterfinal. Bitzer also won the Herb Brooks Award for Class AA in 2012.

105) Alex Funk and Jason Samuelson. Funk scored 11 goals and 10 assists and Samuelson 5 goals and 16 assists as they both finished with 21 points to tie them for seventh all-time among tournament scorers. Funk was all-tourney in 2012 and 2013.

106) Marshall. Representing Section 3 in Class A, the Tigers lost 6-1 to Breck and 4-1 to Duluth Marshall. In 2014, another team from the southwest corner of the state earned the Sec. 3 nod - Luverne. The Cardinals lost both games; 5-2 to Chisago Lakes in the quarterfinals and 4-3 to Totino-Grace in consolation.

107) East Grand Forks, coached by Tyler Palmiscno, who had played in the tournament when his father Tony was coaching the team.

The "Green Wave" beat Hermantown in the finals each year, 7-3 in 2014 and 5-4 in overtime in 2015.

108) 2012. Top-seeded Duluth East fell to Lakeville South 3-2 in overtime; second-seeded Maple Grove lost 5-2 to Hill-Murray; third-seeded Eagan was upset 4-0 by Moorhead, and fourth-seeded Edina lost 3-2 to Benilde-St. Margaret's.

109) Dixon Bowen, Grant Loven, and Tanner Tweten. Bowen led Class A in scoring in 2015 with nine points. Loven had a hat trick in a 5-2 semifinal win over Mahtomedi and Tweten scored two goals, including the overtime winner in the 5-4 win over Hermantown in the finals.

110) St. Cloud Apollo and Breck. The Class A quarterfinal game ended at 5:07 of the first overtime when Brandon Bissitt scored for Apollo. It was the 21st game game in tourney to finish with a 1-0 score but was only the fourth to be scoreless through regulation.

111) Tommy Novak. As a freshman, he recorded two goals and two assists in his first state tourney game as the Cadets blanked Little Falls 7-0.

112) Ryan Kero and Nate Pionk. In the 2015 quarterfinal, each player netted a hat trick and added three assists for six points each in an 8-0 win over Spring Lake Park. Kero tied for the Class A scoring lead with nine points.

113) Justin Kloos. The smallish center had two goals and two assists. Lakeville South won their first-ever trophy with a 2-1 win over Moorhead to claim third after upsetting top-seed Duluth East 3-2 in overtime in the quarterfinals.

114) Phil Beaulieu

115) Wyatt Schmidt, who totaled seven total points in three games. Schmidt, a standout for the Cadet football team, was named the top kicker in the nation his senior season. Matt Perry added two goals and three assists and Jack Stang had four assists in the rout.

116) Dylan Malmquist, who was all-tournament both years. He tied for the scoring lead in both years, also. As a senior in 2015, he was hurt in Edina's 6-4 quarterfinal win over Bemidji and didn't play in the final two games as the Hornets copped third.

117) Jared Kohlquist, whose teams were runners-up to St. Thomas Academy each year. He scored six goals and added three assists in his three-year run at state.

118) Jack Jablonski. A sophomore forward who played on both the varsity and junior-varsity for the Knights, Jack was hit from behind in a junior-varsity game and suffered a spinal-cord injury. His ordeal garnered national attention and his courage helped fuel Benilde-St. Margaret's magical ride to the championship. Jablonksi was present at the Xcel in a second-level suite to witness the Knight victory and was able to celebrate with his teammates in a jubilant locker-room. Jack is now attending USC.

119) Jack, Nick, and Ryan Poehling. Twins Jack and Nick were both all-tournament their junior and senior seasons while younger brother Ryan was their linemate as both a freshman and sophomore. Nick totaled five goals and 11 assists in his tournament career while Jack had seven goals and seven assists.

120) 2013

121) Joey Anderson, who assisted on the tying and winning goals in Hill-Murray's 2-1 semi-final win over Wayzata. Hill-Murray lost to Edina 4-1 in the finals.

122) Goalie David Zevnik, defensemen Wyatt Schmidt and Tony Bretzmen, and forwards Henry Hart, Alex Johnson, and Austin Sattler.

Edina's Bobby Krieger is defended by Warroad's Alan Hangsleben (left), Ed Boucha (center), and Jeff Hallett in a 1970 quarterfinal. (Dave Johnson)

8 Top Players by Decade

The players that appear in this chart all appeared in at least two tournaments. When a player's appearance in the tourney overlapped decades, the fact has been noted. Many players who do not appear here delivered outstanding performances, and in some cases led their teams to the championship, but reached the tournament only once. We recognize here the athletes who demonstrated superior play in more than one tournament.

*1945–1949**
FORWARDS
Rube Bjorkman	John Matchefts	John Mayasich	Dick Peterson
(Roseau)	(Eveleth)	(Eveleth)	(Eveleth)

DEFENSEMEN
Andy Gambucci	Jack McKinnon
(Eveleth)	(Williams)

GOALIE
Willard Ikola
(Eveleth)

*Team shortened due to fewer years of tournament play

1950s

FORWARDS

John Mayasich
(Eveleth)

Oscar Mahle
(Int'l Falls)

Ron Castellano
(Eveleth)

Dave Wensloff
(Roseau)

Mike Castellano
(Eveleth)

Stu Anderson
(St. Paul Johnson)

Jim Stordahl
(Roseau)

Ed Bulauca
(Roseau)

DEFENSEMEN

Bruce Shutte
(Eveleth)

Jim Westby
(Mpls. South)

Ed Mrkonich
(Eveleth)

Bob Schmidt
(St. Paul Johnson)

GOALIES

Tom Wahman
(St. Paul Johnson)

Dick Roth
(Roseau)

• •

1960s

FORWARDS

Doug Woog
(So. St. Paul)

Mike Antonovich
(Greenway)

Tim Sheehy
(Int'l Falls)

Pete Fichuk
(Int'l Falls)

Jim Amidon
(Int'l Falls)

Rob Shattuck
(St. Paul Johnson)

Doug Peltier
(St. Paul Johnson)

Bryan Grand
(Roseau)

DEFENSEMEN

Gary Wood
(Int'l Falls)

Ken Lawson
(Greenway)

Steve Ross
(Int'l Falls)

Terry Abram
(So. St. Paul)

GOALIES

Ron Beck
(Int'l Falls)

Brad Shelstad*
(Mpls. Southwest)

*also '70

177

1970s

FORWARDS

Aaron Broten
(Roseau)

Neal Broten
(Roseau)

Erin Roth
(Grand Rapids)

Todd Lecy
(John Marshall)

John Rothstein
(Grand Rapids)

Bob Krieger*
(Edina)

Scott Kleinendorst
(Grand Rapids)

Dan Lempe
(Grand Rapids)

DEFENSEMEN

Bill Baker
(Grand Rapids)

Craig Norwich
(Edina-East)

Bob Lundeen⁺
(Mpls. Southwest)

Les Auge
(St. Paul Johnson)

GOALIES

Doug Long
(St. Paul Johnson)

Paul Butters
(Roch. John Marshall)

*also, '68, '69: ⁺also, '69

• •

1980s

FORWARDS

Scott Bloom
(Burnsville)

Paul Ranheim
(Edina)

Steve Bianchi
(Bloom. Jefferson)

John Bader *
(Irondale)

Bruce Aikens
(Roch. Marshall)

Jay North
(Bloom. Jefferson)

Dave Maley
(Edina-East, West)

Steve Rohlik
(Hill-Murray)

DEFENSEMEN

Phil Housley
(So. St. Paul)

Larry Olimb
(Warroad)

Mark Osiecki
(Burnsville)

Tom Pederson
(Bloom. Jefferson)

GOALIES

Jon Casey
(Grand Rapids)

Rick Horvath
(Hill-Murray)

* also '79

1990s

FORWARDS

Johnny Pohl
(Red Wing)

Matt Cullen
(Moorhead)

Dave Spehar
(Duluth East)

Nick Checco
(Bloom. Jefferson)

Joey Bianchi
(Bloom. Jefferson)

Ryan Kraft
(Moorhead)

Jamie Langenbrunner
(Cloquet)

Wyatt Smith
(Warroad)

DEFENSEMEN

Mike Crowley
(Bloom. Jefferson)

Jason Godbout
(Hill-Murray)

Nick Angell
(Duluth East)

Dylan Mills
(Duluth East)

GOALIES

Cade Ledingham
(Duluth East)

Randy Koeppl
(Bloom. Jefferson)

· ·

2000s

FORWARDS

Kyle Rau*
(Eden Prairie)

Ben Hanowski
(Little Falls)

Blake Wheeler
(Breck)

Brock Nelson*
(Warroad)

Anders Lee
(St. Thomas, Edina)

Patrick White
(Grand Rapids)

Chris VandeVelde
(Moorhead)

Marshall Everson
(Edina)

DEFENSEMEN

Brian Lee
(Moorhead)

Aaron Ness
(Roseau)

Dano Jacques
(Duluth Marshall)

Joe Stejskal
(Grand Rapids)

GOALIES

John Russell
(Breck)

Andrew Ford
(Eden Prairie)

* Rau played in 2009 and 2011; Nelson played in 2009 and 2010; Ford played in 2009 and 2011

2010-2015

FORWARDS

Tommy Novak
(St. Thomas Academy)

Jake Randolph
(Duluth East)

Dylan Malmquist
(Edina)

Nick Poehling
(Lakeville North)

Alex Funk
(Rochester Lourdes)

Jack Poehling
(Lakeville North)

Dixon Bowen
(E. Grand Forks)

Grant Loven
(E. Grand Forks)

DEFENSEMEN

Jared Kohlquist
(Hermantown)

Jack Sadek
(Lakeville North)

Nate Repensky
(Duluth East)

Jack Daugherty
(St. Thomas Academy)

GOALIES

Charlie Lindgren
(Lakeville North)

David Zevnik
(St. Thomas Academy)

9 The Coaches

1) What coach has the most appearances in the state tournament with 19?

2) What was the real first name of affable and long-time South St. Paul coach "Lefty" Smith?

3) Who are the only coaches to win more than one John Mariucci "Coach of the Year" award (as selected by the state hockey coaches association since 1983)?

4) What coach has won the most consecutive state hockey titles?

5) What former Mariucci "Coach of the Year" won a state title and has served as the President of the Minnesota High School Board of Directors?

6) Have any brothers coached separate teams to state titles as head coaches?

7) Did Herb Brooks ever coach a high school team to a state tournament berth?

8) Who is the only coach to lead his team to the state championship in his first two years as a head coach?

9) Has a coach ever won a state title in his only appearance as a head coach at the tourney?

10) What type of fabric was the hat or fedora that Edina coaching legend Willard Ikola wore behind the bench for Edina and Edina-East? Secondly, just exactly how many different hats did Coach Ikola wear in his 19 years coaching at the state tournament?

11) What three men have coached different teams from different regions of the state to the tournament in consecutive years?

12) Has any University of Minnesota coach ever coached a team to the state high school boys' hockey tournament?

13) What three coaches whose last name starts with a "Z" have coached in the state tourney?

14) Who are the only active coaches, as of 2015, to coach in at least 10 state tournaments?

15) What man coached his high school team to three tourneys and later coached teams to both an NCAA title and a Stanley Cup championship?

16) Who are head coaches who led teams to the state tourney who also played in the National Hockey League?

17) Who was the first coach from a private school to win the state championship?

18) What former University of Minnesota All-American goalie led his teams to 14 state tournament appearances and six titles?

19) What highly-successful head coach of one of the most dominant teams in state annals was also once an All-American goalie at St. Mary's College in Winona in 1932?

20) Has any coach who led a team to the state tournament ever led the United States Olympic team as a head coach?

21) What former South St. Paul and Michigan State star coached both his alma mater and Hastings to the tournament multiple times?

22) What hugely-successful baseball coach, who has won five state titles on the diamond, finally one a hockey crown when his Cretin-Derham Hall team won the 2006 Class AA title with a 7-0 whitewash of Grand Rapids?

23) What state tournament standout, one of the few who have been able to compete in four state tourneys as a player, coached Bemidji to the tourney in both 1985 and 1986?

24) What coach has continued the tremendous tradition at Hill-

Murray by leading his squads to eleven state tourneys since 1999?

25) Who are the only coaches other than Larry Ross to have their teams win three straight titles?

26) Who did former South St. Paul great Doug Woog coach to three state tourneys prior to taking over the University of Minnesota program in the mid-1980's?

27) What wily coach at Alexander Ramsey led the Roseville-based school to tourney appearances seven times?

28) After coaching Thief River Falls to state in 1960, what genial fellow ventured south to Rochester and led John Marshall to three appearances in 1977, 1978, and 1979, including a title in 1977 (4-2 win over Edina-East) and a gut-wrenching double-overtime 4-3 defeat to that same Edina-East team in 1979?

29) Facing cross-city rival Jeff-erson during the regular-season and in the post-season, what coach had Bloomington Kennedy among the upper echelon of state teams and led the Eagles to six tournaments?

Willard Ikola won three titles as a player at Eveleth and eight titles as a coach at Edina. (Photo courtesy Willard Ikola)

30) Who was the head coach at Breck in 2009 and 2010 when they won Class A crowns?

31) Who is the only coach to lead Bloomington Jefferson back to the state tournament since Tom Saterdalen retired?

32) What coach had a sparkling record of 5-0 in state champion-ship games?

33) Grand Rapids won three titles in the single-class era and did it with three different head coaches. Who were they?

34) Who was the highly-successful coach at Mounds View who led the Mustangs to four tourneys (1968, 1969, 1976, 1977) and played in the tourney for St. Paul Murray?

35) What Minneapolis Washburn player from 1959 and 1960 later coached both Apple Valley and Richfield to the tournament?

36) What burly Hibbing mentor brought five Bluejacket teams to state and won the 1973 title?

37) What coach at Greenway-Coleraine led the Raiders to the 1966 consolation title before embarking on a coaching career that led to NCAA titles at Wisconsin and Maine as a trusted assistant?

38) What man has been instrumental in making Holy Angels a force in Minnesota hockey and led the Stars to both the 2002 and 2005 Class AA crowns?

39) What Bemidji High head coach led his team to two state tournaments, finishing second to Edina-East in 1974, and later became noteworthy for his work developing a hockey camp in the Brainerd area and for scouting and working in NHL executive positions?

40) What former International Falls forward coached Moorhead to five state tournaments in the 1990's, winning a trophy on each trip to state?

41) What long-time assistant to Willard Ikola brought Edina-West to its only state berth in 1981 but later replaced the retiring Ikola and won a AA state title with Edina in 1997?

42) Which of the Broten brothers coached their alma mater (Roseau) to the state tourney in 2000?

43) What former North Star defenseman and 14-year NHL veteran became the second former player with the Bloomington-based NHL team to coach a high school team to a state title?

44) Has a coach ever led two schools from the same city to a state tourney berth?

45) What coach, an Eveleth native, led tiny Williams to great heights in 1949, 1950, and 1951 as the Region 3 entrant twice and the Region 8 representative once?

46) What former Eveleth and Gopher puckster coached Albert Lea to the tourney in 2004, 2005, and 2007 in Class A?

47) How many men have coached two different schools to the state tournament?

48) What coach has won the most games at the state tournament?

49) What coach has won the most state championships?

50) Which Eveleth high star and collegiate star at Michigan State won a single-class title with Grand Rapids in 1975 and later coached seven years at UMD?

51) Who coached Minneapolis power Southwest to state tournaments to four state tourneys in the first half of the 1950's?

52) What Rochester Mayo coach broke Willard Ikola's state record for wins on Jan. 15, 2011 with his 617th victory over inter-city rival John Marshall and has led Mayo teams to seven state tournaments?

53) What man became a key assistant at Grand Rapids in 1969 and helped develop a bevy of Division I players but left in 1975 to become an assistant at UMD and later was head coach for the Bulldogs for 18 seasons, winning three WCHA titles?

54) In Class AA in 2004, what coach had a pretty tight defense as his team didn't allow a goal in any of the three tourney games, a total of 153 minutes?

55) What man was the head coach for the Moorhead Spuds for five straight appearances from 2001-05 and again in 2009 and 2012, but witnessed the frustration of seeing his team lose four title games?

56) What brother combination worked as co-head coaches to bring their school five titles in an eight-year span in the 2000's in Class A?

57) What Roseau coach had the tough task of succeeding the legendary Oscar Almquist after the 1967 season and brought the Rams to the tourney in both 1968 and 1969?

58) From 1997 to 2002, this Fergus Falls mentor led his club to the Class A tourney six straight years, with their best finish being third-place in 1999?

59) What Warroad coach brought tenacity and toughness to seven Warrior teams in Class A action in the 1990's and 2000's?

60) What International Falls alumnus became the only coach other than Larry Ross to win a state title for the Canadian-border municipality with a Class A title in 1995?

61) In 2006 and 2007, what coach brought two unheralded Grand Rapids teams to the finals before they succumbed to superior clubs in Class AA?

62) What man led St. Paul Murray to tournament berths in 1949, 1950, and 1951?

63) Which Red Wing coach was a bright strategist in Red Wing's rise to power in Class A in the 1990's?

64) Which Minnesota school has had the most number of men to coach its hockey team to the state tournament with nine?

65) One of the 15 members of the inaugural class of inductees into the Minnesota Hockey Coaches Hall of Fame in 1991, what man directed Minneapolis Washburn to three state tournaments in three different decades?

66) What St. Paul Harding coach was behind the bench for the Knights four times in the tournament in a six-year span?

67) In the 1960's, North St. Paul came to state with two head coaches with the same last name; who were they and were they related?

68) Besides Lefty Smith, who are the other 7 coaches who have taken South St. Paul the short distance to play in the state tourney?

69) Through the 2015 tournament, how many different men have coached teams in the state tournament?

70) What former associate director of the Minnesota State High School League was the coach of Richfield in three straight tournaments (1962-64)?

71) What four former tourney participants went on to be head coach at the U of M?

72) How many coaches that have coached in the state tournament have been inducted into the U.S. Hockey Hall of Fame?

73) What member of the 1976 U.S. Olympic team coached Roseville Area to the Class AA tourney in both 2002 and 2003?

74) Who is the only person to have competed in the tournament and also coached in both the state tournament and NHL levels?

75) Has any coach every played in the tournament and then coached his alma mater to a state championship?

76) Later a coach at North Dakota and a visionary for the sport, who coached Minneapolis Roosevelt to their first tournament in 1956?

77) What coach has led Blaine to the state tournament six consecutive years in Class AA from 2006 to 2011?

78) Perhaps one of the most-respected assistant coaches in state tourney lore, what man was a key advisor to Bloomington Jefferson coach Tom Saterdalen 11 times at the state tournament?

79) What coach oversaw the rise of the central Minnesota school of Little Falls to prominence in Class A over the past decade with six tournament appearances in an eight-year span?

80) What coach has gone the most years between appearances at the state tournament?

81) What coach, who was an assistant to Willard Ikola for 20 years, returned to his hometown to coach and led one of the city school's to the state tournament in 1984?

82) What former Gopher forward coached Roseau to five tournaments in a seven-year span in the late 1970's and early 1980's?

83) What coach brought Benilde-St. Margaret's to state in 1999 and 2001, and won both Class A titles those years, and led the Knights to the AA title in 2012?

84) Who led Eden Prairie to AA titles in both 2009 and 2011 and has brought the Eagles to state on seven occasions?

85) What man has coached six teams to state: Lakeville (2002, 2003, 2004) and Lakeville North (2006, 2010, and 2011) after the district split into two high schools?

86) What coach has a 13-3 record in first-round games at the state tournament and has directed his clubs to trophy wins on 13 occasions?

87) What public-school head coach has butted heads with the strong metro private schools for Class A supremacy for the past decade or so, with 10 top-three finishes in 11 trips to state since 1998?

88) What White Bear Lake coach led the Bears to three tourneys (2003, 2005, and 2011) from Section 4AA and was the winner of the John Mariucci Award winner as Coach of the Year for Class AA in 2011?

89) What former Thief River Falls standout, former Gopher, and 12-year professional player returned as a coach to his high school and helped guide it to tournaments in 2011 and 2012?

90) What Section 8 head coach led heated rivals Warroad and Roseau to state twice each in consecutive years?

91) Selected to the Minnesota State Coaches Hall of Fame in 1996, what Minneapolis South coach brought the Tigers' to state three times in the mid-1950's?

92) What St. Paul Washington coach was the man behind the bench on two of the three occasions when they earned their way to state?

93) Who is the only person to actually coach (on the bench) two different teams in the same tournament? And why?

94) Who are the only men to bring teams to the state tournament ten times or more?

95) Who are the only two men to be the head coach of both a boys' and girls' team from the same school to earn a berth in the state hockey tournament?

96) Both in their first state tournaments in 2015, what coaches won the Class A and Class A John Mariucci award as "Coach of

the Year" chosen by the Minnesota State Boys Hockey Coaches Association?

97) What coach from Lakeville North led the Panthers to a undefeated season (31-0) and the AA title in 2015 after finishing runners-up in 2014?

98) What man led New Prague to its first two state tournaments in 2014 and 2015, taking third-place and fifth place, respectively?

99) A native of Babbitt, what man served as an assistant coach on championship teams for both Apple Valley (AA) in 1996 and Lakeville North (AA) in 2015?

100) Who is the coach that has led the Eagan Wildcats to each of its four state tourneys?

101) Who are the only four men to win a state title as a player and then win a state title as a head coach?

1) Willard Ikola of Edina and Edina-East. Mike Randolph has 16, Tom Saterdalen of Bloomington Jefferson has 15, and Larry Ross of International Falls and Oscar Almquist of Roseau have 14 appearances apiece.

2) Charles. "Lefty" coached eight of the 28 Packer teams that earned their way to state.

3) 5–Bruce Plante (Hermantown) Class A - 1998, 2006, 2007, 2011 (tie); and 2012
   2–Larry Ross (International Falls) 1983, 1985
   George Nemanich (Red Wing) Class A - 1997 and 2002
   Tom Saterdalen (Bloomington Jefferson) 1993, Class AA - 2002
   Cary Eades (Warroad) Class A - 1996, 2003
   Bruce Olson (Roseau) Class AA - 1998, 1999
   Mark DeCenzo (Hibbing) Class AA - 1997; Hibbing/Chisholm, Class A- 2011 (tie)

4) Cliff Thompson of Eveleth won in 1948, 1949, 1950, and 1951. Thompson also holds the mark for most consecutive appearances by a coach at state with 12 (1945-56).

5) Jeff Whisler won a state title as Hill-Murray's head coach in 1993. Whisler presently is the Athletic Director at Mahtomedi. He was inducted into the Hockey Coaches Association Hall of Fame in 2005 and won the Cliff Thompson award for outstanding contributions to the sport of hockey in Minnesota in 2011.

6) Yes. Dennis Rolle won titles in 1954 and 1956 with Thief River Falls and his brother Glenn won a title with Duluth East in 1960.

7) No. Brooks never coached a high school team. His hockey knowledge was reserved for the colleges and the professional ranks, along with the U.S. Olympic team, of course.

8) Bob Gernander (Greenway-Coleraine; 1967 and 1968).

9) Yes. No less than seven men have claimed that honor. They include: Erik Aus - Centennial, 2004 (Class AA); Rod Christiansen - Grand Rapids, 1980; Craig Homola - Eveleth-Gilbert, 1998 (Class A); Bob Kochevar - Eveleth-Gilbert, 1993 (Class A); Todd Manthey - Anoka, 2003 (Class AA); M.J. Urhbom - Hibbing, 1952; and Dennis Fermoyle - Warroad, 2005 (Class A).

10) Hounds-tooth. "Ike" bought what he considered a cheap old hat for $5 in his second year of coaching. The model name, indeed, was called "Champ"! He wore it for 18 before purchasing another similarly-styled hat, which was promptly stolen. He went back to wearing his original hat through his final year of coaching in 1991.

11) John Matchefts, who was coach for Thief River Falls in 1959 and for his alma mater Eveleth in 1960. Mark DeCenzo came to state with Apple Valley in Tier I in 1993 and Hibbing in Tier II in 1994 while Jeff Whisler was the head coach with Hill-Murray in 1991 and Mahtomedi with Tier II in 1992.

12) Yes. Ken Yackel, who coached the Gophers for most of 1971-72 after Glen Sonmor resigned to take over the reigns of the Fighting Saints of the World Hockey Association, led Edina-Morningside to the state consolation title in 1957. Yackel, a three-sport star at the "U" and a standout hockey player, played on the 1952 U.S. Olympic team and played six games for the Boston Bruins in 1959.

Oscar Almquist, legendary Roseau coach, who led the Rams to 4 state titles. (Photo: MSHSL)

13) Peter Zanna (St. Louis Park) in 1948, 1949, 1953, 1956; Ed Zins (St. Cloud Apollo) in 1984 and Joe Zywiec (Henry Sibley) in 1982, 1983.

14) Mike Randolph of Duluth East, Bill Lechner of Hill-Murray, and Bruce Plante of Hermantown. Randolph has been to state 16 times through 2015 and has won two titles (Class AA in both 1995 and 1998) and has also been second on five occasions (1991, 1997, 2000, 2011 and 2015). Lechner has brought the Pioneers to state 11 times and has won one title (2008) and has been second three times. Plante has been to 11 state tourneys with one Class A title, seven runners-up finishes, and two third-place efforts. Curt Giles of Edina has been to state 10 times, nine-

consecutive from 2007-15 and has copped three state titles.

15) Bob Johnson started his coaching career at Warroad and then moved on to Minneapolis Roosevelt and led the Teddies to state in 1958, 1961, and 1963. After coaching at Colorado College, he became "Badger Bob" in 1966 and coached Wisconsin for 16 seasons and won NCAA titles in 1973, 1977, and 1981. He coached six years in the NHL, five in Calgary and one in Pittsburgh, where he won the Stanley Cup in his only season with the Penguins (1999-91). Johnson coached the U.S. Olympic team in 1976.

16) Mike Antonovich (St. Cloud Cathedral - Class A, 1994); Tim Bergland (Fergus Falls - Class A, 2003; Thief River Falls - Class A, 2011, 2012); Scott Bjugstad (Blaine - Class AA, 2000); Aaron Broten (Roseau - Class AA, 2000); Bill Butters (White Bear Lake Area- Class AA, 2001); Curt Giles (Edina - Class AA, 2002, 2007 through 2015); Ken Yackel (Edina-Morningside, 1957)

17) Terry Skrypek. The former Cretin High star coached Hill-Murray of Maplewood to the championship in 1983 when the Pioneers went undefeated (28-0). Skrypek brought 11 teams to state and he also was runner-up on three occasions, in addition to two third-place and two fifth-place finishes.

18) Larry Ross. "Pops" was a Gopher All-American in 1952 and won crowns in 1957, 1962, 1964, 1965, 1966, and 1972. Ross coached International Falls for 31 seasons, winning 566 games and 16 Iron Range Conference titles. Ross had a 28-11 state tourney log.

19) Oscar Almquist, who coached Roseau to four state titles (1946, 1958, 1959, 1961) in 14 tries. He coached 10 teams to state in an 11-year period from 1957-67.

20) Yes. Bob Johnson and Dave Peterson. Peterson, the Minneapolis Southwest coach, led the Indians to 11 state berths, winning the 1970 state title with a 1-0 win over Edina. Peterson coached 27 years at the school. He was the USA coach in both the 1988 Winter Olympics in Calgary and at the 1992 Games in Albertville, France. Johnson coached the 1976 USA team at Innsbruck, Austria, and 4 US National teams (1973-75 and 1981). Johnson coached Minneapolis Roosevelt to 3 tournaments–1958, 1961, and 1963.

21) Russ Welch coached the Packers to five events and the Raiders to four.

22) Jim O'Neill. The Raider coach also coached his alma mater to state in 1988 and 2009.

23) Bryan Grand, who scored five goals and five assists in four years for the Rams and later became a legend playing at Bemidji State under coach Bob Peters.

24) Bill Lechner, who won a AA title in 2008 and was second in three other years.

25) Tom Saterdalen (Bloomington Jefferson, 1992-94); Cliff Thompson (Eveleth, 1948-51); and Greg and Tom Vannelli (St. Thomas Academy, 2011-13).

26) South St. Paul. Woog and the Packers were in the tournament in 1978, 1980, and 1981, when they finished third.

27) Gordy Genz (1963-65, 71-73, and 1987 as Roseville Area)

28) Gene Sack

29) Jerry Peterson, who won a state title in 1987 as Kennedy (25-1) beat Burnsville 4-1.

30) Les Larson, who was a star defenseman for St. Paul Hill in the private school tournament before they joined the MSHSL in 1975. Breck finished fifth in their attempt to three-peat in 2011. Larson brought the

Tom Saterdalen, who led Bloom-ington Jefferson to five state titles. (Photo: Tom Saterdalen)

Mustangs to six Class A tourneys overall in the past seven years.

31) Jeff Lindquist, when the Jaguars finished sixth. Lindquist also coached Blake to the Class A tourney in both 1995 and 1999.

32) Tom Saterdalen, Bloomington Jefferson. The Jaguars earned single-class titles in 1981 and 1989, Tier I crowns in 1992 and 1993, and a Class AA title in 1994. Saterdalen also won two state tennis crowns at Jefferson.

33) Gus Hendrickson (1975), Jim Nelson (1976), and Rod Christiansen (1980).

34) Tom Wegleitner, who scored two goals and added four assists in the '49 tourney when Murray finished in fourth place.

35) Larry Hendrickson, who helped Washburn to second place (4-2 loss to Roseau) in 1950 and a third-place trophy in 1960 (opening round 5-3 loss to eventual-champ Duluth East). Hendrickson's Apple Valley team won the 1996 Class AA title with a 3-2 win over Edina after winning one of the most memorable games in state hockey history with their 5-4 (five-overtime) semifinal triumph over Duluth East.

36) George Perpich, who coached at Hibbing for 29 years and won 401 games. Perpich's teams won at least two games at state on each trip with three third-place trophies and a consolation title besides the one championship. On each of the five trips to state, Perpich had one of his own sons on the team and one of the seven Micheletti boys, too.

37) Grant Standbrook, who was head coach at Dartmouth for five seasons. He became a famous recruiter and valued assistant at Wisconsin for 12 seasons when he and Bob Johnson led the Badgers to three NCAA titles. Thereafter, he was at Maine University for 18 years, where he helped the Black Bears to two national crowns.

38) Greg Trebil, who has been to state five times with the Catholic school from Richfield.

39) Chuck Grillo, who has owned the Minnesota Hockey Camps in Nisswa for over 30 years. Grillo was a scout and the head of player personnel for the North Stars before joining the San Jose Sharks, where he became a well-respected executive.

40) Terry Cullen, whose sons Matt, Mark, and Joe were stars for Moorhead playing for their father in those seasons. Matt has played 17 NHL seasons. Mark and Joe both starred for Colorado College and Mark played 32 NHL games for Chicago and Philadelphia. The elder Cullen twice finished second to Jefferson (Tier I - 1992, Class AA - 1994) and once to Duluth East (AA -1995) and also had two third-place finishes in 1993 (Tier I) and 1997 (AA).

41) Bart Larson. Edina beat Duluth East 1-0 in 1996, a year after losing 3-2 to Apple Valley.

42) Aaron Broten, when Roseau copped the AA consolation title.

43) Curt Giles, when his Edina club won the AA crown with a 4-2 win over top-ranked Minnetonka in 2010. He added a second title in 2013 when the Hornets downed Hill-Murray 4-2 in the finals and a third in 2014 when Edina beat Lakeville North 8-2. Giles, one of the few to effectively execute the hip-check, worked his way into two Stanley Cup finals with the North Stars after playing at UMD. Scott Bjugstad, who was a co-head coach with Steve Larson at Blaine in 2000, is the other former North Star to win a state title as the Bengals won the AA crown.

44) Yes. Brendan Flaherty coached Duluth Central (1996, 2001) and Marshall School (2005–08 and 2012–13) to the tourney and Bruce Frutiger did so at Rochester John Marshall (1996) and Rochester Century (2005, 2007, and 2009). Also, Bart Larson brought Edina-West (1981) and Edina (1995, 1996, 1997, 1998) to state, and Willard Ikola brought Edina to 14 tournaments and Edina-East to five tourneys.

45) Al Braga. Williams, located in Lake of the Woods County, had just 30 students in each grade at the time. The students from Williams now attend Lake of the Woods High, located in Baudette. They lost to Eveleth in the finals in both 1949 and 1950, losing 4-3 in an evenly-contested finale when John Mayasich scored with just 20 seconds left in regulation in the latter year. Braga coached at Williams for just those three years before coaching at Robbinsdale for two seasons.

46) Roy Nystrom, whose team won the Class A consolation crown in 2005. Nystrom has coached for 49 years and has won 683 games through the 2014-15 season. He coached in North Dakota with Grafton (four years) and Grand Forks Central (three years) for seven years and won three state titles and 94 games before his move to Albert Lea for the 1973-74 season. Nystrom has 589 wins with Albert Lea.

47) As of 2015, 18 coaches have brought two different teams to state. The only man to have done so at least four times with two schools is Russ Welch (South St. Paul in 1986, 1987, 1988, 1990, 1994 and Hastings in 1998, 1999, 2000, and 2001). Bernie Broderick coached both Warroad (1948, 1949, 1953) and St. Paul Murray (1957, 1958, 1967) to three tourneys.

48) Willard Ikola with 38 wins in the state tourney. Overall, the legend was 616-149-36 in 33 years of coaching the Hornets from

1958-91. Ikola also won 22 Lake Conference titles. Add together his state titles as a player (3) and this Minnesota icon has been a part of 11 state boys' hockey crowns. He finished with a .791 winning percentage.

49) Willard Ikola, who won eight state titles (1969, 1971, 1974, 1978, 1979, 1982, 1984, 1988) in his amazing career. Larry Ross of International Falls won six and Tom Saterdalen of Bloomington Jefferson and Oscar Almquist of Roseau won five each.

50) Gus Hendrickson, who scored two goals in 1955 and three more in 1956 as Eveleth was fourth and third, respectively, those seasons.

51) Paul Wohlford, who guided the Indians to a runner-up finish in 1955 and third in 1953.

52) Lorne Grosso, who brought the Spartans to state in 1982, 1992, 1994, 1995, 1997, 1999, and 2000 and through the 2015 season has won 694 games. Grosso, who has coached for 47 years, is a cousin to Lou Nanne and played two seasons on the same line with Albert Lea coach Roy Nystrom with the Gophers. Grosso earned his 600th win with a victory over his friend Nystrom, who had earlier earned his 600th win against Rochester John Marshall in 2009. His son, Tony, scored five goals for Mayo in the 1995 AA tournament.

53) Mike Sertich, who was part of Grand Rapids first state crown in 1975.

54) Eric Aus, of Centennial. Aus is the son of Whitey Aus, who brought Frank B. Kellogg of Roseville to the tournament in 1974.

55) Dave Morinville. Moorhead lost 8-1 to Elk River in 2001, 1-0 to Centennial in 2004, 6-4 to Holy Angels in 2005, and 3-0 to Eden Prairie in 2009.

56) Greg and Tom Vannelli of St. Thomas Academy, which won Class A titles in 2006, 2008, 2011, 2012, and 2013. The siblings' first foray into the tourney was in 2005.

57) Francis Macioh, who guided the border city to a consolation title in 1968.

58) Brad Bergstrom, who was a goalie for International Falls in 1983.

59) Cary Eades, whose aggressive teams won Class A titles in 1994, 1996, and 2003.

60) Kevin Gordon, whose Broncos beat Totino-Grace 3-2 in the final in 1995. Under Gordon, they were third in 2000 and lost twice in 2002.

61) Bruce LaRoque. The Thunderhawks lost 7-0 to Cretin-Derham Hall the first year and 5-1 to Roseau the following year. LaRoque played for Grand Rapids in the 1981 tourney and scored a goal as the Indians finished fifth, the eighth straight season they returned home with a trophy.

62) Albert Sandberg. Murray won consolation titles in 1950 and 1951.

63) George Nemanich, whose Wingers were a big factor in the Class A race for five straight years from 1995-1999 and again in 2002. Red Wing completed an undefeated season (28-0) with a 4-3 win over Warroad in 1997 and finished second in 1996 and 2002 and third in 1998.

64) Roseau. Not surprising, as the Rams have had the most appearances at state with 34 through 2015. Besides Oscar Almquist (14), the others to venture to the Twin Cities with the green-clad Rams are Francis Macioh (2), Terry Abram (3), Gary Hokanson (5), Bruce Olson (2), Dean Blais (2), Aaron Broten (1), Scott Oliver (3), and Andy Lundbohm (2).

65) Carl Carlson, who led the Millers to state in 1949, 1959, and 1960. Washburn was fifth in both 1949 and 1960 and second to undefeated Roseau in 1959.

66) Dick Anderson. The best finish for the Knights in all those trips to state was a fourth-place finish in 1973 as the lone win in nine games during that stretch was a 5-3 first-round win over Minneapolis Southwest.

67) Arnie and Wes Bauer, who were brothers. Arnie was the head coach in 1961 and Wes the head coach in 1967. In the early 1960's, the Bauer brothers and long-time tourney fixture John Bartz made up the coaching staff of the Polars.

68) Doug Woog (1978, 1980, 1981), Ralph Page (1947, 1948, 1950), George Karn (1953, 1954, 1955, 1957), Denny Tetu (1969, 1972, 1977), Russ Welch (1986, 1987, 1989, 1990, 1994), Bill Moore (1996) and Jeff Lagoo (2004).

69) 270; of that total, 119 coached in the state tourney just a single year. Thus, 43% of all the head coaches never made it back to state,

an indication of how difficult it is to reach the tourney. Conversely, 47 coaches have been to the tournament at least five times, or 16%.

70) Gene Olive. The best finish for the Spartans during those years was 1964, when they finished fourth. Olive coached Richfield to baseball titles in 1962 and 1965. He played military ball while with the Coast Guard in WWII and then played a couple of seasons with the Memphis Chicks, a minor-league team for the White Sox.

71) Herb Brooks (1972-79); Brad Buetow (1979-1985); Doug Woog (1985-99); and Don Lucia (1999-present).

72) Nine. Oscar Almquist, Aaron Broten, Willard Ikola, Bob Johnson, John Matchefts, Larry Ross, Cliff Thompson, Doug Woog, and Ken Yackel.

73) Steve Sertich. Roseville finished third in 2002 and second in 2003, losing to Anoka 3-1 in the final game. Sertich was a star at Colorado College and scored 71 points in 63 games for the U.S. Olympic team in 1976.

74) Bob Johnson. He played for Minneapolis Central (1949) and coached Mpls. Roosevelt (1958, 1961, 1963) at state and coached both Calgary and Pittsburgh in the NHL. Herb Brooks and Paul Holmgren both played in the state tourney and coached in the NHL but neither even coached a high school team, let alone brought them to the state tourney.

75) Yes. Jeff Whisler played for Hill-Murray (1975, 1976) and then coached them to a title in 1991. Bruce Olson of Roseau played in the tourney in 1975 and coached the Rams to a AA title in 1999. Jim O'Neil coached his alma mater to the AA title in 2006 but he never played in the public tournament. Tyler Palmiscno played for East Grand Forks in the 1998 tournament and won Class A titles in both 2014 and 2015 coaching the Green Wave.

76) Bob May. Roosevelt finished fourth in its initial state tournament experience. May headed to Grand Forks to coach the Sioux and was replaced by future coaching legend Bob Johnson. May led them to a NCAA title in 1959 after finishing second in 1958. His biggest legacy, however, came with his work in promoting women's hockey.

77) Dave Aus. The Bengals finished third in both 2006 and 2009,

losing to eventual-champ Cretin-Derham Hall 4-2 in the semis in 2006 and to eventual-champ Eden Prairie by the same 4-2 score in 2009. His father, Peter Aus, was his co-head coach in the 2009, 2010, and 2011 tournaments.

78) John Bianchi, who not only was a brilliant hockey mind and players' confidante but the father of three talented sons who all were part of a state championship team.

79) Tony Couture (2005-09, 2012). Little Falls, led by Ben Hanowski during four of those trips to state, finished third in 2009 and fifth in 2008 and 2012.

80) Jim O'Neill of Cretin-Derham Hall, who went 18 years between appearances (1988-2006) with the Raiders. Bob Gernander of Greenway-Coleraine went 17 years (1970-1987) as did Gene Sack (Thief River Falls, 1960 and Rochester John Marshall, 1977).

81) Ed Zins of St. Cloud Apollo. It was the first showing by a St. Cloud school since St. Cloud Tech (then just known as St. Cloud) was in the tourney in 1952. St. Cloud public schools didn't even offer hockey from 1953-1971. Apollo, by the way, lost twice in the 1984 tourney (6-2 to Hibbing and 3-0 to Roseau).

82) Gary Hokanson (1978, 1979, 1981, 1983, 1984). The Rams were third in 1978 and 1979.

83) Ken Pauly. The Red Knights beat East Grand Forks 4-2 in 1999 and Rochester Lourdes 2-1 in 2001. In 2012, he led the school to the AA title when the Red Knights downed Hill-Murray 5-1. In between, Pauly coached Minnetonka to the 2006 tournament, when they copped the consolation title.

84) Lee Smith. The Willmar native and Mankato State graduate has an 10-8 record in seven trips to state; his other state berths came in 1999, 2001, 2003, 2014 and 2015.

85) Randy Schmitz, whose best finish came in 2011 when the Panthers earned consolation honors with a 4-3 triple-overtime win over White Bear Lake. Schmitz has coached for 34 years in the Lakeville district, the past 23 as head coach at Lakeville and then Lakeville North since the district split into two schools in 2005. He has also been to five state tournaments as a head softball coach.

86) Mike Randolph of Duluth East. The 26-year Greyhound mentor has a sparkling mark of 29-17 (thru 2015) in state tourney play with two state titles as well as five second-places, four third-places, and two fifth-place finishes. His teams have won trophies on all but three trips to state.

87) Bruce Plante of Hermantown. Plante has a 21-11 record at state and won the 2007 Class A title with a 4-1 win over neighboring rival Duluth Marshall. Hermantown was second in both 2010 (2-1 to Breck) and 2011 (5-4 overtime to St. Thomas Academy), losing both in excruciating fashion. The Cadets beat them again (5-1) in the 2012 final and 5-4 in the 2013 title game. Hermantown lost 7-3 to East Grand Forks in the 2014 title game and 6-5 in overtime to the same team in 2015. The Hawks were third in both 2001 and 2006. Plante's first trip to state in 1998 resulted in a 2-1 loss in the championship game to Eveleth-Gilbert.

88) Tim Sager, whose teams won the consolation crown in both 2003 and 2005. In 2011, the Bears beat sectional rival Hill-Murray in overtime to earn a berth at state, breaking a 14-game losing streak to their long-time nemesis. White Bear Lake would go on to play three straight games in the state tourney in multiple overtimes, the first team to ever do so. They lost to Lakeville North 4-3 in three overtimes to finish sixth.

89) Tim Bergland. The Prowlers claimed third place in 2011 with a 3-0 win over Hibbing/ Chisholm, earning their first trophy since copping fifth place in 1959.

90) Bruce Olson. In 1998 and 1999, he brought Roseau to state and in 2007 and 2008, he guided Warroad to state. Roseau won the AA title under his tutelage in 1999.

91) Rudy Kogi, whose best finish was a third place in 1957.

92) Bob Turner, in 1956 and 1960. Their only other appearance came in 1945.

93) John Rossi. In the 1958 tournament, the St. Paul Harding coach not only coached his club to a second-place finish (1-0 to Roseau) in the Saturday evening finale but he also coached in the consolation title game that afternoon. He replaced St. Paul Murray coach Bernie Broderick, who had fallen ill as Murray fell to Minneapolis Roosevelt 3-2.

94) Willard Ikola (19); Mike Randolph (16); Tom Saterdalen (15); Oscar Almquist (14); Larry Ross (14); Rube Gustafson (12); Cliff Thompson (12); Dave Peterson (11); Terry Skrypek (11); Bruce Plante (11); Bill Lechner (11); and Curt Giles (10).

95) Steve Sertich of Roseville (Girls - 2006; Boys 2002, 2003) and Tom Osiecki of Burnsville (Girls -1996; Boys - 1983-87,1990). Peter Aus, Ray Dahlof, and Jim Scanlan have also coached in both the boys' and girls' tournaments but with different schools.

96) Wade Chiodo of Bemidji (AA) and Tom Benson of Spring Lake Park (A). Unfortunately, each lost both games at state. Bemidji was making their first appearance since 1986 while Spring Lake Park was making their first trip to state in their 43-year history.

97) Trent Eigner, a former Rosemount High star who played collegiately at Miami of Ohio and then in the minors for six seasons. His brother Ty played at Bowling Green and his brother Troy at Army.

98) Chris Lonke. A Proctor native, he also led Simley to a runners-up finish in Class A in 2003 and won the Dave Peterson award in 2015 for his contributions to youth hockey.

99) Bob Altavilla. A long-time assistant at Apple Valley, Altavilla witnessed his son Angelo play in three-straight tournaments for Lakeville North (2013-15). Angelo also won the AA Herb Brooks award award as a senior defenseman and will play baseball at Nebraska.

100) Mike Taylor. Eagan made trips to state in 2006, 2011,2013, and 2014 and brought home the third-place trophy in Class AA in both 2011 and 2014.

101) Willard Ikola won three state titles as a player for Eveleth (1948-50) and eight as head coach of Edina (1969,1971, 1974,1978,1979,1982,1984, and 1988). Wally Chapman won a title as a player with Edina-East in 1982 and then won two Class A titles as Breck's coach in 2000 and 2004. Rod "Buzz" Christensen played for International Falls in 1965 and 1966 and then led Grand Rapids to the title in 1980. Denny Fermoyle was a goalie for Minneapolis Southwest in 1969 and was a co-head coach for Warroad when the Warriors claimed the A title in 2005.

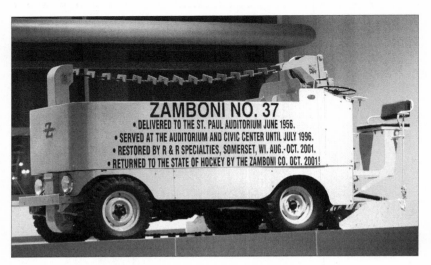

Zamboni #37 (Photo: Kyle Oen)

10 Arenas and Facilities

1) Since its inception in 1945, the state boys hockey tournament was conducted at the same location in St. Paul through 1968. What was the name of the arena?

2) Has the state tourney ever been held in Minneapolis?

3) In what year was the state tournament returned to downtown St. Paul after a seven-year hiatus and in what new facility would the tournament be conducted?

4) Where was the tournament moved for seven years before its return to St. Paul?

5) What is the largest crowd ever to witness an indoor hockey game at any level in Minnesota?

6) What school won the last state title at the St. Paul Auditorium?

7) What was the cause of the gray-white plume that permeated the air at the St. Paul Auditorium during games contested there from 1945-1968?

8) By 1960, how many indoor arenas with artificial ice were located in the entire state of Minnesota besides the St. Paul Auditorium?

9) What was the color scheme of the interior of the St. Paul Civic Center?

10) When was the first year that the tournament was conducted at the Xcel Energy Center?

11) What school won the final title at Met Center and the first at the Civic Center?

12) Has any school won at least one state championship playing at four different venues?

13) What is the official seating capacity of Xcel Energy Center?

14) Who won the final high school tourney game played at the St. Paul Civic Center?

15) Prior to the use of the Zamboni machine, which became prevalent in the 1950s, what system or method did rink workers utilize to clean snow off the ice surface and then put a layer of water on at the St. Paul Auditorium?

16) Who are the only three cities to host the boys' state hockey tournament?

17) What unusual and unique feature did the new St. Paul Civic Center possess when it opened, becoming its trademark and legacy?

18) When was the first year that consolation-round games were contested at the new Mariucci Arena, constructed across the street from the original Williams Arena?

19) What former state tournament participant was literally involved in the design and building of the St. Paul Civic Center, which was finished in January of 1973?

20) What were the dimensions of the ice surfaces of the six arenas that have served as locations for state tournament hockey games?

21) What were or are the capacities of the six arenas that have and are serving as locations for the state hockey tournament?

22) When the St. Paul Civic Center was built adjacent to the former St. Paul Auditorium, what was the original space renamed as a portion of the building still exists?

23) In addition to the high school jersey exhibit at the Xcel Energy Center, what other exhibit was added as a complement to honoring the state high school hockey tournament on the lower level?

24) When Target Center was preparing for their first tournament action in 1992, what interesting scenario ensued as the building was readied for hockey?

Met Center 1974: The start of the title game between Bemidji and Edina-East (MSHSL)

1) St. Paul Auditorium. Thus, the tourney was held in that facility for the first 24 years.

2) Yes. In 1992, with the advent of the Tier I and II format, the Tier II tourney took place at Target Center in downtown Minneapolis. They played semifinal, final, and consolation games at the home of the NBA Minnesota Timberwolves on Friday and Saturday after playing opening-round games at the St. Paul Civic Center on Wednesday. They repeated that scenario in 1993. In 2000, while Xcel Energy Center was being built in St. Paul, championship round games for both Class AA and A were played at Target Center. Also, consolation-round games have been held at Mariucci Arena since 1994.

3) 1976. The St. Paul Civic Center was constructed for the local World Hockey Association team, the Minnesota Fighting Saints. The team played in the old St. Paul Auditorium early in the 1972-73 season and moved into the new building on Jan. 1, 1973. The original WHA team played there through 1976 and a second contingent played there for most of the 1976-77 season before disbanding.

4) Metropolitan Sports Center, located in Bloomington, which was home to the Minnesota North Stars of the National Hockey League. The building was constructed in 1967 in preparation for the franchise's initial season in 1967-68.

5) The 2008 Class AA semifinals drew a crowd of 19,547 to watch Edina beat Benilde-St. Margaret's 5-4 in overtime and eventual-champion Hill-Murray dispatch Roseau 6-2.

6) Greenway-Coleraine beat South St. Paul 6-1 in the finals, their second straight title.

7) Smoke, from the paying customers.

8) Sixteen (16). The other four located within the confines of the Twin Cities area were Williams Arena (Minneapolis), Golden Valley Ice Arena, the Minneapolis Auditorium, and DuPont Arena (Minneapolis). By 1970, there were 60 indoor rinks in Minnesota and 25 in the Twin Cities. In 1982, there were 130 state-wide and 60 in the Twin Cities metro area. As of 2015, there are over 200 indoor arenas and a total of 275 ice-sheets.

9) Harvest-gold, orange, and purple.

10) 2001

11) Grand Rapids

12) Yes. Roseau won four state titles at the St. Paul Auditorium (1946, 1958, 1959, and 1961) and one each at the Civic Center (1990), the Target Center (1999), and Xcel Energy Center (2007).

13) 18,539

14) Duluth East. The Greyhounds won the Class AA title over Anoka 3-1 in 1998.

15) A large sled with metal skis with a large container of water atop was used to clean the ice. A drip pipe off the back-end flooded the ice surface.

16) St. Paul, Minneapolis, and Bloomington

17) Clear, plexi-glass boards. At the time it was only one of two arenas in the world (the other being the 1972 Olympic rink in Sapporo, Japan) that had the transparent boards, allowing fans sitting in the first few rows to see the puck and action close to the boards.

18) 1994

Xcel Energy Center (photo: Kyle Oen)

19) Len Lilyholm, who played for Robbinsdale in the 1959 tourney and scored five goals with an assist in earning all-tournament laurels for the Robins. Lilyholm was an architect working on the project while he was playing for the Fighting Saints, who played in the facility.

20) St. Paul Auditorium (85 x 200); Metropolitan Sports Center (85 x 200); St. Paul Civic Center (85 x 200); Target Center (80 x 190); Mariucci Arena (100 x 200); and the Xcel Energy Center (85 x 200).

21) St. Paul Auditorium (7,500); Metropolitan Sports Center (14,989); St. Paul Civic Center (16,188); Target Center (17,500); Mariucci Arena (10,000); and the Xcel Energy Center (18,539).

22) Roy Wilkins Auditorium, in honor of the civil rights leader from St. Paul. Today, the Wilkins complex also connects to the River Centre Convention Center and the Xcel Energy Center.

23) Headlines from the *St. Paul Pioneer Press* from 18 selected tournaments are displayed on eight support pillars that surround the lowel level. The exhibit begins with the very first event in 1945 and includes representations from both the boys' and girls' tourney, which began in 1995.

24) The lines were properly painted on the ice but the blue lines on the boards were not aligned with the blue lines on the ice so the boards had to be painted over and then painted to match with the lines on the ice.

11 Non-Playing Personnel

1) What man served as a tournament referee in the 1940's, 1950's, and 1960's?

2) What man has served for 28 years as a Game Manager at the state tournament and has also served as a goal judge, timer, penalty-box attendant and referee?

3) What public-address announcer started his state tournament job in 1976, the year that the tourney returned to St. Paul at the Civic Center and also was the main P.A. announcer for the North Stars from 1981 until they left for Texas in 1993?

4) What man, certainly one of the pioneering giants of high school hockey in Minnesota, worked in some capacity as a state tournament employee every year from 1945-91?

5) What St. Paul Washington grad refereed high school hockey for 32 years and had a 30-year association with the state tournament, as a referee (12), as a tournament director (16), and as an associate director of the Minnesota State High School League?

6) What fellow serves as both an official scorer and a public-address announcer and has done so since 2004 and has also done radio play-by-play work since 1992?

7) What former tournament participant oversaw the tournament as its director for six years in a 21-year career as an associate director of the MSHSL and also served as the director of the Herb Brooks Foundation for six years and is now on its Board of Directors?

8) What man has served as the Supervisor of Officials at the tourney for the past 24 years?

9) Who sold programs at the state tournament for over 40 years?

10) Who served as one of the main public-address announcers for the tournament for nearly 40 years?

11) What man spent 26 years as the head trainer for the state boys' hockey tournament from 1976-2001, apart from his job as the head trainer at the University of Minnesota?

12) What two senior gentlemen and good friends spent many years manning the penalty box at the state tourney as attendants?

13) What man was very instrumental in organizing and establishing the tournament as a legitimate enterprise along with Gene Aldrich and served as on-ice official and in other tournament capacities for many years and, in fact, was the first man to propose the idea of a state high school hockey tournament?

14) What school's principal also served as the dynamic leader of the band appearing with the team whenever they earned a tourney berth?

15) In what year were referees and linesman required to wear helmets?

16) What father and son tandems have worked as on-ice officials at the state tournament?

17) What Detroit native and St. Thomas University graduate witnessed his first tournament game in 1971 and started working as a public-address announcer in 1992?

18) What gentleman has served as a goal-judge and a penalty-box attendant since 1991?

19) What current *St. Paul Pioneer Press* reporter, who is the beat writer for the hometown Minnesota Wild, has also covered the state hockey tourney extensively?

20) Who has been the designer of the tournament program for the past 15 years?

21) What gentleman, the founder of "Let's Play Hockey", did play-by-play of the tourney on the radio in the 1950's and later served as the public-address announcer when the games were played at Met Center from 1969-75?

22) What veteran Orono High coach was a regular officiating games at the state tourney from the 1950's to the 1970's?

23) What man was a referee in the most championship games in tourney history?

24) What man has done yeoman work as an official scorer for the past 36 years?

25) Which rink attendant drove the Zamboni machine resurfacing the ice for 24 years at both the St. Paul Auditorium and the Civic Center?

26) Currently, who is the tournament director for the state boys' hockey tournament?

27) What two gentlemen officiated more than a decade together as a team at the tourney and have served as video replay judges for the past nine years?

28) Which two officials refereed in two classic overtimes games in the 1970 event, the five-overtime quarterfinal between Greenway and St. Paul Johnson and the title contest between Edina and Minneapolis Southwest?

29) The sports editor at ABC Newspapers in Anoka, what veteran sportswriter has served as a statistician from 1987 to 2014?

30) Which former Edina player is now working as one of the public-address announcers?

31) In 2011, what brothers became the first three-brother combination to officiate a game together when they called the Breck-Thief River Falls quarterfinal in Class A?

32) What two U.S. Hockey Hall of Fame members were referees in the 1963 classic title-game showdown between two-time defending champion International Falls and St. Paul Johnson, which won a 4-3 overtime thriller?

33) What former tournament referee now serves as the Assistant Supervisor of Officials?

34) What former tournament official became the first full-time executive director of the United States Amateur Hockey Association in 1972 and helped it become a professional organization (now known as USA Hockey) with his brilliant leadership for 15 years?

35) What Eveleth native and St. Cloud State player and coach was a referee in 15 of the first 16 state tournaments?

36) What two fellows served as goal judges for 17 straight seasons with one another?

37) What man acted as a game timer for 19 years from 1976-94?

38) After Larry Larson served as the head of Media Services for the Minnesota State High School League (1975-1989), what man succeeded him and continued in that capacity for the next 25 years?

39) What Greenway-Coleraine all-tourney forward (1962) and future UMD stalwart was a well-respected on-ice official in 14 tournaments in the 1970's and 1980's?

40) What physician served as the tournament doctor for 15 years from 1977-1991?

41) Who served as a penalty timer at the tournament from 1976-95?

42) All-tournament for Thief River Falls in 1959 after scoring five goals for the 5th-place Prowlers, who is this man who later was a referee in seven tournaments in the 1970's?

43) Who has served as a head timer at the tournament since 1996 and for nine years as an official scorer?

44) Who are the only referees to officiate in at least nine straight tournaments?

1) John Gustafson, who was an official in the first-ever tournament in 1945. Gustafson also was a game timer for several tournaments.

2) Ken Kosel

3) Dick Stanford, who worked the tourney microphone for 33 years and announced his final tournament in 2008. No wonder his diction and syntax were so smooth, he was an English and Speech teacher at St. Paul Johnson! Besides working the hockey tournaments, he also worked the Prep Bowl, the girls' basketball tournament, and the state track and field meet.

4) John Neihart, who worked a total of 47 consecutive tournaments. John was a referee, a goal judge, a game manager, and a team host.

5) John Bartz, who was an assistant coach for North St. Paul in 1961 and 1967 and is now the executive secretary for the Suburban East Conference. Bartz attended his first state tournament in 1948 and has seen every one since then, except for his time in military service (which allowed him an opportunity to see the U.S. hockey team play in the 1956 Olympics in Cortina d'Ampezzo, Italy). Bartz continues to work at the tournament as a Game Manager along with Ken Kosel, another long-time official at the tourney.

6) Rick Benson. A former hockey player at Minneapolis Edison, Benson was the public-address announcer for the Gopher women's program for the first 10 years and also did a year with the men's program.

7) Skip Peltier, who worked for the League from 1985-2005. Peltier was a sophomore on the 1963 state champion St. Paul Johnson and as a junior had a goal and three assists as the Governors finished second. In his third and final year in the tourney, Peltier added a goal as his team finished third. Peltier's brothers Ron, Doug, and Bob all later starred for the east-siders. Peltier also coached Park-Cottage Grove and was the athletic director at both Park-Cottage Grove and Woodbury.

8) Bill Kronschnabel, a Cretin graduate, who has served in that capacity since 1991. Bill officiated in four straight tourneys (1987-90), including two championship games in a 35-year career as a referee. He also worked 24 years as an NCAA Division III referee and was the NCHA Commissioner for several years.

9) Art Tysk

10) Bob Reid, who worked the hockey tournament from 1966-2003. Reid announced high school tournaments for a total of 42 years and never missed an assignment. He handled eight different sports tournaments (wrestling, baseball, softball, boys basketball, girls basketball, boys hockey, girls hockey, and football) and is in the MSHSL Hall of Fame. Reid worked as a Master of Ceremonies and a P.A. announcer even in high school at St. Louis Park. Reid worked only consolation games for boys hockey and when the Tier II and Class A tourneys began, he covered all of their games. Reid was the public-address announcer for Gopher hockey and baseball and was one of the first employees of the North Stars in 1967.

11) Jim Marshall, who spent 42 years as a trainer for the Gopher athletic program. He succeeded Lloyd "Snapper" Stein at the U of M, a fellow who had also worked the state hockey tournament for many years prior to Marshall.

12) Hank Frantzen and Herb Brooks, Sr. The latter gentleman was the father of Herb Brooks, the former St. Paul Johnson and Gopher player who later went on to even greater fame as a coach, of course. They worked together from 1976-1984 and Frantzen, who was a referee in several title games in the early years, continued on until 1989 as an attendant.

13) John Neihart. "Big John", 6'6", coached high school hockey at Harding, Humboldt, Johnson and St. Agnes and was head coach at Hamline University from 1948-73. He officated or coached at least 100 games a year for 35 years and was President of the St. Paul Hockey Officials Association for 11 years. He refereed for 37 years overall, from high school to semi-pro. Neihart was the tournament's Supervisor of Officials for over 20 years, and was a state tourney referee for many years. He also served as a goal judge for the North Stars for 21 years at Met Center, in addition to serving in the same capacity at the state tournament.

14) Hill-Murray's Frank Asenbrenner, who served as principal at the Maplewood Catholic school from the school's inception in 1971 when Hill H.S. (boys) merged with Archbishop Murray H.S. girls) until 1991. He was the band director from 1971 until 1994. Asenbrenner directed the band for a few private tournaments and first directed in the public tourney in 1975, as Hill-Murray became the first non-public school to earn a berth in the tournament. He

directed his school's band for 15 tournaments, including two titles in 1983 and 1991. All eight of Asenbrenner's children attended Hill-Murray.

15) 1989

16) Buzz Olson (father) and J.B. Olson (son); Scott Parker (father) and John Parker (son).

17) Dave "Stats" Wright, who first worked consolation games at Mariucci Arena when the Tier I-II tourney was played there in 1992. Wright, a voice of St. Thomas sports for 40 years, now mostly announces "day" games at the state tournament during the A and AA tourney but has also served as an official scorer. A long-time employee of the St. Paul Saints, he wrote a book about the Twins in 2010 entitled, "162-0."

18) Jim "Cisco" Davis, a former Cretin goalie in the 1960s, who also works as a timer.

19) Bruce Brothers, who worked the tournament for the *Minneapolis Tribune* from 1972-83 and for *Minnesota Hockey Magazine* in 1986-87. Brothers has also covered Gopher men's and women's hockey.

20) David Swanson, who has been employed by both Gopher State Litho and Carlson Print Group in the design and production of the program.

21) Bob Utecht

22) Leo Goslin. Leo will forever be remembered in tourney lore for his dedication and persistence to the game. Wearing the ubiquitous black pants as is the custom for all officials, he had the misfortune to rip his pants...and severely. Goslin finished out the period and with the aid of safety pins and black tape, he was back at it the next period looking...black! Leo won the Cliff Thompson Award in 1989.

23) John Bartz, who worked a total of seven title games. Bartz wrote the first National Rules Federation handbook for ice hockey and was the chairman of the national committee for several years. Bartz was also the Supervisor of Officials at the tournament from 1981-90.

24) John Vosejpka, who has also worked the boy's basketball tournament for over 30 years and the girl's basketball

tournament for over 10 years. Vosejpka, currently an Athletic Facilitator for the St. Paul schools, worked his first state hockey tourney in 1979.

25) Mike Nedeau, who drove the Zamboni from 1963-1986 at both arenas. Nedeau operated and maintained Zamboni #37, which was used at both the Auditorium and Civic Center from June of 1956 to July of 1996. It is now prominently displayed at Xcel Energy Center near the Kellogg and West 7th entrance gate. Nedeau has worked in guest services at the Xcel since the Wild started playing there in 1999.

26) Craig Perry, who has been in charge of running the tourney since 2006. A Fort Frances, Ontario native, Perry played college hockey at North Dakota.

27) Jerry Krieger and Greg Shepherd, who worked 30 years as a pair refereeing high school and college hockey, including the WCHA.

28) Swede Lund and Ray Olson

29) Tom Yelle, who has witnessed every state tournament since 1969. Yelle has worked as an official scorer, press box announcer, and in various other capacities for 28 years.

John Bartz, long-time on-ice official and tournament director. (Photo courtesy John Bartz)

30) Jim Carroll, who has been working the tourney since 2005 and was one of the state's top players in 1986 for the Hornets. Carroll, who played at Michigan Tech, is now the public-address announcer for the Vikings.

31) Rick, Gary, and Brad Larsen. Their grandfather, Hank Frantzen, was also an official in the tourney in the 1950's and 1960's and also refereed three consecutive NCAA title games from 1951-53. Frantzen also led Macalester to four MIAC hockey titles. Rick and Brad played for St. Paul Johnson in the 1984 and 1991 tourneys, respectively. The father of the three brothers, Jack, played on the

1963 Johnson team that beat International Falls 4-3 in 1963 to win their fourth and final state title and officiated high school games with Rick and Gary before ending his own 25-year officiating career.

32) Hal Trumble and Don Wheeler. The game was dramatic because it not only was Rube Gustafson's last as coach for the champion Governors but it was the first title game to go to overtime and kept the Broncos from completing an undefeated season.

33) Rick Tibesar, who was an official in eight tournaments and has been serving in his current capacity for 25 years. Tibesar, a 28-year St. Paul policeman, was a high school and college referee for 35 years.

34) Hal Trumble. He not only worked several state tournaments but became a college and international referee and refereed the gold-medal game at the 1968 Olympics. Trumble was the General Manager of three U.S. National teams and managed the 1972 U.S. Olympic team to a silver medal. Hal, who was also an international baseball and softball umpire, was inducted into the U.S. Hockey Hall of Fame in 1985.

35) Roland Vandell. A defenseman who played in front of Frankie Brimsek with the Huskies, Vandell later coached his alma mater in the 1940s and 1950s and also was a college referee for 20 years.

36) Jack Larsen and Dale Carmichael, who were mainstays from 1976-92. Carmichael was a goal judge for 30 years (1976-2005) at three different venues. Arnie Bauer was also a goal judge along with the previous two from 1976-89.

37) Bud Bodin

38) Howard Voigt, who worked his 25th state hockey tournament in 2014.

39) Mike Tok, who was from Bovey.

40) Dr. James Priest

41) Ted Olson

42) Dale Wennberg

43) Mark Wahman, who is now the head timer.

44) John Bartz (1972-80) and Bill Mason (1990-98).

12 Media

1) What national sports celebrity and ABC sportscaster appeared during the broadcast of the 1979 tournament when the rights to the event were owned by KSTP, their local affiliate?

2) What former Gopher All-American and former North Star player, coach, and general manager has been a color analyst for the tournament broadcast since 1964?

3) What group is responsible for selecting the all-tournament teams for both Class AA and A, since it was re-introduced for the 1990 tournament?

4) What player, the Mr. Hockey award winner in 1992, never made it to the state tournament that season but did appear as a commentator for KMSP-TV in his senior season?

5) What veteran NHL broadcaster did play-by-play of the 2014 tournament?

6) What television station was the first to broadcast the tournament, when was the first year it was broadcast, and what viewers had access to it?

7) What Ch. 5 (KSTP) political reporter has handled the pre-game, post-game, and between games "hosting" for the state boys hockey tournament for the past eleven years?

8) In 1983, what national publication did a feature story on the state boys hockey tourney, entitled, "The Thrill of a Lifetime"?

9) What Warroad native has written features for the tournament

program and now writes and does radio spots about hockey at the high school, college, and pro levels?

10) In 1968, what man composed *Minnesota State High School Hockey Tournament History*, a compilation of the tourney's records, statistics, and summaries of the tournament's first 24 years?

11) In 2003, John Rosengren's book, *Blades of Glory: The Story of a Young Team Bred to Win*, chronicled the 2000-01 season of what school?

12) What former *Minneapolis Tribune* writer, who was a long-time beat writer for the Gopher hockey team and the author of *Herb Brooks, The Inside Story of a Hockey Mastermind*, has written about the tournament in some capacity for more than fifty years?

13) In 1984, what national daily newspaper had a reporter at the tournament?

14) What play-by-play broadcaster in the 1960's was the primary play-by-play man when WTCN-TV owned the broadcast rights for the high school tournament?

15) In 1987, ESPN featured the boys state hockey tourney on which of its signature programs?

16) What year was the tournament first broadcast by radio?

17) What author wrote a book on the highlights of the Minnesota State Hockey Tournament in 1982, entitled, *Skate for Goal*?

18) What *St. Paul Pioneer Press* writer, who wrote for the paper for 33 years, annually worked the tournament doing special features and notes?

19) What television station covered the tournament when it expanded into a two-tier arrangement and then a two-class set-up during the 1990's?

20) What local author and former Fairmont High player, who has published more than 50 books (mainly about Minnesota sports), highlighted the boys state hockey tournament in two books?

21) What television station became the first to televise all of the

tournament's games?

22) What world-renowned newspaper completed a feature on the tournament in advance of the 1989 tournament?

23) What veteran Minneapolis photographer took photos at the state tourney for the *Star and Tribune* for nearly 30 years?

24) A *St. Paul Pioneer Press* writer from 1983-2006, what scribe played in the 1965 tourney for Minneapolis Southwest?

25) What local artist has provided the cover art for the state boys' hockey tournament program since 1998?

26) What was the name of the documentary filmed in 2004 featuring the hockey tournament?

27) What ardent supporter of high school athletics has written about the tournament since 1984, when he was attending St. Thomas University?

28) What Hockey Hall of Fame broadcaster worked tourney games on radio for KSTP?

29) Who has served as the exclusive corporate sponsor for the Minnesota State High School League for the past two decades and has presented the all-tournament awards since 1990?

30) What *Pioneer Press* columnist predicted that St. Paul Harding would upset Edina-East in the 1974 quarterfinals at Met Center?

31) What Thief River Falls announcer from KTRF and long-time tournament broadcaster was enshrined in the Minnesota State Hockey Coaches Association Hall of Fame in 1992?

32) What television analyst once climbed on to the Zamboni machine between periods and interviewed the driver while he was resurfacing the St. Paul Auditorium ice?

33) Which former KSTP sports broadcaster had a son who was a steady performer for the Breck Mustangs' on their Class A title teams of 2009 and 2010?

34) A sturdy center for Edina in 2007 and 2008, what Hornet player's father served 24 years as a sports reporter and investigative reporter for

Edina-East coach Willard Ikola is interviewed during the 1979 tourney by Channel 5 reporter Ed Karow and ABC broadcaster Howard Cosell. (Photo courtesy Willard Ikola)

KSTP-TV Channel 5 and played as a backup goalie for Minneapolis Southwest in the 1975 tournament.

35) A book titled *River of Champions*, written by Mary Halverson Schofield, chronicled the hockey season of what Minnesota school and community?

36) What Princeton native started broadcasting the boys' state tournament in 2006 and has won three Upper Midwest regional Emmy's for his work covering the tournament in 2006, 2007 and 2008?

37) What Fox Sports North host and Wild play-by-play voice has worked at the state tournament on either radio or local cable for over 20 years?

38) What two broadcasters did play-by-play and color commentary, respectively, for WTCN in the 1970's?

39) The present play-by-play announcer for Gopher hockey on 1500ESPN, this gentleman did 15 tournament broadcasts from 1991 to 2005, often working alongside color-analyst Lou Nanne. Can you name him?

40) What current KSMP-TV sports director has been a big booster of high school hockey and the state tournament during his sports broadcasting career?

41) When KSTP owned the broadcast rights to the tournament, who was the owner of the station who was so passionate about supporting the game of hockey?

42) What former Twin Cities journalist and Pulitzer Prize winner (2000) wrote a feature on the state tournament in 2004 for *Sports Illustrated* entitled, "High School Heaven"?

43) What *Minneapolis Star Tribune* photographer has covered the state tournament for the past 40 years?

44) What local station has the current rights to broadcast the boys' state hockey tourney?

45) What *Minneapolis Star Tribune* reporter, responsible for the entertaining section "2Days 2Cents", the "2-Do List", and "The Game Plan" on page two of the sports page each day, has covered the tournament since 2001?

46) When WCCO gained the broadcast rights to the tourney in the 1980s, what man working for "Hockey Night in Canada" was brought in to do play-by-play for the telecasts?

1) Howard Cosell. "The Mouth", made famous on ABC's "Monday Night Football" telecasts alongside the late Don Meredith and Frank Gifford, was present because KSTP owner Stanley Hubbard wanted to make a big splash as his local station had just switched national affiliations from NBC to ABC. KSTP had the broadcasts for four seasons (1979-82).

2) Lou Nanne. The Canadian transplant (Sault St. Marie, Ontario) would even stay in town to do interviews during the Thursday first-round games and then fly out the next day to wherever the North Stars were playing in time for their next game.

3) Originally, members of the press voted for the all-tournament team. Later, a committee of hockey coaches was established to select the twelve players in each class. Presently, a combination of sportswriters/broadcasters and a coaches panel now determines the all-tourney teams.

4) Brian Bonin of White Bear Lake, a future All-American and Hobey Baker winner.

5) Gary Thorne, who called NHL games for ESPN, ESPN2, and NBC.

6) WTCN, the only independent station, broadcast the first tourney in 1954 in the Twin Cities area but just the third-place and championship games and continued broadcasting the games until 1978. Twin City Federal was the paying sponsor for WTCN during those years. In the early years, the only bid to broadcast the tourney came from WTCN.

7) Tom Hauser, who played his youth hockey in Edina and graduated from Edina-West.

8) *Sports Illustrated*. The 11-page spread was written by hockey writer E.M. Swift and described his observations of the previous year's tournament.

9) Jess Myers, who writes for *USA Hockey Magazine* and *InsideHockey.com* and is on the committee that selects the Hobey Baker award. He also covers the Wild on 1500ESPN.

10) Art Solz, Jr., whose father and three brothers owned Arthur's Four Seasons restaurant on University Avenue in Minneapolis. Solz won 11 letters at Minneapolis Edison, including one in hockey.

Lou Nanne (left) and Clay Matvick are shown broadcasting during the 2011 tournament. (Kyle Oen)

He began the Edison High Sports Hall of Fame and was inducted into it three days before his death in 1991.

11) Bloomington Jefferson. The Jaguars, however, did not make the 2000-01 state tourney as they were beaten 2-1 in the Section 5 semifinals by Eastview.

12) John Gilbert, who witnessed his first tourney action in 1963 and has covered the state tournament ever since. Gilbert wrote for 30 years for the *Minneapolis Star Tribune* and was selected to the Minnesota State Coaches Association Hall of Fame in 2003.

13) *USA Today*

14) Frank Buetel, who also did work for the Twins in the 1960's. Buetel, who is enshrined in the Minnesota Museum of Broadcasting Hall of Fame, also did hockey play-by-play for the Gophers, North Stars, and Fighting Saints.

15) *Scholastic Sports America*

16) 1947. Roseau had all three of its games in the tourney broadcast throughout northwest Minnesota. The Rams lost 2-1 to St. Paul Johnson in the championship game.

17) Gary L. Phillips

18) Gregg Wong, who covered the tournament from 1969-2002.

19) KMSP-TV (Channel 9), which owned the rights from 1992-2004. In 1992, the station paid $151,000 for broadcast rights for the first year of Tier I and II and $180,998 in 1994 for the first year of two-class hockey.

20) Ross Bernstein. He was "Goldy," the Gopher hockey mascot whose humorous antics at the old Mariucci Arena mesmerized the fans. He wrote his first book called, *Gopher Hockey by the Hockey Gopher*, published in 1992. His book on all levels of Minnesota hockey, *Frozen Memories*, was published in 1999 and *More Frozen Memories* was printed in 2007. Both books had extensive coverage of the state tournament.

21) WCCO-TV (Channel 4) in 1983. The station did 40 pre-taped pieces and was on the air for 24 hours of coverage that year. WCCO paid $150,000 a year for three years to earn the rights to air the broadcasts. WCCO broadcasted the event from 1983-91. In the last of their three three-year contracts, WCCO paid $1,580,000 to broadcast the games from 1989-91.

22) The New York Times

23) John Croft, who started at the *Minneapolis Tribune* in 1957 and shot sports exclusively for more than 10 years before branching out to also do other assignments. Croft spent 40 years with the *Star Tribune*.

24) Mike Fermoyle. A reserve goalie for Dave Peterson's team, Fermoyle played at the end of a consolation-round game against Alexander Ramsey. Trailing 4-1, the Indians pulled starter Bruce Nelson and inserted Fermoyle with 2:04 remaining. Fermoyle left the ice for a sixth attacker and Bob Cronk scored to pull Southwest to within two goals with 30 seconds left. Rick Wickre of Ramsey then scored into an empty net with just three seconds left. At that time, goals were counted against the goalie pulled for the sixth attacker, so Fermoyle, who didn't face a shot, has a goals-against-average of 17.42. Fermoyle worked for the Rochester Post-Bulletin for three years during the heydays of John Marshall. He also became an accomplished amateur golfer and was named to the Minnesota Golf Association Hall of Fame in 2011.

25) Terrence Fogarty

26) "Ice Dreams", an hour-long show that was produced by Fox Sports Net and received rave reviews.

27) Tim Leighton

28) Al Shaver, the legendary North Star radio voice who worked all 26 seasons the North Stars were located in Bloomington from 1967-93. Shaver, who was inducted into the Hockey Hall of Fame in 1993 as a Foster Hewitt Memorial winner, did play-by-play of the Gophers for three seasons after the Stars left for Dallas.

29) Wells Fargo. The awards recognize student-athletes who demonstrate exceptional sportsmanship, team commitment, athletic ability, and leadership.

30) Don Riley. In the "Eye-Opener" the St. Paul columnist had a feeling the hometown Knights, coached by Richard Anderson, would knock off Ikola's boys. It didn't work out that way as Edina-East won 9-0, outshooting Harding 49-13.

31) Don Olson

32) Lou Nanne, who did so in the mid-1960's with WTCN. In another rink-side interview during that era, the former Gopher and North Star player had his microphone cord severed by the Zamboni.

33) Eric Gislason, who has worked the tourney for 28 years either on television or radio (16 years as a sports anchor at Ch. 5). His son Ben was all-tournament in 2010.

34) Matt Leer, who scored a goal and two assists in 2007 when the Hornets' took fifth place and a goal and an assist in 2008 when Edina was second. His father, Robb, covered all the hockey tournaments during his tenure at Channel 5 and also the North Stars for 14 seasons. Robb played in the 1975 tournament for Minneapolis Southwest and made five saves as a reserve goaltender in a 6-1 finals loss to Grand Rapids. Robb's son Nick also played in the 2011 and 2012 tourneys for Edina.

35) Thief River Falls, which won the state crown that year.

36) Clay Matvick, who broadcasted the play-by-play of all championship-round games in both Class A and AA for seven years. He formerly worked for FSN for five years in the metro and has been employed by ESPN since 2006 and is now doing not

225

Tom Hauser (left), Mike McGraw (center), and Dave Palmquist (right) shown between periods working the 2011 tourney for KSTC-TV. (Kyle Oen)

only college hockey but basketball and football, too.

37) Anthony LaPanta. The versatile LaPanta worked radio broadcasts for various local stations starting in 1991, including championship games for KFAN from 2006-10.

38) Joe Boyle and Roger Buxton

39) Wally Shaver, the son of legendary broadcaster Al Shaver. Wally's son, Jason, is a third-generation announcer as he is doing play-by-play for the Chicago Wolves of the IHL. Wally also did a few years of radio work of the prep tournament.

40) Jim Rich, who previously worked at KBJR-TV in Duluth.

41) Stanley Hubbard, who played at Breck and then at Minnesota in the 1950's.

42) George Dohrmann, who previously had worked for the *St. Paul Pioneer Press* from 1997-2000 and won his Pulitzer for his work uncovering the academic fraud scandal in the Gopher men's basketball program.

43) Bruce Bisping, who also did marvelous work photographing the North Stars.

44) KSTC-TV. Channel 45 is owned and operated by Hubbard Broadcasting, which also owns the local ABC affiliate, KSTP (Channel 5). The original contract was through 2015 but was extended to 2021 in 2009 and includes webcasting. The MSHSL Board of Directors accepted KSTC's bid in 2004, including the right to televise girls' hockey, and boys' and girls' basketball. KSTC provides on-air promotions, community involve- ment/public service messages, website elements, special events marketing, and outside media support.

45) Michael Rand

46) Chris Cuthbert, who now works for TSN cable network doing play-by-play in Canada.

13 Team Records

1) Which school has won the most state titles with nine?

2) What school has the most state tourney appearances with 34?

3) Who are the only teams to play into overtime in all three games in a single tourney?

4) What legendary program holds the all-time mark for most overall wins in the history of the tournament?

5) Which school holds the record for most consecutive state hockey titles?

6) Who is the only school to score at least 10 goals in a championship game?

7) Which hockey power has suffered the most overtime losses?

8) Which school has allowed the most goals all-time?

9) What school holds the mark for best won-lost percentage (minimum 15 games)?

10) Which two teams combined to score the most goals ever scored in a single game with 17 in a consolation final in 1984?

11) What school has recorded the most shutouts with 10?

12) On how many occasions has a team scored at least 10 goals in a tournament game?

13) What school has established a tradition for playing excellent hockey in the state tournament but has dealt with the frustration of losing all seven title games they have participated in?

14) What school has lost the most tournament games with 46?

15) What four schools have scored seven goals in one period?

16) What is the only school to compete in six straight title games?

17) Which school became the first located south of the Twin Cities metro area to win the state title?

18) What school has won the most overtime contests?

19) Which school holds the record for the longest winning streak in Minnesota state boys' hockey history?

20) Which school is the only one in tourney history to win consecutive titles by shutout?

21) What team holds the mark for most goals scored in a single tournament?

22) Who are the only two schools to appear in the tournament in each decade (not counting 2010 - 2015 as a new decade)?

23) Which school has the most second-place finishes with eight?

24) Which proud hockey programs share the most third-place finishes with six?

25) Which two schools have claimed the most consolation trophies?

26) Which is the last Minnesota boys' team to finish the season with a perfect record?

27) Which school holds the honor of earning a state berth with the lowest enrollment?

28) Through 2015, what school has scored the most goals in tournament history?

29) Amazingly, what tournament regular once played a stretch over three years where they played five consecutive overtime games?

30) What school holds the record for the most tourney appearances since the single-class era ended in 1991 with 16?

31) What school holds the tournament record for consecutive wins with 14?

32) In an incredible irony, what school played in an overtime championship game and then played the same opponent in the quarterfinals the next year and then repeated the same scenario with another opponent the following year?

33) Which are the only two schools to score ten goals in consecutive games?

34) Unfortunately, what school has lost all 18 (yes, all 18) of their quarterfinal games?

35) Which is the only school to play two consecutive games into at least two overtimes and, in fact, played all three state tourney games into at least the second overtime?

36) Which school has the most consecutive second-place finishes in tourney annals with six?

37) Which school has the most consecutive third-place finishes over the past 71 years?

38) Has any school ever won three consecutive consolation titles?

39) Truly, one of the great accomplishments in state hockey history is the record of one school winning a trophy in eight straight state tournaments. What prominent hockey power enjoyed this phenomenal streak of outstanding play?

40) Who are the only four schools to win a state championship while achieving 30 wins or more?

41) What school holds the record for scoring the fastest two goals in a game?

42) Which school set a record that will never be broken and will be very difficult to tie as they gave up exactly zero (0) goals in a single tournament?

43) What school has had the most appearances in the tourney without winning a title?

44) What school holds the record for the most consecutive appearances with 12?

International Falls, the 1962 State Champions.

45) Has any team besides Eveleth ever won at least three straight championships?

46) What two schools have won state hockey titles in three different formats (single-class, Tier I or II, or Class AA or A)?

47) Has any school ever won a state title more than once by winning in overtime?

48) Have two teams ever faced each other in a championship game three years in a row?

49) Besides tourney powerhouses Edina, Eveleth, International Falls, and Roseau, who are the other five schools to win at least four state championships?

50) Which school has the best winning percentage in tourney history (10 games minimum)?

51) What school set a tourney record when 16 different players recorded a point in a 12-0 rout of St. Cloud Apollo in a Class quarterfinal in 2013?

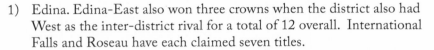

1) Edina. Edina-East also won three crowns when the district also had West as the inter-district rival for a total of 12 overall. International Falls and Roseau have each claimed seven titles.

2) Roseau. South St. Paul is second with 28 appearances. Edina has made 26 appearances with Edina-East making five, so some say the Hornets have been in 31. Hill-Murray has been in 27 tournaments in the 41 years they have been eligible to compete.

3) Edina (1970), Greenway-Coleraine (2001), Duluth East (2011), and White Bear Lake (2011).

4) Roseau has been victorious 55 times. Edina (50) and Edina-East (12) would combine for 62 total if the two were added together. Hill-Murray (40), Duluth East (39) Warroad (38), St. Paul Johnson (35), Duluth East (35), South St. Paul (34), and International Falls (33) follow.

5) Eveleth, with four straight from 1948-51 with Cliff Thompson at the helm.

6) Warroad. The Warriors beat Red Wing 10-3 in the Class A final in 1996. The two teams combined to score the most goals ever by both teams in a title game, also, with 13.

7) Hill-Murray, with ten sudden-death defeats. White Bear Lake and Minneapolis Roosevelt have each lost seven overtimes games.

8) Roseau with 287; South St. Paul has allowed 270.

9) St. Thomas Academy (.814) with a 22-5 mark in nine appearances and five Class A state titles. In their first foray into Class AA in 2015, the Cadets took the consolation title. Edina-East went 12-3 (.800) in five forays into the state tournament in their short nine-year history with two state titles (1978, 1979) to boot. Eveleth, including two years as Eveleth-Gilbert, is third at .750 with a 33-11 mark in 15 seasons. Breck is fourth at .718 with a 23-9 record in 11 appearances.

10) Roseau beat Burnsville 9-8 in overtime with Sean Bucy scoring the game-winner. Burnsville's John Borrell had three goals and two assists and Paul Broten two goals and two assists for the Rams. Andy Luckraft had 29 saves for the Braves and Roseau's Troy Olson

had 26 saves for the winners. All told, 17 goals were tallied on just 72 shots, a rather gaudy shooting percentage for both squads.

11) Eveleth, with two each in both 1949 and 1950. Willard Ikola had half of them, too!

12) 24; Eveleth has done it five times and St. Thomas Academy three times.

13) Moorhead. The Spuds, who have maintained one of the top high school and youth programs over the past 20 years, came closest in 2004, when they lost a 1-0 heart-breaker to Centennial in a AA finale. Other runners-up finishes came in 1992 (Tier I), 1994 (AA), 1995 (AA), 2001 (AA), 2005 (AA), and 2009 (AA).

14) South St. Paul. The Packers have lost 46 games and won 34 in 80 total games.

15) Eveleth (1945), Hill-Murray (1991), Breck (2010), and St. Thomas Academy (2011). Eveleth scored seven in the second period of their 16-0 thrashing of Granite Falls in a quarterfinal with Milan Begich scoring the hat trick and adding an assist. Meanwhile, Hill-Murray reached their total in the second period of their 11-4 semifinal romp over Grand Rapids. Mark Strobel started the furious onslaught with two goals in 25 seconds. In 2010, Breck scored seven times in the second period of their 11-1 quarterfinal romp over New Ulm as Tyson Fulton had a goal and two assists. In 2011, St. Thomas thumped New Ulm 13-2 in the first round, with nine different Cadets scoring. All four teams went on to claim the state title.

16) Hermantown (2010-15). Unfortunately, the Hawks lost each and every one of their Class A title games during that stretch. Four were one-goal losses and two came in overtime. International Falls (1962-66) and Eveleth (1948-52) were both in five title games in a row and both the Broncos and Golden Bears won four of those tilts.

17) Rochester John Marshall. The Rockets beat Edina-East 4-2 in 1977.

18) Edina has won nine games in overtime but Hill-Murray has played in the most with 17.

19) Eveleth. The dominating Golden Bears won 79 consecutive games from 1948-52 with four straight state titles (1948-51) before losing to Hibbing in the Region 7 finals. Hibbing beat Eveleth again, to prove it was no fluke, by a 4-3 margin in the state finals after Eveleth entered the tourney as the Region 3 representative.

20) International Falls. Larry Ross' powerhouse whipped Bloomington 7-0 in 1965 and Roseau 5-0 in 1966.

21) Eveleth scored 30 goals in 1945 on their way to the first-ever state championship.

22) Roseau and South St. Paul

23) Hill-Murray. Moorhead has been runners-up seven times without a title. Hermantown has also lost seven championship games but won a Class A crown in 2007. Warroad has been second six times while Grand Rapids, Duluth East, and Roseau all have five.

24) South St. Paul and Duluth East.

25) Edina (7). Roseau (6) and White Bear Lake (5) follow.

26) Red Wing (28-0 in 1997). The Wingers won the Class A crown with a 4-3 win over Warroad. Hermantown was 29-0-1 in 2007 and Warroad was 27-0-2 in 2005.

27) Williams, which had an enrollment of 90 for grades 10-12 from 1949-51.

28) Roseau (321 goals scored).

29) Edina. The Hornets won the 1969 title in overtime, played all three games in 1970 past regulation, and played their first-round game in 1971 into overtime.

30) Duluth East. The Greyhounds have copped two Class AA crowns, four second-place trophies, five third-place trophies, and two consolation titles since 1992.

31) Eveleth. In 1947, the Bears lost 5-3 to Minneapolis West in a third-place game. They then swept three games each of the next four years in becoming the first dynasty as the streak stood at 12. In the 1952 tourney, they extended their winning streak to 14 with wins over Thief River Falls and St. Paul Humboldt. The skein would end with a 4-3 loss to Hibbing in the finals. Bloomington Jefferson won 13 in a row in the late 1980's and early 1990's and St. Thomas Academy won 13 in a row from 2007-2013.

32) Edina. The Hornets beat Warroad 5-4 in overtime in the 1969 title game and then beat Warroad 3-2 in the 1970 quarterfinals.

The Breck Mustangs, 2009 Class A champions. (Kyle Oen)

After losing to Minneapolis Southwest 1-0 in an extra-session in that year's finals, Edina then beat Southwest 4-3 in the first round in 1971.

33) Eveleth and St. Thomas Academy. Eveleth did it twice (1945 and 1951). In the first tourney, Eveleth routed Granite Falls 16-0 and St. Paul Washington in its first two games. The John Mayasich-led Bears beat Williams 12-1 and Minneapolis Southwest 11-5 in its first two games six years later. In 2013, the Cadets downed St. Cloud Apollo 12-0 and East Grand Forks 11-0 in the first two rounds in Class A.

34) White Bear Lake. Even worse, the last seven losses have come by a single goal, and that includes a 4-3 double-overtime loss to Duluth East in the 2011 AA event.

35) White Bear Lake, in 2011. The Bears lost their quarterfinal to Duluth East 4-3 in two overtimes before edging Blaine 4-3 in the consolation semis in two overtimes. In the AA consolation title game, they fell to Lakeville North 4-3 just 15 seconds into the third overtime. Minnetonka (1985) and Edina (2000) both played two multiple overtime games but not in succession.

36) Hermantown in Class A (2010, 2011, 2012, 2013, 2014 and 2015), with three of the losses coming to St. Thomas Academy and two to East Grand Forks. Duluth Marshall lost three in a row (2006,

2007, 2008), also in Class A, with two coming at the hands of St. Thomas.

37) Duluth East, Hill-Murray, Roseau, and Breck have each won two in a row.

38) No. However, no less than five schools have won two-straight (St. Paul Murray (1950-51), Roseau (1967-68), Hill-Murray (1977-78), East Grand Forks (2001-02), and Rochester Lourdes (2009-10).

39) Grand Rapids (1974-81), which eclipsed Eveleth's mark of seven (1948-54).

40) St. Paul Johnson (34-1 in 1947); Roseau (30-0 in 1959, Centennial (30-0-1 in 2004) and Lakeville North (31-0 in 2015).

41) Thief River Falls. In the 1954 title game, Lyle Guttu and Marv Jorde scored just six seconds apart (at 9:40 and 9:46 of the second period) as the Prowlers claimed the state crown with a 4-1 win over Eveleth. Both Guttu and Jorde scored twice.

42) Centennial (2004)

43) South St. Paul. The Packers have been to "The Show" 28 times without winning it all. They have been runners-up twice (1961, 1968) and have been third six times.

44) Eveleth (1945-56); the Golden Bears brought home trophies in 10 of those years. Roseau (1961-69) is second with nine and Grand Rapids (1974-81) is third with eight.

45) Yes, Bloomington Jefferson won three-straight in 1992 (Tier I), 1993 (Tier I), and 1994 Class AA); and St. Thomas Academy won three in a row in Class A (2011, 2012, 2013).

46) Eveleth and Bloomington Jefferson. Eveleth won five one-class titles (1945, 1948, 1949, 1950, 1951), a Tier II title in 1993 as Eveleth-Gilbert, and a Class AA title as Eveleth-Gilbert in 1998. Jefferson won single-class crowns in '81 and '89, Tier II titles in 1992 and 1993, and the first Class AA title in 1994.

47) Yes. In fact, Edina-East won consecutive titles in 1978 (5-4 over Grand Rapids in two overtimes) and 1979 (4-3 over Rochester John Marshall). There have been only eight other occasions when a title game has needed an extra-session. John Marshall is the only team to have lost more than one title game (the other being a 5-4 loss to Bloomington Jefferson in the 1989 final).

48) Yes, St. Thomas Academy beat Hermantown in the Class A finals in 2011, 2012, and 2013. On four other occasions, the same two teams have met in title games in consecutive years: Eveleth and Williams (1949 and 1950); International Falls and St. Paul Johnson (1963 and 1964); Burnsville and Hill-Murray (1985 and 1986); and Red Wing and Warroad (1996 and 1997, Class A).

49) Bloomington Jefferson (5), St. Thomas Academy (5), St. Paul Johnson (4), Warroad (4), and Breck (4). Edina/Edina-East has 12 crowns while Eveleth, International Falls, and Roseau all have seven.

50) Benilde-St. Margaret's (.917%). The Red Knights are 11-1 in four tourney trips, with two titles in Class A and one in AA.

51) St. Thomas Academy

14 Individual Records

1) Who is the all-time leading scorer in state tournament history?

2) Who is the only player with 10 assists in a single tournament?

3) What goaltender holds the career tourney mark for most shutouts with five?

4) What noteworthy Minnesota playmaker holds the record for most assists in one period?

5) What players have been the leading scorer in the tournament more than once?

6) Who holds the record for most saves by a goaltender in a regulation game?

7) Which two players hold the record for most assists in a single game with six?

8) What player has scored the fastest two goals in succession?

9) What player and future Gopher All-American had a record 17 assists in 12 games?

10) Who holds the record for most points compiled during a single tournament with 18?

11) What well-known figure had the fewest saves in an entire tournament (three games)?

12) Who are the only goalies in tourney history to be the starting netminder (playing all three games) for schools that won at least two state championships?

Karl Goehring (Apple Valley), making one of a record 65 saves in a 5-4 overtime win over Duluth East in 1996. The five-overtime victory was the longest in tournament history. (Photo: Rick Orndorf, *Dakota County Tribune*)

13) What goalkeeper has held the record for most stops in a single tournament since 1970?

14) What player scored an incredible 36 goals over the duration of his four-year high school state tourney career?

15) Who is the only goalie to record three straight shutouts in a single tourney and, obviously, helped his team win a state championship?

16) Who are the only two players to record hat tricks in each of three tourney games in a single state boys' hockey tournament?

17) What clutch goaltender made a record 17 saves in a single overtime?

18) What player has recorded the fastest "pure" hat trick (three consecutive goals)?

19) Who are the only players to win the Herb Brooks award (since 2004) and also claim the state title in the same year?

20) Who is the only player to score more than ten goals in one tournament?

21) What player has scored in the most games in tournament history?

22) What is the mark for the fastest goal from the start of a game?

23) What goalie holds the record for the fewest saves in a game?

24) What player holds the record for most consecutive games with an assist?

25) What goalie once played two periods in a row without facing a shot from the opposition?

26) Who is the only player to score overtime winners in consecutive games?

27) What player set records for most points (8) and goals (7) in a game in the same tilt?

28) What netminder holds the career mark for most tournament games played?

29) Who is the only player to compete in five state tournaments?

30) What goalie holds the record for most saves in a single period of play?

31) Who is the only player to win four state titles as a player?

32) Which player holds the mark for most points in a period?

33) Which player holds the record for most games played?

34) What tourney competitor holds the mark for most goals scored in one period?

35) Which player holds the records for the most games recording an assist?

36) Who is the only player to record at least six goals in two consecutive games?

37) What netminder played the most minutes in one tournament?

38) Who holds the record for most goals scored in a championship game?

39) What goaltender and former tourney coach holds the career record for most saves?

40) Which players have been named all-tournament three times?

41) What player scored a hat trick in the shortest duration in tournament history?

42) Who are the only six players to total double-digit goals and assists in tourney history?

◄ ANSWERS TO CH 14 – INDIVIDUAL RECORDS ►

1) John Mayasich of Eveleth, who totaled 46 points in four tourneys from 1948-51. He averaged nearly four points per game in an era when regulation play was limited to 36 minutes (12-minute periods), meaning he registered a point about every nine minutes. Dave Spehar of Duluth East is second in career points with 29 with Johnny Pohl of Red Wing and Little Falls' Ben Hanowski tied for third with 28. John Matchefts of Eveleth is fifth with 26.

2) Jamie Langenbrunner of Cloquet with 10 in the 1993 Tier I tourney. Langenbrunner also played in the 1992 Tier I tourney, scoring a goal and an assist as Cloquet was fourth. He didn't play his senior year at Cloquet, opting to play junior hockey in Canada. He made his NHL debut in 1995 and has played over 1,000 games, mostly with Dallas and New Jersey and is now with St. Louis. He has been on two U.S. Olympic teams and was captain of the 2010 team that captured silver at Vancouver.

3) Willard Ikola. The Eveleth High goalie had one in 1947, two more in 1949, and another in 1950.

4) Neal Broten. The Roseau center had four assists in the first period of a third-place game against Mounds View in 1978, a 5-3 Rams win.

5) Rube Bjorkman of Roseau (1946, 1947); John Matchefts of Eveleth (1947, 1948); John Mayasich of Eveleth (1949, 1950, 1951); Jim Amidon of International Falls (1962, 1963); Mike Antonovich of Greenway-Coleraine (1968, 1969); Aaron Broten

of Roseau (1978, 1979); Dave Spehar of Duluth East (1995, 1996 Class AA); Johnny Pohl of Red Wing (1996, 1998 Class A); Ben Hanowski of Little Falls (2008, 2009 Class A); and Dylan Malmquist of Edina (2013, 2014 Class AA).

6) Mason Campion. The Marshall goalie had 58 saves in a 4-1 loss to Duluth Marshall in a consolation game in 2013. Alex Kangas of Rochester Century held the previous record with 50 stops in a fifth-place game against White Bear Lake in 2005. Kangas completed his four-year career with the Gophers in 2011.

7) Chris Locker of Duluth East (1996) and Dom Talarico of Proctor/Albrook, Saginaw (1997).

8) Wally Grant of Eveleth, who tallied twice within seven seconds in the third period of a 10-0 semifinal win over St. Paul Washington in 1945. Grant's two goals gave him a natural hat trick. Teammate Neil Celley recorded one in the first period and Pat Finnegan's third goal finished the scoring. In the title game that season, Grant scored twice within 59 seconds in tallying both the tying and winning markers in the 4-3 triumph over Thief River Falls. Finnegan scored two goals within 1:25 earlier.

9) Johnny Pohl. The Red Wing sensation, who led the Wingers to the Class A title in 1997, had two as a freshman, two as a sophomore, five as a junior, and eight as a senior.

10) John Mayasich. As a senior, the Eveleth star totaled 18 points in 1951 as the Bears wrapped up their fourth consecutive state title.

11) Ralph Engelstad of Thief River Falls, who had only 14 for the Prowlers in 1945. Engelstad, who later went to play for North Dakota, had two against White Bear Lake in the quarterfinals, three versus St. Cloud in the semis, and nine in the 4-3 title-game loss to Eveleth. Engelstad is the guy who donated $110 million to North Dakota to build the arena named in his honor in Grand Forks for the Sioux and another $10 million for an arena in his hometown.

12) Willard Ikola (Eveleth–1948, 1949, 1950); Dick Roth (Roseau–1958, 1959); Ron Beck (International Falls–1965, 1966); John Russell (Breck–2009, 2010), and Andrew Ford (Eden Prairie–2009, 2011); and David Zevnik (St. Thomas Academy - 2011, 2012, 2013). Randy Koeppl of Bloomington Jefferson started two games in 1992 and all three games in 1993 for the Jaguars and Jake Schuman of Benilde-St. Margaret's started one

Brothers Johnny (left) and Mark Pohl were major cogs in Red Wing's drive to the Class A state title in 1997. (Photo courtesy Jim Pohl.)

game in 1999 and all three for the Red Knights in 2001.

13) Doug Long. The St. Paul Johnson stalwart made 124 saves for the Governors in one of the most impressive displays of netminding in tourney history in 1970. He had 61 in a 5-4 (5 OT) game win over Greenway-Coleraine in his first game, 52 more in a 2-1 overtime loss to Edina in the semis, and 11 more in a 3-1 loss to before being replaced by reserve Bob Schoenrock in a 4-1 consolation final loss against Hibbing early in the second period. Schoenrock finished with 18 saves without allowing a goal.

14) John Mayasich. The incomparable Eveleth Golden Bear, still holds 10 major scoring records 50 years after he established them.

15) Greg Stutz of Centennial in 2005.

16) John Mayasich of Eveleth (1951) and Dave Spehar of Duluth East (1995). Mayasich scored four goals in the first game, seven in the semis, and all four goals in the 4-1 title game triumph over St. Paul Johnson in 1951. Spehar had three goals in each game, including the go-ahead and insurance goals in the 5-3 win in the championship game over Moorhead in 1995.

17) Karl Goehring. The diminutive Apple Valley goalie was spectacular in the fourth overtime of the classic 1996 Class AA semifinal thriller against Duluth East.

18) Brandon Sampair. The Mahtomedi freshman wing scored three goals in a 2:26-span in the first period of a 7-2 Class A third-place win over St. Cloud Cathedral in 1994. All of the goals were assisted by his senior linemate and brother, Jesse, who totaled five assists in the game. Adam Johnson of Hibbing/Chisholm, a sophomore forward, tallied his pure hat trick in 3:29 in a 6-4 semifinal Class A loss to Hermantown in 2011. Eveleth legend John Mayasich took 3:52 to score three straight goals in a 6-0 win over White Bear Lake in 1949. Lake of the Woods center Mark Amundsen garnered a pure hat trick in 4:19 in a 7-4 quarterfinal win over Totino-Grace in 1993. Meanwhile, Joe Bianchi of Bloomington Jefferson is next at 4:52 and he did it in the limelight of the 1992 Tier I title game against Moorhead. In a 2-2 tie game in the second period, Bianchi scored three straight goals to give his team a lead in a 6-3 win for the Jaguars.

19) Joe Phillippi of Hill-Murray (Class AA in 2008); A.J. Reid of St. Thomas Academy (Class A-2011); Chad Huttel of Hermantown (Class A-2007); Greg Flynn of Centennial (Class AA-2004), Dixon Bown of East Grand Forks (Class A - 2015) and Angelo Altavilla of Lakeville North (Class AA - 2015).

20) John Mayasich, who did it twice. As a junior, he scored 11 goals to lead Eveleth to the title, and in his final season for Eveleth High, he recorded an incredible 15 goals.

21) John Mayasich, who scored in all 12 games he played from 1948-51.

22) Seven seconds. St. Cloud Cathedral's Josh Wolke scored the Crusaders' only goal in a 4-1 loss to Henry Sibley in a 1993 Tier II consolation title game.

23) Ron Drobnick of Eveleth, who made a single third-period save when the powerful Bears demolished Granite Falls 16-0 in the third game ever played in 1945. His counterpart between the pipes, Gorman Velde, had 15 saves.

24) Johnny Pohl. He had assists in all three games in 1997 and 1998 and also had two games with assists in 1995 and one in 1996.

25) Ron Drobnick of Eveleth. In a 1945 quarterfinal blasting of Granite Falls (16-0), Drobnick didn't make a save until the third period and it was the only one he registered.

John Mayasich (Eveleth 1948-1951), still holds many scoring marks fifty years after he created them. He is the only individual to play on four championship teams. (Photo: U.S. Hockey Hall of Fame Museum)

26) Adam Hoaglund of Simley. In the Class A tourney in 2003, the senior forward scored in the first extra-session to beat St. Louis Park 2-1 in the first round. In the semis versus Rochester Lourdes, he struck again in the second overtime as the Spartans won 3-2. Hoaglund didn't get a chance to score another, however, as Warroad beat them in regulation, 3-1, to earn the title.

27) John Mayasich, who set the mark in a 1951 semifinal against Mpls. Southwest and goalie Denny Sullivan. Mayasich had hat tricks in both the first and third periods as Eveleth won 11-5. In the 4-2 clinching win over St. Paul Humboldt, Mayasich scored all four goals for the winners, who clinched their fourth straight hockey crown. In the opening 12-1 win over Williams, Mayasich scored all four of his goals in the first period and added an assist to set another tourney record for most goals and most points in a stanza.

28) Willard Ikola of Eveleth, who played in 12 games in four years

of state tourney play. In his final three seasons (1948, 1949, 1950), Ikola was all-tournament and his team won the state championship on each occasion.

29) Anders Lee, who played in every single tournament from 2005-09. The fleet center played for St. Thomas Academy as an eighth-grader in 2005 and then scored two goals and two assists as a freshman when the Cadets won their first Class A crown in 2006. As a junior, Lee scored a goal and an assist as STA finished third in 2007. In 2008, he played for Edina, his hometown residence, and recorded an assist as the Hornets lost to Hill-Murray in the finals. As a senior at Edina, his top-ranked club had to settle for the consolation title as Moorhead upset them 5-2. Lee, however, was the leading scorer in the tourney with a goal and eight assists for nine points.

30) Mason Campion of Marshall had 28 stops in the third period of a 4-1 loss to Duluth Marshall in the Class A consolation semifinals in 2013.

31) John Mayasich (Eveleth; 1948-51). Sixteen players have been on three title teams, including seven from the early Eveleth squads (1948-51), five from International Falls powerhouse (1964-66), and four from Bloomington Jefferson's dynasty (1992-94).

32) John Mayasich (5) of Eveleth had four goals and an assist in the first period of a 12-1 quarterfinal win over Williams in 1951.

33) Anders Lee (15). Lee played in three games for St. Thomas Academy in 2005, in 2006, and again in 2007 in Class A. He also played in three games for Edina in Class AA in both 2008 and 2009.

34) John Mayasich of Eveleth scored four goals in a little more than 10 minutes in the first period of a 12-1 win over Williams in a 1951 first-round game.

35) Johnny Pohl of Red Wing had assists in nine games and also holds the all-time mark with 17 during his Class A career (1995-98).

36) John Mayasich of Eveleth scored six in a game in the 1950 event and seven in 1951, both semifinal victories for the Bears.

37) Jared Schletty of White Bear Lake played 199 minutes and 25 seconds in the 2011 event. His back-up, Michael Jordan, played 7:02 as the Bears played a total of 206 minutes and 53 seconds in

playing three straight multiple overtimes games with 26 seconds of empty-net play. Duluth East's JoJo Jeanetta played 195:56 as his team also played three overtime games in 2011.

38) Grant Besse scored five goals in 2012 when Benilde-St. Margaret's downed Hill-Murray 5-1 in the 2012 AA final. John Mayasich scored all four of Eveleth's goals in a 4-1 win over St. Paul Johnson in 1951. A total of 12 other players have scored hat tricks in the championship game, including Mayasich in the 1950 final.

39) Jim Nelson of Roseau (252). As a sophomore, Nelson had 56 saves in losses to Int'l Falls (39) and Greenway (17). His junior year, Nelson recorded 119 saves (30 against Greenway, 50 against Johnson, and 39 against International Falls). In his final season, Nelson had 77 more (27 versus North St. Paul, 16 against Edina, and 34 against Roosevelt). He coached Grand Rapids to the title in 1976.

40) John Matchefts (Eveleth: 1947-49); Willard Ikola (Eveleth: 1948-50); John Mayasich (Eveleth: 1948-51); Doug Woog (South St. Paul: 1959, 1961, 1962); Bob Lillo (Roseau: 1961-63); Gary Wood (International Falls: 1963-65); Tim Sheehy (International Falls: 1964-66); Mike Antonovich (Greenway-Coleraine: 1967-69); Bobby Krieger (Edina: 1968-70); Matt Cullen (Moorhead : 1993-95); Dave Spehar Duluth East: 1994-96); Dan Carlson (Edina: 1995-97); Tom Moore (Red Wing:1996-98); Johnny Pohl (Red Wing: 1996-98), Jared Kolquist (Hermantown: 2010-12) and David Zevnik (St. Thomas Academy: 2011-13).

41) Stu Anderson. The St. Paul Johnson forward scored three goals in just 2:07 in the first period of a 5-3 third-place victory over South St. Paul in the 1954 tournament. However, the Packers' Richard Lick had scored between Anderson's first and second tallies, erasing his chance for a natural hat trick. Anderson led the tourney with six goals as he also scored twice in a 7-0 win over Wayzata and once in a 3-2 loss in the semis to Eveleth.

42) John Mayasich (36 goals, 10 assists) - Eveleth, 1948-51; John Matchefts (14 goals, 12 assists) - Eveleth, 1948-50; Mike Antonovich (12 goals, 10 assists), Greenway-Coleraine, 1967-69; Aaron Broten (10 goals, 10 assists) - Roseau, 1978-79; Johnny Pohl (11 goals, 17 assists) - Red Wing, 1995-98; Alex Funk (11 goals, 10 assists) - Rochester Lourdes, 2010-13

15 Potpourri

1) What school won a state title, believe it or not, despite losing not just one but twice in post-season and then went on to be victorious by five goals in the state tourney final?

2) Did the Warroad Warriors ever win a single-class state tournament (1945-1991)?

3) In the first few decades of the state tournament, teams were represented not by sections but by what categorical term?

4) In what northern suburb is Centennial High located, the 2004 Class AA champion?

5) Without question, one of the most dominant programs in Minnesota state boys hockey tournament history has been International Falls. When they won the Class A state title in 1995, what other school district were they in a cooperative with?

6) What school actually had their band regularly perform on the ice...on skates?

7) What hockey conference has won the most state titles?

8) What two Roseau players became the first brother duo to earn all-tourney status in the same season?

9) How many private schools have won the Class A title since the tourney split into two classes by enrollment in 1994?

10) The largest attendance for any single tournament is 135,618. What year was it?

11) Twelve Minnesota-born-and-bred hockey players were on the 1980 U.S. Olympic team that won the gold medal in Lake Placid. Which ones also played in both the state high school hockey tournament and the NHL?

12) Has a team ever won a state title by either having a losing record overall or a tie record for all its games, including state tournament competition?

13) Due to concerns about disrespecting the heritage of Native-Americans, several schools switched nicknames over the past few decades. What were the nicknames of the Burnsville Blaze and the Grand Rapids Thunderhawks prior to those changes?

14) What are the official colors of the Bloomington Jefferson Jaguars?

15) All of the following individuals were among the best players to ever perform in the state tournament: John Mayasich, Mike Antonovich, Neal Broten and Mike Crowley. Were they all right-handed or all left-handed?

16) How many schools located within the confines of the city of St. Paul have won a state title besides the Johnson Governors?

17) What is the common nickname for these schools that have won a state title: Apple Valley (AA-1996), Bloomington Kennedy (1987), Eden Prairie (AA-2009, 2011) and Totino-Grace (A- 2002)?

18) What are the two smallest schools in enrollment to earn a state tourney berth?

19) In what year did the officials start using video replays to determine whether goals were legitimate?

20) Did any of the Carlson brothers from Virginia, made famous in the classic hockey movie, "Slapshot", ever play in the state hockey tournament?

21) In what year did the single-class or one-class tourney end?

22) When the tournament switched venues to the Met Center, what tradition did the North Stars begin as a treat for the teams that earned berths in the tourney?

23) From 1945-1956, how many maximum players were on the state tournament roster for each participating school?

24) What were the lengths of state tournament periods from 1945-1970?

25) Which schools have lost championship games in consecutive seasons?

26) What coach won four championship games and also lost four championship games?

27) Who are the only two schools from southern Minnesota (south of the Twin Cities metro area) to win a state hockey title?

28) In what year did the state boys' hockey tourney split into two classes (A and AA) based on enrollment of students in grades 10-12?

29) What school won a state title with the nickname of...."HAWKS"?

30) Tim Sheehy, Henry Boucha, Dave Spehar, and Johnny Pohl were stars for their teams at the state hockey tournament? Were they all left-handed or all right-handed?

31) Two of the most storied programs in the history of the boys' state hockey tournament are St. Paul Johnson and South St. Paul, who share the same two colors on their uniforms. What are they?

32) What former Gopher and North Star winger, who played for Irondale in the 1981 event, won a state AA title as co-coach of the Blaine Bengals in 2000?

33) Which of the following schools have participated in the state tournament over the long history of the event: Winona, Staples, Owatonna, Park-Cottage Grove, Brainerd, Columbia Heights, Forest Lake, Marshall, and Shakopee?

34) What former Minnesota Governor was a strong player for his tradition-laden school and played for Minnesota and the U.S. Olympic team but never made it to a state tourney?

35) On how many occasions has a state title game gone into sudden-death overtime?

36) How many times has a Minneapolis school won a state title?

37) Incredibly, what school has been in just four tournaments with a 4-7 overall record but has suffered six overtime losses in those appearances?

38) In what year (single-class) were only 42 goals scored in a total of 11 games?

39) What fellow served as a public-address announcer for some of the games in the 2008 tournament but also was an on-ice official for the Roseau-Hill Murray game?

40) Have any teams ever played in the tournament and been eliminated after two games by being blanked in both games?

41) How many goals have been scored in the history of the state tournament?

42) Has a tournament every been played where over half of the games were won by shutout?

43) How many overtime games have been played in tournament history?

44) In what year did the top four seeds in each class (AA and A) start getting seeded by the coaches whose teams were to play in the tournament?

45) How many total games have been played in the history of the state tournament?

46) On how many occasions has a team won a state title by entering the tourney through the so-called "Back Door"?

47) Besides the Broten brothers (Neal, Aaron, and Paul), there are four other families who have had brothers that have played both in the NHL and in the state tournament; who are they?

48) What two teams played in the longest game (by minutes) in state tourney annals?

49) What was the brand name for the long pants that became fashionable for the players to wear in the early 1980's?

50) What school used an unusual ploy when a delayed penalty was called on an opponent in the 1960's?

51) Until the 1968-69 season, where was the only place on the ice surface where body-checking was allowed?

52) In what year did tournament attendance reach 100,000 for the first time?

53) What suburban school was the first to win a state title?

54) What was the profit for the first tournament in 1945?

55) What seven players have won the Hobey Baker Award, given to the best collegiate player in the nation, after playing in the Minnesota state boys' high school hockey tournament?

56) Begun in 2004, an award is given to a player in each class who best represents the values, characteristics, and traits of what Minnesota hockey icon?

57) What is the latest (or earliest, depending on your point of view) time that a game has ever lasted into the evening/morning?

58) What school holds the record for the most consecutive years representing the same region/section?

59) How many players have ever won a state title with their father as the head coach?

60) What school within the past decade brought a team to the state tournament with two eighth-graders, both of whom are now playing in the NHL?

61) When tournament periods were just 12 minutes from 1945-1970, how long of a duration were penalties?

62) What brand of puck is used for tournament games?

63) After being a key part of the award ceremony following the championship game from 1945-72, the MSHSL reintroduced all-tournament teams in what year?

64) Since the MSHSL starting registering season-ticket holders in 1956, how many of the original accounts (four tickets maximum)

Greenway-Coleraine goalie Bill Joy (right) picks up a high-sticking penalty attempting to screen Hibbing goalie Andy Micheletti and defenseman Ron Olson during a delayed penalty on Hibbing in Greenway's 4-3 semifinal victory during the 1967 tourney.

are still active?

65) Who is the only player to win a state high school hockey title with his prep team at the same venue where his college team won an NCAA title?

66) What are the school colors of the International Falls Broncos?

67) Who became the first player to play in the state tournament and make the NHL?

68) What was the mantra bellowed by Greenway-Coleraine players after winning the first Tier II crown in 1992?

69) What is the earliest calendar date for the first day of the boys' state hockey tourney and what is the latest calendar date for the first day of a boys' hockey tourney?

70) What was and is the nickname for the athletic teams at East Grand Forks, which has made ten appearances at state (three in the single-class era and seven in Class A)?

71) What former NHL goaltender has served as the goalie coach for the Edina Hornets in their recent appearances at state?

72) How many players that have competed in the tournament in the past 71 years have been inducted into the U.S. Hockey Hall of Fame in Eveleth?

73) In Class AA in 2013, how many players tied for the scoring lead?

74) In the early years of the tournament, what was the name of the skate shop located across the street from the St. Paul Auditorium?

75) In what Olympic year did the U.S. squad have eight players who once participated in the Minnesota state high school boys hockey tournament?

76) Who is the only player to play in at least two tournaments with two different schools?

77) How many schools have won a state hockey championship?

78) What tournament hero married Minnesota hockey heroine Krissy Wendell?

79) What noteworthy Minnesota hockey coach, who won a state title with two of his sons playing for the team, was drafted by the Washington Redskins after playing college football at Georgetown?

80) How many different private schools have won a state hockey title since they were admitted into the tournament 41 years ago?

81) In what suburbs are private school hockey powers St. Thomas Academy, Hill-Murray, Benilde-St. Margaret's, and Breck located, respectively?

82) With the advent of the Tier I and II experiment in 1992, coaches in each section ranked the teams in their own sections. The top eight competed in Tier I with all others to play in Tier II, regardless of enrollment. What two teams were ranked the highest of the eight that played in the Tier II tournament?

83) Who is the only player besides the iconic John Mayasich of Eveleth (36) to score at least 20 goals in state tourney history?

84) From all appearances, photographs taken of state tournament entrants indicate that forwards and defensemen didn't start wearing shoulder pads until what year?

85) What face protection did Duluth East goalies wear in tourney action in 1960 and 1961?

86) What family had six of their sons play for Edina's Willard Ikola?

87) Has anyone ever played in a state tourney, been an assistant coach in the event, been a head coach in the state tournament, and also been a referee in the tourney?

88) Duluth Marshall, a top Class A program over the past decade or two, has a nickname made famous by the previous school that was located at the top of the hill on the central entrance to Duluth. What was that school?

89) In the early years of the tournament, where were the tournament schools housed?

90) What school had the ironic twist of having played three tournament games that all finished with the identical score of 4-3?

91) How many players who have participated in the state tournament have played in the NHL?

92) What two teams played in the longest championship game in the 71-year history of the tournament on March 12, 2011?

93) On how many occasions have the same teams played in a championship game three years in a row?

94) In the history of the state boys' hockey tournament, how many different schools have earned a berth to the "big dance"?

95) Which of the two Twin Cities has had more of its public schools earn berths in the state tournament - St. Paul or Minneapolis?

96) What conference do perennial state powers Moorhead, Roseau, and Warroad play in?

97) What woman, a sister to a Gopher All-American, has attended every one of the 71 boys' hockey tournaments?

98) Of schools that have made a minimum of 10 appearances in the state tournament, which one has the highest percentage of winning a trophy?

99) Considering only schools that have made at least 10 appearances in the tourney, which four schools have the best winning percentages?

100) What tournament goalie holds the highest saves-per-game average (five games minimum) with 33 per game?

◀ **ANSWERS TO CHAPTER 15 - POTPOURRI** ▶

1) Greenway-Coleraine (1968). The Raiders beat South St. Paul 6-1 in the title game after beating Mounds View and then St. Paul Johnson. They lost to Hibbing 2-0 in the finals of District 28 play but both teams advanced to the Region VII tourney, where Greenway lost in overtime to International Falls 1-0. With the rules in effect at the time, the Raiders played the Section 8 runner-up to determine the Section 3 champion (also known as the Back Door) and Greenway beat Thief River Falls 4-1 to earn the berth.

2) No. Warroad, however, finished second three times (1948, 1953, and 1969). They have won four Class A crowns (1994, 1996, 2003, and 2005) and have been second three times in A in 1997, 2000, and 2009.

3) Regions

4) Circle Pines. Centennial also takes in students from Lino Lakes, Lexington, Blaine, and Centerville. Erik Aus' club became the only team to ever win a state crown by winning all three games by virtue of a shutout. In 1995, the school changed their nickname from Chiefs to the present one of Cougars.

5) Littlefork-Big Falls. This arrangement was no longer in force for the last two Broncos' appearances in 2000 and 2002. International Falls/Littlefork-Big Falls beat Totino-Grace 3-2 in that 1995 Class A championship with Kevin Gordon as their head coach.

6) St. Paul Murray. The Pilots were in the tourney in 1950, 1951, 1957 and 1958.

7) Iron Range with 22, including 13 of the first 24 years of the single-class format. International Falls (7), Eveleth (5), Eveleth-Gilbert (2), Grand Rapids (3), Hibbing (2), Greenway-Coleraine (2), Greenway-Coleraine/Nashwauk-Keewatin (1).

8) Jim and Larry Stordahl in 1959, who helped the Rams win their second straight title.

9) Four: St. Thomas Academy five, Breck four, Benilde-St. Margaret's three and Totino-Grace one. Benilde-St. Margaret's (2012) and Cretin-Derham Hall (2006) have each won Class AA titles and Hill-Murray won AA in 2008 while Holy Angels won the AA crown in both 2002 and 2005.

10) 2015. The previous record was 129,643 attendees in 2008.

11) Bill Baker (Grand Rapids), Mike Ramsey (Mpls. Roosevelt), Neal Broten (Roseau), Rob McClanahan (Mounds View), Steve Christoff (Richfield). Two played in the tournament but never in the NHL (Steve Janaszak of Hill-Murray and Phil Verchota of Duluth East). Mark Pavelich of Eveleth, John Harrington of Virginia, Buzzy Schneider of Babbitt, David Christian of Warroad and Eric Strobel of Rochester Mayo never made it to state; however, Christian and Pavelich both played in the NHL.

12) Yes. Eveleth-Gilbert, in 1993, beat Lake of the Woods 3-2 in two overtimes to win the Tier II title. The Bears record was 14-14.

13) Burnsville (Braves) was changed to Blaze for the 1993-94 season. Burnsville High opened in 1957 and they were originally known as the Bulldogs. Grand Rapids (Indians) made the switch to Thunderhawks for the 1995-96 season.

14) Columbia blue and silver

15) Left-handed

16) One. Cretin-Derham Hall won the AA title with a 7-0 win over Grand Rapids in 2006.

17) Eagles. The only other common nicknames of schools to win a state title include: Raiders (Greenway-Coleraine - 1967, 1968 and Cretin-Derham Hall - AA 2006); Indians (Grand Rapids - 1975, 1976, 1980 and Mpls. Southwest - 1970); and Hornets (Edina - 1969, 1971, 1982, 1984, 1988, 1997, 2010 and Edina-East - 1974, 1978, 1979).

18) Williams and Hallock, both schools from Region 8 in northwest Minnesota.

19) 2006

20) No. Neither Jeff or Jack nor Steve played in the tournament as the Blue Devils never made it to the single-class tourney in the 1970's when the three Carlson's played high school hockey. Virginia, which is now in a cooperative with Mt. Iron-Buhl, has been in three Class A tournaments—2005, 2009, and 2010.

21) The final year of the single-class or one-class tournament was in 1991. In 1992 and 1993, the MSHSL approved a two-year experiment (Tier I and Tier II) where teams were ranked either among the top eight teams per section by the coaches (Tier I) and those ranked lower than eighth were slated to play in Tier II.

22) The North Stars, starting in 1969, would schedule a home game early in the week of the tournament so the high-schoolers could attend, then go on the road to vacate the building for the tournament.

23) 12; from 1957-69, the roster limit was 15; and from 1970-75, it was 17. Starting with 1976, there were 18 on a roster until it was expanded to 20 in 1983.

24) 12 minutes; in 1971, the periods were expanded to 15 minutes and to 17 minutes in 2004.

25) Williams (1949, 1950); Hill-Murray (1985,1986); Moorhead (1994, 1995 and 2004, 2005); Grand Rapids (2006, 2007); Duluth Marshall (2007, 2008). Hermantown is the only team to lose six in a row (2010–2015).

26) Oscar Almquist. The Roseau legend won crowns in 1946, 1958, 1959, 1961 and lost title tilts in 1947, 1957, 1962, and 1966. Almquist won 406 games in his coaching career.

27) Rochester John Marshall (1977) and Red Wing (Class A -1997)

28) 1994; the first winners of this format were Bloomington Jefferson (AA) and Warroad (A).

29) Hermantown (Class A - 2007)

30) Right-handed

31) Maroon and white

32) Scott Bjugstad, who worked with Steve Larson.

33) Brainerd, Forest Lake, and Park-Cottage Grove have never played in a state tourney while Columbia Heights (1983), Owatonna (1998-AA), Shakopee (2005-A), Staples (1945), Marshall (2013), Luverne (2014), and Winona (1952) have all made one appearance each.

34) Wendell Anderson, who played at St. Paul Johnson in the 1950's for the Governors. Anderson was a stellar player for John Mariucci at Minnesota and played for the U.S. in the 1956 Olympics in Italy. Tim Pawlenty only played on the junior-varsity for South St. Paul in the late 1970's while present Governor Mark Dayton played goalie for Blake in the 1960's but played in the independent tourney and later for Yale.

35) Eleven. Seven have ended in a single overtime and four in multiple overtimes. In 1978, Edina-East beat Grand Rapids 5-4 in two overtimes; in 1993, Eveleth-Gilbert won the Tier II title with a 3-2 double-overtime win over Lake of the Woods/Baudette; in 2005, Warroad edged Totino-Grace 4-3 in two overtimes, and in 2011, Eden Prairie beat Duluth East 3-2 in triple-overtime.

36) Once. Minneapolis Southwest beat Edina 1-0 in overtime to win the 1970 state tourney. Southwest was second twice, in 1955 and 1975.

37) North St. Paul. The Polars, who lost twice each in extra periods in 1961 and 1970, also won two games in overtime, so eight of their 11 state tourney games went past regulation.

38) 1946

39) Jim Carroll

40) Yes, on nine occasions. In fact, White Bear Lake was blanked in two separate years (1951 and 1970). Other teams to be held without a goal are St. Louis Park (1958), Hallock (1957), St. Paul Johnson (1959), Henry Sibley (1997), Hutchinson (2000), Lakeville South (2008), and Spring Lake Park (2015).

41) 6,635 goals (through 2015)

42) Yes, in both 1945 and 1957, six of the 11 tournament games ended in shutouts. There have been seven years when there were no shutouts.

43) 153. Ninety-six have been single overtimes, 39 were double overtime, 12 were triple-overtime, 3 were four overtimes, 2 were five overtimes, and 1 was eleven overtimes.

44) 2007. The top four seeds are selected in each class and then a random draw determines their opponent. The top seed and the fourth seed are in the same bracket and the second and third seed are in the other bracket. Prior to this arrangement, the bracket structure was set on an alternating basis, where one section would be pre-determined to play seven different sections in a seven-year cycle.

45) 1,045 (as of games through 2015)

46) Four. From 1949-74, the Region 3 representative came from either Region 7 (Iron Range Conference and Duluth Schools) and Region 8 (northwest Minnesota). For 16 years (1949-64), the loser from either region final got the nod. From 1965-1974, the losers of the Region 7 and 8 title games played for the right to be the Region 3 team. On all four occasions, it was a Region 7 team that overcame a loss in the finals to win state (Duluth East, 1960), International Falls (1964), Greenway-Coleraine (1968), and Hibbing (1973).

47) Matt and Mark Cullen of Moorhead; Joe and Pat Micheletti of Hibbing; Jon and Todd Rohloff of Grand Rapids; and Jeff and Kirk Nielson of Grand Rapids.

48) Apple Valley beat Duluth East 5-4 in five overtimes in a historic semifinal on March 8, 1996. The game lasted a record 93 minutes and 12 seconds. The 11-overtime saga won by Minneapolis South 3-2 over Thief River Falls in a 1955 quarterfinal is the second-longest with 87:50. Overtimes in 1955 were just five minutes; thus, explaining the discrepancy. The third-longest occurred in 2010, when Minnetonka bested Hill-Murray 2-1 in four overtimes (86:21).

49) Cooperalls. Instead of breezers and socks, the players wore the single pant-style bottoms. The first team to wear them in the tourney was South St. Paul in 1981.

50) Greenway-Coleraine. In the 1960's, Bob Gernander's goaltenders were given clear instructions when the opposing team had committed an infraction and his own team was in possession of the puck. Instead of heading to the bench for a sixth attacker, as

was and is the usual custom in hockey, the Raider goalie was to skate down ice and, hopefully, screen the opposing goalie. In fact, Joy picked up more than one penalty that season for interference in just that manner. It is now outlawed as goalies cannot venture past the red line and it was changed because of Greenway's practice.

51) Defensive zone (inside your own blue line). Checking in the neutral zone or in the offensive zone was a penalty (illegal check). By the 1969-70 season, checking was allowed all over the ice.

52) 1979 (total attendance was 100,902)

53) Edina. The Hornets beat Warroad 5-4 in overtime in the 1960 title game. Bloomington Jefferson (1981), Burnsville (1985), and Bloomington Kennedy (1987) became the next suburban schools to win it all.

54) $135.06. Tournament director Gene Aldrich turned this money over to the State High School League, which started operating the tournament in 1946.

55) Neal Broten (Roseau) - 1981; Tom Kurvers (Bloomington Jefferson) - 1984; Robb Stauber (Duluth Denfeld) - 1988; Chris Marinucci (Grand Rapids) - 1994; Brian Bonin (White Bear Lake) - 1996 and Jack Connolly (Duluth Marshall) - 2012; and Drew LeBlanc (Hermantown) - 2013. Kurvers, Marinucci and Connolly all won their college honor at UMD. Broten, Stauber, and Bonin won as Minnesota Gophers and LeBlanc as a St. Cloud Husky.

56) Herb Brooks. The Herb Brooks Foundation has presented the awards to the two players earning the lofty award during the awards presentation, either with Herb's son Danny or his daughter Kelly presenting the award or both.

57) The classic 1996 AA semifinal between Apple Valley and Duluth East ended at 1:39 a.m. with Apple Valley prevailing 4-3 in the fifth overtime.

58) Roseau represented Region VIII nine straight years (1961-69).

59) Steve Ross - father Larry (Int'l Falls-1964, 1965, 1966)
Matt Ikola- father Willard (Edina-East - 1974)
Steve Ikola - father Willard (Edina-East -1978)

George, Jr. and Jim Perpich - father George (Hibbing - 1973)
Mark Osiecki - father Tom (Burnsville - 1985, 1986)
Tim Manthey - father Todd (Anoka - 2003)
Nick Oliver - father Scott (Roseau - 2007)
Rob Vannelli - father Tom (St. Thomas Academy - 2006, 2008)

60) St. Thomas Academy, with Anders Lee and Jordan Schroeder, in 2005 when the Cadets finished fourth in Class A. Schroeder had a goal and four assists and became the youngest player to ever earn all-tournament.

61) One minute and 30 seconds (1:30) for minor infractions and three minutes for majors.

62) Bauer

63) 1991. The teams were re-introduced as one of the benefits for the League's new premier corporate partner at the time, First Banks, which later became U.S. Bank, and is now Wells Fargo.

64) Approximately, 200 through the 2015 state tournament. These tickets are solely for Class AA. For the 2015 tourney, there were 4,173 season-ticket accounts.

65) Mike Montgomery, who was a forward for Centennial when they copped the AA title at the Xcel Energy Center in St. Paul in 2004 and a senior defenseman for UMD when Bulldogs earned their first-ever national title at the same rink in April of 2011. Mike was a junior when he scored the only goal of the game in Centennial's 1-0 win over Moorhead in the prep game and he was a steady all-around performer and captain for Scott Sandelin's club as the Bulldogs beat Michigan 3-2 in overtime.

66) Purple and gold. International Falls, by the way, did not have an official nickname for its athletic teams for 30 years. In 1941, athletic director Walt Sheela won a contest sponsored by the local newspaper to name their sports teams and the name "BRONCOS" won out, a terrific way to honor hometown football star Bronko Nagurski, the former Gopher All-American and NFL legend with the Chicago Bears.

67) Henry Boucha. After appearing with Warroad in the 1969 tournament, Boucha became the first-ever tournament participant to play in the NHL when he made his debut with the Detroit Red Wings in the 1971-72 season. He played three seasons for the

Kyle Kohlquist, Duluth East netminder, cannot stop this shot by Apple Valley defenseman Aaron Dwyer in the 1996 Class AA semifinal. (Photo: Rick Orndorf)

Wings before a season with the North Stars (1974-75) and then finished up with Kansas City and Colorado. Boucha scored 56 goals and added 49 assists in 247 NHL games.

68) "We're Number 65," a sarcastic reference to the fact that the top 64 teams were selected to play in the Tier I tourney (eight teams for eight sections). Greenway, under .500 when the playoffs began, finished 16-12.

69) February 13, 1945 and March 17, 1977. From 1945-69, the tourney was always competed during February but starting with March 5-7, 1970, all of the tourneys have been contested during the month of March.

70) Green Wave. The "East Side", as they are known in hockey circles in that area, were in the tourney in 1971, 1980, and 1982 and then again four times in a five-year span in Class A (1998, 1999, 2001, 2002) and again three more times from 2013-15. They won the Class title for the first time in 2014 and repeated as champs in 2015.

71) Don Beaupre, the former North Star goaltender and teammate of head coach Curt Giles.

72) Twenty-two. Jeff Sauer (2014), Aaron Broten (2007), Keith Christiansen (2005), Phil Housley (2004), Dick Dougherty (2003), Doug Woog (2002), Mike Ramsey (2001), Neal Broten (2001), Mike Curran (1998), Bill Nyrop (1997), Tim Sheehy (1997), Reed Larson (1996), Henry Boucha (1995), Wally Grant (1994), Dave Langevin (1993), Bob Johnson (1991), John Matchefts (1991), Herb Brooks (1990), Willard Ikola (1990), Roger Christian (1989), Billy Christian (1984), and John Mayasich (1976).

73) Seven, all with five points. (Zach Lavalle of Hill-Murray; Alex Toscano of Duluth East; Grant Weiss, Thomas Carey, and Aaron Herdt of Moorhead; and Connor Hurley and Dylan Malmquist of Edina).

74) Strauss Skate

75) 1956. They included Willard Ikola, John Matchefts, and John Mayasich of Eveleth, Jack Petroske of Hibbing, Dick Dougherty of International Falls, Gordon Christian of Warroad, Gene Campbell of Minneapolis South, and Dick Meredith of Minneapolis Southwest.

76) Anders Lee. Now playing for the New York Islanders, Lee competed in three for St. Thomas Academy (2005, 2006, 2007) and two for Edina (2008, 2009).

77) 31; 20 schools have won at least two titles. With just one champion from 1945-1991 and two champions since 1992, there have been 93 champions crowned through 2015.

78) Johnny Pohl, who wed the former Park Center star in 2007. Pohl played in the state tournament four times with Red Wing, leading the Wingers to the A title in 1997 and later was an All-American at Minnesota. Wendell, who helped her Park Center team to the girls' hockey title in 2000, was also an All-American at Minnesota and captured the Patty Kazmaier trophy, emblematic of the top female college player in 2005. Johnny (head coach) and Krissy (assistant coach) now are in charge of the Cretin-Derham Hall girls' hockey program.

79) George Perpich. The gregarious giant from Hibbing won a state title in 1973. Perpich never played for Washington but did play for the Brooklyn Dodgers and the Baltimore Colts in the All-American Conference in 1946 and 1947, as a tackle.

80) Seven. St. Thomas Academy (5), Breck (4), Hill-Murray (3), Benilde-St. Margaret's (3), Holy Angels Academy (2), Totino-Grace (1) and Cretin-Derham Hall (1). All but Breck are Catholic schools.

81) Mendota Heights (St. Thomas Academy), Maplewood (Hill-Murray), St. Louis Park (Benilde-St. Margaret's) and Golden Valley (Breck).

82) Greenway-Coleraine was ranked 11th and Rosemount 12th in their respective sections. No other team that earned their way into Tier II play ranked higher than those two and those two teams met in the finals.

83) Dave Spehar of Duluth East (1994-96). The little Greyhound sniper scored twice as a sophomore and then bagged nine goals each as both a junior and senior.

84) 1963

85) In 1960, Duluth East goalie Don Hilsen didn't wear a facemask while tending goal for the state titlists. In 1961, Greyhound netminder Jon Birch wore a fiberglass mask on his face but with no protection on the top or side of his head. By 1962, most of the goalies in the state tournament were wearing fiberglass masks. A decade later, many goalies were wearing wire-cage masks and helmets that protected the entire head.

86) Carroll. Mike, Steve, Tom, Pat, Dan, and Jim all played for the Hornets. Tom was on back-back state titlists in 1978 and 1979 for Edina-East and Dan was on the 1982 Edina winner while Steve was the starting goalie on the 1977 team that lost to Rochester John Marshall 4-2 in the finals.

87) Yes. Lou Cotroneo played for St. Paul Johnson in the 1947 tourney, was an assistant under Rube Gustafson for seven trips to state, brought seven teams to state as a head coach at his alma mater, and also was an on-ice official.

88) Duluth Cathedral, which was a private Catholic school that was one of the dominant teams of the 1960's throughout all of Minnesota under coach Del Genereau. Marshall School was founded in 1972 by a group of civic and religious leaders after the Diocese of Duluth could no longer afford to sustain the school. In 1987, the name of the school was renamed...The Marshall

TV cameramen take a break between overtimes in a 1970 quarterfinal game won by St. Paul Johnson 4-3 over Greenway-Coleraine in five overtimes. (Photo credit: Dave Johnson)

School...to highlight its independent status and remains the only college preparatory school in northern Minnesota.

89) St. Paul Hotel and Lowry Hotel, adjacent to the St. Paul Auditorium. Interestingly, the school's were housed according to their regional number. Thus, Roseau, the Region 8 representative, had rooms for their teams on the 8th floor.

90) White Bear Lake (2011). In the quarterfinals, they lost to Duluth East in two overtimes and then downed Blaine in the consolation finals in two overtimes. In the fifth-place game, the Bears lost to Lakeville North in three overtimes.

91) 108, including 33 active players through the 2014-15 NHL season.

92) Eden Prairie beat Duluth East 3-2 in three overtimes in a game that lasted 80 minutes and 43 seconds.

93) Once. St. Thomas Academy and Hermantown conducted three battle royales in 2011, 2012, and 2013 in Class A. Each time, the Cadets prevailed over the Hawks.

94) 137 (128 if counting cooperative programs). Incidentally, 40 of the schools have made just one appearance.

95) Minneapolis (8) and St. Paul (6). Minneapolis Southwest made 15 appearances and St. Paul Johnson made 22 appearances. Sadly, the change in demographics in those two major cities have left Minneapolis with one consolidated team and St. Paul with just Como Park, Highland Park, and Johnson as public schools still playing varsity hockey.

96) Mariucci, named after the legendary Eveleth native and former Gopher coach.

97) Lucille Korsman of Farmington. A native of Virginia, she attended the first tourney as a high school senior and cheered for neighboring Eveleth. Her family has had four tickets ever since. Lucille now attends just the first day (Thursday) Class AA session with her duaghter, Sue, so she can witness all the teams play. Her brother, Harold "Babe" Paulsen, was a Gopher All-American in 1940 and was their all-time leading scorer until the mid-1960's. Paulsen coached at Roseau and Thief River Falls before starting the Michigan State program.

98) Grand Rapids (.857%). The Indians/Thunderhawks has been to the tournament 14 times and have won 12 trophies. Hibbing (.846) is second by virtue of taking home 11 trophies in 13 tries.

99) Eveleth (.750), which has won 33 of 44 all-time games. Breck (.719) is second with a 23-9 log in 11 trips. Grand Rapids (.690) is third; International Falls (.679) is fourth. St. Thomas Academy (.814) is 22-5 at state but has only nine appearances.

100) Terry Smith of Bloomington, who had 166 saves in five games in action for the Bears in 1964 and 1965. Jim Nelson of Roseau averaged 31.5 saves for the Rams in eight games from 1965-67.

16 All Tournament Teams

1945

John Okoneski – St. Paul Washington
Bob Baker – Thief River Falls
Jim Doyle – Thief River Falls
Wes Hovie – Thief River Falls
Clem Cossalter – Eveleth
Neil Celley – Eveleth
Pat Finnegan – Eveleth
Wally Grant – Eveleth

1946

Clark Wilder – Rochester
Bob Harris – Roseau
Rube Bjorkman – Roseau
John Rosenthal – White Bear Lake
Jim Renstrom – St. Paul Johnson
Francis Tholl – St. Cloud
Andy Gambucci – Eveleth
Ron Martinson – Eveleth

1947

Steve Badalich – So. St. Paul
Jim Goit – Minneapolis West
John Matchefts – Eveleth
Vern Johnson – Roseau
Rube Bjorkman – Roseau
Orv Anderson – St. Paul Johnson
Jim Renstrom – St. Paul Johnson
Dave Reipke – St. Paul Johnson

1948

Willard Ikola – Eveleth
Orv Korstad – Warroad
Gene Klun – Eveleth
Gene Lowe – St. Paul Harding
Max Oshie – Warroad
John Matchefts – Eveleth
Dick Peterson – Eveleth
Harley Woog – South St. Paul

1949

Willard Ikola – Eveleth
Jack McKinnon – Williams
Sam Gibbons – Warroad
Chet Lundsten – Williams
Buster Oshie – Warroad
John Matchefts – Eveleth
John Mayasich – Eveleth
Tom Wegleitner – St. Paul Murray

1950

Willard Ikola – Eveleth
Ron Castellano – Eveleth
John Mayasich – Eveleth
Dan Voce – Eveleth
Dick Dougherty – Int'l Falls
Ray Beauchamp – Williams
Chet Lundsten – Williams
Jack McKinnon – Williams

1951

Warren Strelow – St. Paul Johnson
Bob Schmidt – St. Paul Johnson
Dick Meredith – Mpls. Southwest
Jack Erickson – Thief River Falls
Ron Castellano – Eveleth
John Mayasich – Eveleth
Ed Mrkonich – Eveleth
Dan Voce – Eveleth

1952

Jack Petroske – Hibbing
Don Vaia – Hibbing
George Jetty – Hibbing
Mike Castellano – Eveleth
Dave Hendrickson – Eveleth
Dave Shutte – Eveleth
Bob Schmidt – St. Paul Johnson
Don Berg – Mpls. Southwest
Mel Sobaski – So. St. Paul

1953

Gene Picha – St. Paul Johnson
Roy Karnuth – St. Paul Johnson
Gary Shea – St. Paul Johnson
Rog Christian – Warroad
Harlan Meek – Warroad
Mike Castellano – Eveleth
Dave Rodda – Eveleth
Pete Passolt – Mpls. Southwest
Bruce Weber – St. Paul Humboldt

1954

Marv Jorde – Thief River Falls
Joe Poole – Thief River Falls
Jack Hoppe – Thief River Falls
Mike McMahon – Thief River Falls
Dave Rodda – Eveleth
Bob Kochevar – Eveleth
Ed Oswald – Eveleth
Richard Lick –So.St. Paul
Stu Anderson –St. Paul Johnson
Dick Jinks – St. Paul Harding

1955

Stu Anderson – St. Paul Johnson
Tom Wahman – St. Paul Johnson
Rod Anderson – St. Paul Johnson
Jack Holstrom – St. Paul Johnson
Larry Alm – Minneapolis South
Henry Metcalf – So. St. Paul
Joe Poole – Thief River Falls
John Delmore – Roseau
Rog Rovick – Mpls. Southwest
Bob Began – Eveleth

1956

Duane Glass – Thief River Falls
Jack Poole – Thief River Falls
Glen Carlson – Thief River Falls
Jerry Norman – Eveleth
Elmer Walls – Eveleth
Larry Carlson – Edina
Murray MacPherson – Edina
Larry Cronkhite – Int'l Falls
Oscar Mahle – International Falls
Gary Olin – Mpls. Roosevelt

1957

Oscar Mahle – International Falls
Dave Frank – International Falls
Tom Neveaux – International Falls
Jim Whereley – International Falls
Neal Johnson – Roseau
Ed Baulaca – Roseau
Dave Wensloff – Roseau
Harold Vinnes – St. Paul Johnson
Mark Skoog – St. Paul Johnson
(continued next page)

1957 (cont)

Jim Ekberg – Mpls. South
Maurice Kallman – Mpls. South
Jim Emerson – Edina

Rick Alm – Mpls. South
Bob Anderson – Mpls. South
Jerry Zeller St. Paul Murray

1958

Keith Brandt –Roseau
Dick Roth – Roseau
Dave Wensloff – Roseau
Ed Baulaca – Roseau
Larry Anderson – Roseau
Mike Mathis – St. Paul Harding
Doug McClellan – St. Paul Harding
Jim Olszewski – St. Paul Harding
Arnie Johnson – St. Paul Harding
Jerry Bergstrom – Mpls. Roosevelt
Vic Quale – Mpls. Roosevelt
Dick Kalb – International Falls
Bob Reith – St. Louis Park
Jim Arendt – St. Paul Murray
Ken Pedersen – So. St. Paul

1959

Dale Olson – Roseau
Jim Stordahl – Roseau
Don Ross – Roseau
Larry Stordahl – Roseau
Dick Roth – Roseau
Ken Hanson – Mpls.Washburn
John Simus – Mpls.Washburn
Tom Gould – Mpls.Washburn
Doug Woog – So. St. Paul
Rich Brown – So. St. Paul
Dan Cullen – Internatioinal Falls
Tom Morse – International Falls
Dale Wennberg – Thief River Falls
Len Lilyholm – Robbinsdale
Don Laine – Mpls. Patrick Henry

1960

Jim Ross – Duluth East
Mike Hoene – Duluth East
Bill Sivertson – Duluth East
Dick Fischer – Duluth East
Jeff Sauer – St. Paul Washington
Don Norqual – St. Paul Washington
John Finandaca – St. Paul Washington
John Simus – Mpls. Washburn
Jim Nyholm – Mpls. Washburn
Don Laine – Mpls. Patrick Henry
Jim Anderson – Mpls. Patrick Henry
Rich Brown – So. St. Paul
Bill Beiber – Edina
Frank Judnick – Eveleth
Archie Schnieder – Thief River Falls

1961

Bob Lillo – Roseau
Jerry Swenson – Roseau
Chuck Oseid – Roseau
Bob Magie – Duluth East
Dick Fischer – Duluth East
Jon Birch – Duluth East
Gary McAlpine – So. St. Paul
Vince Egan – So. St. Paul
Doug Woog –So. St. Paul
Pat Goff – North St. Paul
Steve Kopesky – North St. Paul
Rolf Vinnes – St. Paul Johnson
Craig Falkman – St. Paul Johnson
Darrell Nichols – Bloomington
Jon Hall – Mpls. Roosevelt

1962

Mike Curran – International Falls
Keith Christiansen – Int'l Falls
Don Milette – International Falls
Glen Blumer – International Falls
Jim Amidon – International Falls
Bob Lillo – Roseau
Paul Rygh – Roseau
Gary Grugel – Roseau
Frank Zywiec – So. St. Paul
Doug Woog – So. St. Paul
John Lothrop – Greenway, Coleraine
Mike Tok – Greenway, Coleraine
Jim Branch – Richfield
Bill Ronning – Mpls. Washburn
Mike McRoberts – Edina

1963

Greg Hughes – St. Paul Johnson
Rob Shattuck – St. Paul Johnson
Ron Evenson – St. Paul Johnson
Hank Remachel – St. Paul Johnson
Jim Amidon – International Falls
Gary Wood – International Falls
Dick Haugland – International Falls
Bob Lillo – Roseau
Larry Skime – Roseau
Brick Anderson – Alexander Ramsey
Bob Boysen – Alexander Ramsey
Greg Page – St. Paul Murray
Mark Thompson – St. Paul Murray
Ken Smith – Richfield
Jon Hall – Mpls. Roosevelt

1964

Tim Sheehy – International Falls
Gary Wood – International Falls
Larry Roche – International Falls
Pete Fichuk – International Falls
Greg Hughes – St. Paul Johnson
Mike Crupi – St. Paul Johnson
Rob Shattuck – St. Paul Johnson
Bill Ersbo – Mpls. Patrick Henry
Dick Subject – Mpls. Patrick Henry
Tim Bergstrom – Roseau
Carson Hedlund – Roseau
Kip Myre – Richfield
Barry Bloomgren – Richfield
Rick Wickre – Alexander Ramsey
John McKay – Duluth East

1965

Tim Sheehy – International Falls
Tony Curran – International Falls
Gary Wood – International Falls
Pete Fichuk – International Falls
Ron Beck – International Falls
Terry Smith – Bloomington
Dave Roddy – Bloomington
Pat McKusky – St. Paul Johnson
Gary Lamotte – St. Paul Johnson
Bob Olein – Alexander Ramsey
Jerry Christensen – Alexander Ramsey
Bob Hocking – So. St. Paul
Terry Abram – So. St. Paul
Jerry Klema – Roseau
Bob Stanley – Mpls. Southwest

1966

Tim Sheehy – International Falls
Ron Beck – International Falls
Steve Ross – International Falls
Ron Weum – International Falls
Bryan Grand – Roseau
Jim Nelson – Roseau
Mike Baumgartner – Roseau
Ryan Brandt – Roseau
Jim Carter – So. St. Paul

1967

Mike Antonovich – Greenway, Coleraine
Ken Lawson – Greenway, Coleraine
Bill Joy – Greenway, Coleraine
Mick Metzer – Greenway, Coleraine
Ron Peltier – St. Paul Johnson
Doug Peltier – St. Paul Johnson
Glenn Goski – St. Paul Johnson
Craig Sarner – North St. Paul
Frank Sanders – North St. Paul

1966 (cont)

Jim Quirk – So. St. Paul
Bob Tok – Greenway, Coleraine
Kent Nyberg – Greenway, Coleraine
Bill Matschke – White Bear Lake
Phil DeHate – St. Paul Johnson
Ron Docken – Mpls. Roosevelt

1968

Mike Antonovich – Greenway
Ken Lawson – Greenway, Coleraine
Terry Casey – Greenway, Coleraine
Dave Stangl – Greenway, Coleraine
Mark Kronholm – So. St. Paul
Dale Abram – So. St. Paul
Joe Bonk – So. St. Paul
Scott Franzen – St. Paul Johnson
Doug Peltier – St. Paul Johnson
Phil Anderson – St. Paul Johnson
Tim Tyson – Mounds View
Bart Buetow – Mounds View
Earl Anderson – Roseau
Mike Lundbohm – Roseau
Jim King – Mpls. Southwest

1970

Bob Lundeen – Mpls. Southwest
Paul Miller – Mpls. Southwest
Doug Robbins – Mpls. Southwest
Bruce Carlson – Edina
Bob Krieger – Edina
Bill Nyrop – Edina
Dennis Fearing – Hibbing
John Perpich – Hibbing
Mike Polich – Hibbing
Neal Barrette – St. Paul Johnson
Doug Long – St. Paul Johnson
Fran McClellan – St. Paul Johnson
Dan Griffin – No. St. Paul
Steve Nordquist – No. St. Paul
Alan Hangsleben – Warroad
Lyle Kvarnlov – Warroad
Tom Peluso – Greenway, Coleraine

1967 (cont)

Bill Baldrica – Hibbing
Bob Collyard – Hibbing
Bruce Falk – Roseau
Mike Baumgartner – Roseau
Steve Hall – Mpls. Roosevelt
Bob Gustafson – Edina

1969

Earl Anderson – Roseau
Mike Antonovich – Greenway
Henry Boucha – Warroad
Rick Fretland – Edina
Jeff Hallett – Warroad
Alan Hangsleben – Warroad
John Harris – Roseau
Doug Hastings – Edina
Jim Knutson – Edina
Bob Krieger – Edina
Mark Kronholm – So.St.Paul
Marv Kvarnlov – Warroad
Gene Mortel – So.St.Paul
Tom Peluso – Greenway, Coleraine
Dixon Shelstad – Mpls. Southwest

1971

Dave Bremer – Edina
Tim Carlson – Edina
Dave Geving – Edina
Dave Otness – Edina
Mitch Brandt – Roseau
Mike Broten – Roseau
Tim Delmore – Roseau
Robbie Harris – Roseau
Mike Dalton – International Falls
John Prettyman – International Falls
Les Auge – St. Paul Johnson
Doug Long – St. Paul Johnson
Jerry Meier – Hastings
Dean Talafous – Hastings
Pat Phippen – Alexander Ramsey
Bob Lundeen – Mpls. Southwest
Tim Schroeder – East Grand Forks

1972

Paul Brown – International Falls
Craig Dahl – International Falls
Jim Knapp – International Falls
Peter Waselovich – Int'l Falls
Dan Benzie – Grand Rapids
Kelly Cahill – Grand Rapids
Doug Christy – Grand Rapids
John Taft – Mpls., Southwest
Steve Eichorn – Edina
Steve Short – Alexander Ramsey
John Shewchuk – So. St. Paul
Tom Sundberg – St. Paul Harding

1991 **

Mark Strobel – Hill-Murray
Matt Mauer – Hill-Murray
Wade Salzman – Duluth East
Rusty Fitzgerald – Duluth East
Kevin Rappana – Duluth East
Jason Christopherson – Burnsville
Chris Porter – Burnsville
Kelly Fairchild – Grand Rapids
Darby Hendrickson – Richfield
Brandon Steege – Richfield
John Rushin – Bloomington Kennedy
Corey Howe – Roseau

1992 (Tier I)

Joe Bianchi – Bloomington Jefferson
Tim McDonald – Bloomington Jeff.
Dan Trebil – Bloomington Jefferson
Jason Blake – Moorhead
Jim Jacobson – Moorhead
Rhett Marsten – Moorhead
Jon Hillman – Blaine
Dutch Barrett – Cloquet
Brad Chartier – Cloquet
Mike O'Connell – Apple Valley
Brent Godbout – Hill-Murray
Jason Godbout – Hill-Murray

1992 (Tier II)

Jason Alto – Greenway, Coleraine
Jeff Antonovich – Greenway, Coleraine
Jason Koski – Greenway, Coleraine
Mike Vekich – Greenway, Coleraine
Chris Hvinden – Rosemount
Jeremy Stier – Rosemount
Tim George – Orono
Tim Sweezo – Orono
Jason Ziebarth – Cambridge
Jason Bennett – Mpls. Roosevelt
Scott Lynch – Mpls. Roosevelt
Andy Semlak – Mahtomedi

1993 (Tier I)

Nick Checco – Bloomington Jefferson
Mike Crowley – Bloomington Jeff.
Jon De St. Hubert – Bloomington Jeff.
Randy Koeppl – Bloomington Jeff.
Brent Godbout – Hill-Murray
Jason Godbout – Hill-Murray
Josh Arnold – Moorhead
Matt Cullen – Moorhead
Jamie Langenbrunner – Cloquet
Rick Mrozik – Cloquet
Aaron Novak – Cloquet
Sergei Petrov – Cloquet

1993 (Tier II)

Eric Thorson – Eveleth-Gilbert
Damian Sabetti – Eveleth-Gilbert
T. J. Thomas – Eveleth-Gilbert
Zach Young – Eveleth-Gilbert
Mark Amundsen – Lake of the Woods
Eric Larson – Lake of the Woods
Ryan Usiski – Lake of the Woods
Ryan Nosan – Lake of the Woods
Troy Ricci – Lake of the Woods
George Awada – Henry Sibley
Brian Rolig – Henry Sibley
Bryan Benedict – Orono

** All-tournament teams were re-introduced in 1991 after being discontinued following the 1972 tournament. The Minnesota State High School League's new premier corporate partner at the time, First Banks (later U.S. Bank) sponsored the awards.

1994 (Tier I)

Joe Bianchi – Bloomington Jefferson
Mike Crowley – Bloomington Jeff.
Jeff Heil – Bloomington Jefferson
Josh Arnold – Moorhead
Matt Cullen – Moorhead
Rob Gramer – Moorhead
Ryan Kraft – Moorhead
Clint Johnson – Duluth East
Dave Spehar – Duluth East
Ryan Huerta – So. St. Paul
Jesse Rooney – White Bear Lake
Matt Jeffers – Osseo

1994 (Tier II)

Andy Fermoyle – Warroad
Tom Lund – Warroad
Wyatt Smith – Warroad
Brian Bolf – Hibbing
Joe Lolich – Hibbing
Brandon Sampair – Mahtomedi
Jesse Sampair – Mahtomedi
Benji Wolke – St. Cloud Cathedral
Ryan Karasek – Hermantown
Brian McDonald – Hermantown
Billy Birminghan – Mpls. Edison
Herbie Nivala – Farmington

1995 (Class AA)

Cade Ledingham – Duluth East
Chris Locker – Duluth East
Dave Spehar – Duluth East
Troy Bagne – Moorhead
Matt Cullen – Moorhead
Ryan Frisch – Moorhead
Joel Jamison – Moorhead
Tony Grosso – Rochester Mayo
Matt Leimbek – Rochester Mayo
Jason Noterman – Rochester Mayo
Mike Anderson – Blmtn Jefferson
Dan Carlson – Edina

1995 (Class A)

Jon Austin – International Falls
Paul Hilfer – International Falls
Todd Sether – International Falls
Aaron Ratfield – Totino-Grace
Ryen Ratfield – Totino-Grace
Jake Searles – Totino-Grace
Zach Hallett – Warroad
Wyatt Smith – Warroad
Bryce Barry – Red Wing
Jay Barry – Red Wing
Ryan Dolder – Hutchinson
Christian Peterson – Blake

1996 (Class AA)

Brad DeFauw – Apple Valley
Aaron Dwyer – Apple Valley
Karl Goehring – Apple Valley
Chris Sikich – Apple Valley
Erik Westrum – Apple Valley
Kyle Kolquist – Duluth East
Chris Locker – Duluth East
Dave Spehar – Duluth East
Andy Wheeler – Duluth East
Peter Armburst – Edina
Dan Carlson – Edina
Jay Kopishcke – Alexandria

1996 (Class A)

Zach Hallett – Warroad
Tanner Martell – Warroad
Kaine Martell – Warroad
Aaron Stodgell – Warroad
Matt Ulwelling – Warroad
Bryce Barry – Red Wing
Seth Larson – Red Wing
Tom Moore – Red Wing
Johnny Pohl – Red Wing
Christopher Hicks – Breck
Jon Maruk – Breck
Troy Urhdahl – Litchfield

1997 (Class AA)

Dan Carlson – Edina
Sam Cornelius – Edina
Jeff Hall – Edina
Ben Stafford – Edina
Nick Angell – Duluth East
Ryan Coole – Duluth East
Kyle Kohlquist – Duluth East
Matt Mathias – Duluth East
Dylan Mills – Duluth East
Mark Cullen – Moorhead
Brian Nelson – Moorhead
Brandon Sampair – Hill-Murray

1998 (Class AA)

Nick Angell – Duluth East
Adam Coole – Duluth East
Pat Finnegan – Duluth East
Kevin Oswald – Duluth East
Ryan Johnson – Anoka
Dan Scott – Anoka
Rick Talbot – Anoka
Lee Brooks – Bloomington Jefferson
Dave Hergert – Bloomington Jefferson
Jeff Taffe – Hastings
Ben Tharp – Hastings
Dan Welch – Hastings

1999 (Class AA)

Jake Brandt – Roseau
Derrick Byfuglien – Roseau
Mike Klema – Roseau
Jesse Modahl – Roseau
Derek Garcia – Hastings
Jeff Taffe – Hastings
Dan Welch – Hastings
Mitch Glines – Elk River
Paul Martin – Elk River
Trevor Frischmon – Blaine
Matt Hendricks – Blaine
Ryan LaMere – Holy Angels

1997 (Class A)

Joe Edstrom – Red Wing
Tom Moore – Red Wing
Johnny Pohl – Red Wing
Travis Trembath – Red Wing
Mark Carlson – Warroad
Justin Ferguson – Warroad
Adrian Hasbargen – Warroad
Matt Ulwelling – Warroad
Dom Talarico – Proctor
Jim Dahl – Breck
Jon Maruk – Breck
Nathan Kirschner – Mora/Hinckley

1998 (Class A)

Dan Heitzman – Eveleth-Gilbert
Andy Sachetti – Eveleth-Gilbert
Pete Samargia – Eveleth-Gilbert
Nick Dolentz – Hermantown
Jon Francisco – Hermantown
B.J. Knapp – Hermantown
Chris Oppel – Hermantown
Brian Cashman – Red Wing
Tom Moore – Red Wing
Johnny Pohl – Red Wing
Jace Anders – St. Louis Park
Tyler Palmiscno – East Grand Forks

1999 (Class A)

Mike Grobe – Benilde-St. Margaret's
Luke Irwin – Benilde-St. Margaret's
Jake Riddle – Benilde-St. Margaret's
Troy Riddle – Benilde-St. Margaret's
Joe Schuman – Benilde-St. Margaret's
Shawn Bartlette – East Grand Forks
Sam Brown – East Grand Forks
Tommy White – East Grand Forks
Kevin Ackley – Fergus Falls
Anthony Blumer – St. Thomas Academy
Mark Pohl –Red Wing
Jon Francisco – Hermantown

2000 *(Class AA)*

Brandon Bochenski – Blaine
Scott Foyt – Blaine
Matt Hendricks – Blaine
Matt Moore – Blaine
Tom Allen – Duluth East
Ross Carlson – Duluth East
Dan Hoehne – Duluth East
Nick Licari – Duluth East
Travis Kieffer – Hastings
Chris Kapsen – Edina
Josh Grahn – Roseau
Andy Canzenello – Rochester Mayo

2000 *(Class A)*

Jake Brenk – Breck
Josh Haller – Breck
Todd O'Hara – Breck
Nick Marvin – Warroad
Brian McFarlane – Warroad
Cory Monshaugen – Warroad
Tony Selvog – Warroad
Jayme Fisher – International Falls
Brady Fougner – International Falls
Derrick Zirips – International Falls
Nathan Raduns – Sauk Rapids-Rice
Mark Stuart – Rochester Lourdes

2001 *(Class AA)*

Chris Nathe – Elk River
Kelly Plude – Elk River
Trevor Stewart – Elk River
Chad Beiswenger – Moorhead
Mark Buchholz – Moorhead
James Marcy – Moorhead
Gino Guyer – Greenway, Coleraine
Andy Sertich – Greenway, Coleraine
Travis Kieffer – Hastings
Adam Welch – Hastings
Andrew Panchenko – Eastview
Eric Aarnio – White Bear Lake

2001 *(Class A)*

Danny Charleston – Benilde-St. Margaret's
Tony Grannes – Benilde-St. Margaret's
Ricky Hopkins – Benilde-St. Margaret's
Jake Schuman – Benilde-St. Margaret's
Brandon Harrington – Rochester Lourdes
Dan Smith – Rochester Lourdes
Jake Taylor – Rochester Lourdes
Dan Knapp – Hermantown
B.J. Radovich – Hermantown
Ryan Miller – Fergus Falls
Nick Bydal – East Grand Forks
Per Wimmercranz – Mound Westonka

2002 *(Class AA)*

Jimmy Kilpatrick – Holy Angels
Dan Kronick – Holy Angels
Ben Luth – Holy Angels
Kevin Rollwagen – Holy Angels
Tony Ciro – Hill-Murray
Matt Czech – Hill-Murray
Garrett O. Regan – Hill-Murray
Collin Cody – Roseville/St. Anthony
Nick Klaren – Roseville/St. Anthony
Mark Van Guilder – Roseville/S.A.
Andy Dirlam – Bloomington Jefferson
Barnabas Birkeland – Elk River

2002 *(Class A)*

Dan McCauley – Totino Grace
Kevin Piper – Totino-Grace
Tim Serie – Totino-Grace
Reid Cashman – Red Wing
Adam Hendel – Red Wing
Joe Laplant – Red Wing
Mike Pohl – Red Wing
Tom Pohl – Red Wing
Charlie Cobb – Rochester Lourdes
Brandon Harrington – Rochester Lourdes
Marcus Rezka – Rochester Lourdes
Ryan Miller – Fergus Falls

2003 (Class AA)

Sean Fish – Anoka
Ben Hendrick – Anoka
Tim Manthey – Anoka
Kyle Olstad – Anoka
Neal Carlson – Roseville Area
Andy Carroll – Roseville Area
Pat Eagles – Roseville Area
Jerad Kaufmann – Roseville Area
Jack Hillen – Holy Angels
Kevin Huck – Holy Angels
Josh Frider – Moorhead
Dustin Mercado – White Bear Lake

2003 (Class A)

Gabe Harren – Warroad
Andrew Hasbargen – Warroad
T.J. Oshie – Warroad
Tony Selvog – Warroad
Troy Davenport – Simley
Adam Hoaglund – Simley
Dan Ohmann – Simley
Ryan McClure – Orono
Brad Kern – Hibbing
Drew Walters – Hibbing
Josh Duncan – Rochester Lourdes
Dan Perry – Fergus Falls

2004 (Class AA)

R. J. Anderson – Centennial
Tom Gorowsky – Centennial
Tim Ornell – Centennial
Greg Stutz – Centennial
Jon Ammerman – Moorhead
Brian Lee – Moorhead
Cory Loos – Moorhead
Chris Johnson – Duluth East
Rob Johnson – Duluth East
Mike Carman – Holy Angels
Joey Miller – Wayzata
B.J. O'Brien – Lakeville

2004 (Class A)

Marcus Bellows – Breck
Jordan Fulton – Breck
Blake Wheeler – Breck
Pat Dynan – Orono
Peter Engebretson – Orono
Anders Peterson – Orono
Glenn Ylitalo – Orono
Drew Walters – Hibbing
Shea Walters – Hibbing
Andrew Hasbargen – Warroad
Eric Olimb – Warroad
Alex Stalock – So. St. Paul

2005 (Class AA)

Jay Bariball – Holy Angels
Tyler Hawkins – Holy Angels
Jared Hummel – Holy Angels
Lathan Logan – Holy Angels
Jon Ammerman – Moorhead
Matt Becker – Moorhead
Brian Lee – Moorhead
Chris VandeVelde – Moorhead
Cade Fairchild – Duluth East
Chris Sall – Duluth East
Eric Schultz – Tartan
Alex Kangas – Rochester Century

2005 (Class A)

Kyle Hardwick – Warroad
Eric Olimb – Warroad
T.J. Oshie – Warroad
Dan Malone – Totino-Grace
Dave Norling – Totino-Grace
Brian Schack – Totino-Grace
Mark Thiele – Totino-Grace
Chris Connolly – Duluth Marshall
Scott Kozlak – Duluth Marshall
Jordan Schroeder – St. Thomas Academy
Matt Niskanen – Virginia/Mt. Iron-Buhl
Jon Breuer – Albert Lea

2006 (Class AA)

Ben Hause – Cretin-Derham Hall
Chris Hickey – Cretin-Derham Hall
Ben Kinne – Cretin-Derham Hall
Ryan McDonagh – Cretin-D.H.
Reidar Jensen – Grand Rapids
Jared Smith – Grand Rapids
Joe Stejskal – Grand Rapids
Patrick White – Grand Rapids
Nick Larson – Hill-Murray
Derek McCallum – Hill-Murray
Jack Paul – Minnetonka
Matt Olson – Blaine

2006 (Class A)

Jack Baer –St. Thomas Academy
Aaron Crandall – St. Thomas Academy
Jordan Schroeder – St. Thomas Academy
Rob Bordson – Duluth Marshall
Bob Gutsch – Duluth Marshall
Kevin Jones – Duluth Marshall
Matt Letourneau – Duluth Marshall
Jason Paul – Duluth Marshall
Karl Gilbert – Hermantown
Ryan Hill – Hermantown
Jason Paul – Hermantown
Michael Benedict –Thief River Falls

2007 (Class AA)

Sam Carr – Roseau
Mike Lee – Roseau
Dustin Moser – Roseau
Aaron Ness – Roseau
Kurt Weston – Roseau
Reidar Jensen – Grand Rapids
Zach Morse – Grand Rapids
Joe Stejskal – Grand Rapids
Patrick White – Grand Rapids
Joe Faupel – Rochester Century
Garrett Grimstad – Rchstr Century
Tyler Barnes – Burnsville

2007 (Class A)

Nathan Hardy – Hermantown
Chad Huttel – Hermantown
Joe Krause – Hermantown
Drew LeBlanc – Hermantown
Jack Connolly – Duluth Marshall
Bob Gutsch – Duluth Marshall
Dano Jacques – Duluth Marshall
Ian Stauber – Duluth Marshall
Aaron Crandall – St. Thomas Academy
Jon Schreiner – St. Thomas Academy
Aaron Marvin – Warroad
Jared Festler – Little Falls

2008 (Class AA)

Dan Cecka – Hill-Murray
Ryan Furne – Hill-Murray
Joe Phillippi – Hill-Murray
Dan Sova – Hill-Murray
Derick Caschetta – Edina
Marshall Everson – Edina
Joe Gleason – Edina
Zach Budish – Edina
Matt Berglund – Benilde-St. Mrgrts
Chris Student – Benilde-St. Mrgrts
Tyler Landman – Roseau
Aaron Ness – Roseau

2008 (Class A)

Kurt Altrichter – St. Thomas Academy
James Saintey – St. Thomas Academy
Jon Schreiner – St. Thomas Academy
Rob Vannelli – St. Thomas Academy
Ryan Walters – St. Thomas Academy
Dano Jacques – Duluth Marshall
Zach Mausolf – Duluth Marshall
Willie Paul – Duluth Marshall
Mark McDonald – Warroad
Bryce Ravndalen – Warroad
Ben Hanowski – Little Falls
Stephen Rindelaub – St. Cloud Cathedral

The 2008 Class AA All-Tournament Team (Photo: Kyle Oen)

2009 (Class AA)

Nick Leddy – Eden Prairie
Kyle Rau – Eden Prairie
Taylor Wolfe – Eden Prairie
Jordan Doschadis – Moorhead
Trent Johnson – Moorhead
Logan Marks – Moorhead
Brendan Baker – Edina
Marshall Everson – Edina
Mark Alt – Cretin-Derham Hall
Ben Walsh – Cretin-Derham Hall
Nick Bjugstad – Blaine
Tony Larson – Blaine

2009 (Class A)

Reid Herd – Breck
Mike Morin – Breck
Joe Rehkamp – Breck
John Russell – Breck
Jason Goldsmith – Warroad
Brett Hebel – Warroad
Brock Nelson – Warroad
Michael Pieper – Warroad
Izaak Berglund – Little Falls
Ben Hanowski – Little Falls
Jordan Palusky – St. Cloud Cathedral
Nate Schmidt – St. Cloud Cathedral

2010 (Class AA)

Ryan Cutshall – Edina
Max Everson - Edina
Connor Girard - Edina
Charlie Taft - Edina
Max Gardner - Minnetonka
Justin Holl - Minnetonka

Jim Kruger – Minnetonka
Andrew Prochno – Minnetonka
Chris Casto – Hill-Murray
Willie Faust – Hill-Murray
Jack Walsh – Hill-Murray
Hudson Fasching – Apple Valley

2010 (Class A)

Tyson Fulton - Breck
Ben Gislason - Breck
Mike Morin - Breck
John Russell - Breck
Charlie Comnick - Hermantown
Jared Kohlquist - Hermantown

Jeff Paczynski - Hermantown
Andy Foster - Warroad
Brett Hebel - Warroad
Brock Nelson - Warroad
Ben Marshall - Mahtomedi
Brandon Zurn - Mahtomedi

2011 (Class AA)

Andrew Ford – Eden Prairie
Dan Molenaar - Eden Prairie
Kyle Rau - Eden Prairie
Nick Seeler – Eden Prairie
Hunter Bergerson – Duluth East
Jake Randolph – Duluth East
Nate Repensky – Duluth East
Dom Toninato – Duluth East
Nick Kuchera – Eagan
Will Merchant – Eagan
Charlie Lindgren – Lakeville North
Brandon Wahlin – White Bear Lake

2011 (Class A)

A.J. Reid – St. Thomas Academy
Zach Schroeder – St. Thomas Academy
David Zevnick – St. Thomas Academy
Jared Kohlquist – Hermantown
Connor Lucas– Hermantown
Garrett Skrbich – Hermantown
Jared Thomas – Hermantown
Nick DeCenzo – Hibbing
Adam Johnson – Hibbing
Matt Audette – Thief River Falls
Austin Rudnick – Breck
Rory Vesel – Rochester Lourdes

2012 (Class AA)

Grant Besse – Benilde-St. Mrgret
Christian Horn – Benilde-St. Mrgret
Dan Labosky – Benilde-St.Margaret
Justin Quale.Benilde – St. Margaret
Sam BeckerHill - Murray
Blake Heinrich – Hill-Murray
Conrad Sampair – Hill-Murray
Nate Repensky – Duluth East
Dom Toninato – Duluth East
Michael Bitzer –Moorhead
Justin Kloos – Lakeville South

2012 (Class A)

Andrew Commers – St. Thomas Academy
Tom Novak – St. Thomas Academy
Eric Shurhamer – St. Thomas Academy
David Zevnik – St. Thomas Academy
Jared Kohlquist – Hermantown
Jared Thomas –Hermantown
Jake Zeleznikar – Hermantown
Jake Kenney – Breck
Grant Opperman – Breck
Chris Forney – Thief River Falls
Joey Hanowski – Little Falls
Alex Funk – Rochester Lourdes

2013 (Class AA)

Connor Hurley – Edina
Andy Jordahl – Edina
Dylan Malmquist – Edina
Parker Reno – Edina
Sam Becker – Hill-Murray
John Dugas – Hill-Murray
Zach LaValle – Hill-Murray
Mitch Slattery – Hill-Murray
Phil Beaulieu – Duluth East
Meirs Moore – Duluth East
Alex Toscano – Duluth East
Jacob Dittmer – Moorhead

2014 (Class AA)

Miguel Fidler – Edina
Dylan Malmquist – Edina
Tyler Nanne – Edina
Andrew Rohkohl – Edina
Jack Poehling – Lakeville North
Nick Poehling – Lakeville North
Alex Strand – Roseau
Zach Yon – Roseau
Phil Beaulieu – Duluth East
Luc Snuggerud – Eden Prairie
Nick Wolff – Eagan
Andrew Lindgren – Eagan

2015 (Class AA)

Ryan Edquist – Lakeville North
Jack McNeely – Lakeville North
Jack Poehling – Lakeville North
Nick Poehling – Lakeville North
Jack Sadek – Lakeville North
Ash Altmann – Duluth East
Gunnar Howg – Duluth East
Alex Spencer – Duluth East
Ryan Peterson – Duluth East
Peter Tufto – St. Thomas Academy
Seamus Donohue – St. Thomas Academy
Garrett Wait – Edina

2013 (Class A)

Jack Daugherty – St. Thomas Academy
Matt Per – St. Thomas Academy
Wyatt Schmidt – St. Thomas Academy
David Zevnik – St. Thomas Academy
Chris Benson – Hermantown
Travis Koepke – Hermantown
Neal Pionk – Hermantown
Adam Smith – Hermantown
Tommy Hajicek – East Grand Forks
Colton Poolman – East Grand Forks
Matt Colford – Breck
Alex Funk – Rochester Lourdes

2014 (Class A)

Tye Ausmus – East Grand Forks
Colton Poolman – East Grand Forks
Tanner Tweten – East Grand Forks
Josh Weber – East Grand Forks
Zach Kramer – Hermantown
Nate Pionk – Hermantown
Daniel Bailey – St. Cloud Cathedral
Zach Fritz – St. Cloud Cathedral
William Hammer – St. Cloud Cathedral
Ben Henderson – Totino-Grace
Austin Isaacson – New Prague
Gunnar Olson – Luverne

2015 (Class A)

Dixon Bowen – East Grand Forks
Grant Loven – East Grand Forks
Trevor Selk – East Grand Forks
Tanner Tweten – East Grand Forks
Josh Weber – East Grand Forks
Wyatt Aamodt – Hermantown
Eric Gotz – Hermantown
Ryan Kero – Hermantown
Luke Olson – Hermantown
Nate Pionk – Hermantown
Jack Becker – Mahtomedi
Tanner Breidenbach – St. Cloud Apollo

17 Hockey Lists

 ## TOURNAMENT CHAMPIONS

Year	Champion	Runnerup	Score	Third-Place	Consolation
1945	Eveleth	Thief River Falls	4-3	St. Paul Washington	White Bear Lake
1946	Roseau	Rochester	6-0	Eveleth	St. Cloud
1947	St. Paul Johnson	Roseau	2-1	Minneapolis West	So. St. Paul
1948	Eveleth	Warroad	8-2	St. Cloud	St. Paul Harding
1949	Eveleth	Williams	4-1	Warroad	Minneapolis Washburn
1950	Eveleth	Williams	4-3	International Falls	St. Paul Murray
1951	Eveleth	St. Paul Johnson	4-1	Thief River Falls	St. Paul Murray
1952	Hibbing	Eveleth	4-3	Mpls. Southwest	Thief River Falls
1953	St. Paul Johnson	Warroad	4-1	Eveleth	St. Paul Humboldt
1954	Thief River Falls	Eveleth	4-1	St. Paul Johnson	St. Paul Harding
1955	St. Paul Johnson	Mpls Southwest	3-1	So. St. Paul	Thief River Falls
1956	Thief River Falls	International Falls	3-2	Eveleth	St. Paul Johnson
1957	International Falls	Roseau	3-2	Minneapolis South	Edina
1958	Roseau	St. Paul Harding	1-0	So. St. Paul	Minneapolis Roosevelt
1959	Roseau	Mpls Washburn	4-2	International Falls	Thief River Falls
1960	Duluth East	St. Paul Washington	3-1	Mpls Patrick Henry	Minneapolis Washburn
1961	Roseau	So. St. Paul	1-0	Duluth East	St. Paul Johnson
1962	International Falls	Roseau	4-0	So. St. Paul	Edina
1963	St. Paul Johnson	International Falls	4-3 OT	Roseau	Alexander Ramsey
1964	International Falls	St. Paul Johnson	7-3	Mpls. Patrick Henry	Roseau
1965	International Falls	Bloomington	7-0	St. Paul Johnson	Alexander Ramsey
1966	International Falls	Roseau	5-0	South St. Paul	Greenway-Coleraine
1967	Greenway	St. Paul Johnson	4-2	Hibbing	Roseau
1968	Greenway	So St. Paul	6-1	St. Paul Johnson	Roseau
1969	Edina	Warroad	5-4 OT	South St. Paul	Greenway-Coleraine
1970	Mpls Southwest	Edina	1-0 OT	Hibbing	North St. Paul
1971	Edina	Roseau	1-0	International Falls	Hastings
1972	International Falls	Grand Rapids	3-2	Mpls. Southwest	Edina
1973	Hibbing	Alexander Ramsey	6-3	International Falls	Mpls. Southwest
1974	Edina East	Bemidji	6-0	Grand Rapids	Hibbing
1975	Grand Rapids	Mpls Southwest	6-1	Hill-Murray	Duluth East
1976	Grand Rapids	Richfield	4-3	Hill-Murray	Bloomington Kennedy
1977	Roch John Marshall	Edina East	4-2	Grand Rapids	Hill-Murray
1978	Edina East	Grand Rapids	5-4 2OT	Roseau	Hill-Murray
1979	Edina East	Roch John Marshall	4-3 OT	Roseau	Grand Rapids
1980	Grand Rapids	Hill-Murray	2-1	Bloom Jefferson	Irondale
1981	Bloomington Jefferson	Irondale	3-2	South South Paul	Grand Rapids
1982	Edina	White Bear Mariner	6-0	Hibbing	Cloquet
1983	Hill-Murray	Burnsville	4-3	Henry Sibley	Edina
1984	Edina	Bloom. Kennedy	4-2	Hibbing	Roseau
1985	Burnsville	Hill-Murray	4-3	Anoka	Hibbing
1986	Burnsville	Hill-Murray	4-1	Duluth Denfeld	Bemidji
1987	Bloom. Kennedy	Burnsville	4-1	Greenway-Coleraine	So. St. Paul
1988	Edina	Hill-Murray	5-3	Bloom-Jefferson	Duluth Denfeld
1989	Bloom. Jefferson	Roch. John Marshall	5-4 OT	Duluth Denfeld	Edina
1990	Roseau	Grand Rapids	3-1	Minnetonka	White Bear Lake

1991	Hill-Murray	Duluth East	5-3	Burnsville	Richfield
1992-I	BloomJefferson	Moorhead	6-3	Blaine	Apple Valley
1992-II	Greenway,Coleraine*	Rosemount	6-1	Orono	Mpls Roosevelt
1993-I	Bloomington Jefferson	Hill-Murray	4-0	Moorhead	Cloquet/Esko/Carlton
1993-II	Eveleth-Gilbert	Lake-of-Woods*	3-2 2OT	Henry Sibley	Orono
1994AA	Bloom Jefferson	Moorhead	3-1	Duluth East	White Bear Lake Area
1994A	Warroad	Hibbing	5-3	Mahtomedi	Minneapolis Edison
1995AA	Duluth East	Moorhead	5-3	Edina	Bloom Jefferson
1995A	Int'l Falls	Totino-Grace	3-2	Warroad	Hutchinson
1996AA	Apple Valley	Edina	3-2	Duluth East	Alexandria
1996A	Warroad	Red Wing	10-3	Breck	Simley
1997AA	Edina	Duluth East	1-0	Moorhead	Anoka
1997A	Red Wing	Warroad	4-3	Proctor*	Breck
1998AA	Duluth East	Anoka	3-1	Bloom Jefferson	Hastings
1998A	Eveleth-Gilbert	Hermantown	2-1	Red Wing	East Grand Forks
1999AA	Roseau	Hastings	4-0	Elk River Area	Blaine
1999A	Benilde-St. Margaret's	East Grand Forks	4-2	Fergus Falls	St. Thomas Academy
2000AA	Blaine	Duluth East	6-0	Hastings	Roseau
2000A	Breck	Warroad	3-2	International Falls	Farmington
2001AA	Elk River Area	Moorhead	8-1	Greenway*	Eastview,Apple Valley
2001A	Benilde-St. Margaret's	Rochester Lourdes*	2-1	Hermantown	East Grand Forks
2002AA	Holy Angels	Hill-Murray	4-2	Roseville Area	Elk River Area
2002A	Totino-Grace	Red Wing	3-2	Rochester Lourdes*	East Grand Forks
2003AA	Anoka	Roseville Area	3-1	HolyAngels	White Bear Lake Area
2003A	Warroad	Simley	3-1	Orono	Hibbing
2004AA	Centennial	Moorhead	1-0	Duluth East	Holy Angels
2004A	Breck	Orono	7-2	Hibbing	Warroad
2005AA	Holy Angels	Moorhead	6-4	Duluth East	White Bear Lake Area
2005A	Warroad	Totino-Grace	4-3 2OT	Duluth Marshall	Albert Lea
2006AA	Cretin-Derham Hall	Grand Rapids	7-0	Blaine	Minnetonka
2006A	St. ThomasAcademy	Duluth Marshall	4-3	Hermantown	Blake School
2007AA	Roseau	Grand Rapids	5-1	Rochester Century	Edina
2007A	Hermantown	DuluthMarshall	4-1	St. Thomas Academy	Orono
2008AA	Hill-Murray	Edina	3-0	Benilde-St. Margaret's	Woodbury
2008A	St. Thomas Academy	Duluth Marshall	5-1	Warroad	Little Falls
2009AA	Eden Prairie	Moorhead	3-0	Blaine	Edina
2009A	Breck	Warroad	7-3	Little Falls	Rochester Lourdes*
2010AA	Edina	Minnetonka	4-2	Hill-Murray	Duluth East
2010A	Breck	Hermantown	2-1	Warroad	Rochester Lourdes*
2011AA	Eden Prairie	Duluth East	3-2 3OT	Eagan	Lakeville North
2011A	St. Thomas	Hermantown	5-4 OT	Thief River Falls	Breck
2012AA	Benilde-St. Margaret's	Hill-Murray	5-1	Lakeville South	Duluth East
2012A	St. Thomas	Hermantown	5-1	Breck	Little Falls
2013AA	Edina	Hill-Murray	4-2	Duluth East	Moorhead
2013A	St. Thomas	Hermantown	5-4	Breck	Duluth Marshall
2014AA	Edina	Lakeville North	8-2	Eagan	Roseau
2014A	East Grand Forks	Hermantown	7-3	New Prague	Totino-Grace
2015AA	Lakeville North	Duluth East	4-1	Edina	St. Thomas Academy
2015A	East Grand Forks	Hermantown	5-4 OT	Mahtomedi	New Prague

*Denotes cooperatively sponsored program:
International Falls/Little Fork-BigFalls;Proctor/Albrook,Saginaw; Greenway, Coleraine/Nashwauk-Keewatin;
Rochester Lourdes/Stewartville/Plainview(20001,2002); Rochester Lourdes/Stewartville/Chatfield(2009);
Lake of the Woods, Baudette, Minnesota/Rainy River,Ontario,Canada

Leading Scorers by Year

Year	Name	School	Goals	Assists	Points
1945	Wally Grant	Eveleth	9	4	13
	Pat Finnegan	Eveleth	8	5	13
1946	Rube Bjorkman	Roseau	4	1	5
	Bob Harris	Roseau	3	2	5
1947	Rube Bjorkman	Roseau	6	0	6
	Dave Reipke	St. Paul Johnson	5	1	6
	Francis Tholl	St. Cloud	4	2	6
	Jim Broker	St. Cloud	4	2	6
	John Matchefts	Eveleth	3	3	6
1948	John Matchefts	Eveleth	9	5	14
1949	John Mayasich	Eveleth	7	4	11
1950	John Mayasich	Eveleth	11	1	12
	Ray Beauchamp	Williams	5	7	12
1951	John Mayasich	Eveleth	15	3	18
1952	Jack Petroske	Hibbing	3	8	11
1953	Roger Bertelson	St. Paul Johnson	4	1	5
	Jack Stoskopf	Warroad	4	1	5
	Mike Castellano	Eveleth	3	2	5
	Gerald Palkovich	Eveleth	2	3	5
1954	Dick Jinks	St. Paul Harding	8	0	8
1955	Merv Meredith	Mpls. Southwest	5	1	6
1956	Cliff Strand	Thief River Falls	4	3	7
1957	Oscar Mahle	International Falls	7	1	8
1958	Ken Pederson	So. St. Paul	6	2	8
1959	Dan Cullen	International Falls	6	1	7
	Jim Stordahl	Roseau	4	3	7
1960	Bill Sivertson	Duluth East	5	1	6
	Jim Ross	Duluth East	3	3	6
1961	Craig Falkman	St. Paul Johnson	5	0	5
	Jon Hall	Mpls. Roosevelt	0	5	5
	Tom Brindley	St. Paul Johnson	2	3	5
1962	Glen Blumer	International Falls	3	3	6
	Jim Amidon	International Falls	2	4	6
	Doug Woog	So. St. Paul	2	4	6
1963	Jim Amidon	International Falls	4	4	8
1964	Rob Shattuck	St. Paul Johnson	3	4	7
1965	Pete Fichuk	International Falls	4	3	7
1966	Bob Tok	Greenway, Coleraine	5	3	8
1967	Craig Sarner	North St. Paul	2	9	11
1968	Mike Antonovich	Greenway, Coleraine	3	6	9
1969	Mike Antonovich	Greenway, Coleraine	7	1	8
1970	Paul Miller	Mpls. Southwest	4	2	6
	Leo Marshall	Warroad	3	3	6
	Frank Krahn	Warroad	1	5	6
1971	Jerry Meier	Hastings	3	2	5
	Dave Otness	Edina	2	3	5

Leading Scorers by Year (cont)

Year	Name	School	Goals	Assists	Points
1972	John Shewchuck	So. St. Paul	2	4	6
	Warren Miller	So. St. Paul	2	4	6
1973	Joe Micheletti	Hibbing	7	4	11
1974	John Rothstein	Grand Rapids	5	2	7
1975	Erin Roth	Grand Rapids	3	7	10
1976	Steve Christoff	Richfield	5	4	9
1977	Scott Lecy	Rochester Marshall	5	2	7
	Scott Kleinendorst	Grand Rapids	4	3	7
1978	Aaron Broten	Roseau	4	3	7
1979	Aaron Broten	Roseau	6	6	12
1980	Jay North	Bloom. Jefferson	4	3	7
	Scott Richart	Irondale	6	1	7
	John Bader	Irondale	2	5	7
1981	Tony Kellin	Grand Rapids	3	6	9
1982	Steve Bianchi	Bloom. Jefferson	1	6	7
	Jim Johannson	Rochester Mayo	5	2	7
1983	Todd Okerlund	Burnsville	2	6	8
1984	Paul Ranheim	Edina	4	3	7
1985	Tod Hartje	Anoka	3	3	6
	Pat Marolt	Hibbing	4	2	6
1986	Scott Bloom	Burnsville	5	5	10
1987	Jason Miller	Bloom. Kennedy	6	2	8
	John Young	So. St. Paul	2	6	8
1988	Larry Olimb	Warroad	2	4	6
	Kevin Degel	Bloom. Jefferson	0	6	6
	Chris Marinucci	Grand Rapids	1	5	6
1989	Sean Rice	Bloom.Jefferson	5	3	8
1990	Chris Gotziaman	Roseau	4	2	6
	Justin McHugh	Minnetonka	4	2	6
1991	Mark Strobel	Hill-Murray	4	3	7
1992-I	Joe Bianchi	Bloom. Jefferson	6	1	7
	Tim McDonald	Bloom. Jefferson	4	3	7
	Jon Hillman	Blaine	3	4	7
	Mike O'Connell	Apple Valley	3	4	7
1992-II	Scott Lynch	Mpls. Roosevelt	4	5	9
1993-I	Jamie Langenbrunner	Cloquet	3	10	13
	Sergei Petrov	Cloquet	6	7	13
1993-II	Mark Amundson	Lake of the Woods	6	4	10
1994-AA	Ryan Kraft	Moorhead	8	1	9
1994-A	Brian Bolf	Hibbing	2	8	10
	Jesse Sampair	Mahtomedi	4	6	10
1995-AA	Dave Spehar	Duluth East	9	0	9
1995-A	Ryan Dolder	Hutchinson	7	2	9
1996-AA	Dave Spehar	Duluth East	9	4	13

Leading Scorers by Year (cont)

Year	Name	School	Goals	Assists	Points
1996-A	Josh Heppner	Warroad	1	6	7
	Kaine Martell	Warroad	2	5	7
	Johnny Pohl	Red Wing	5	2	7
1997-AA	Brian Nelson	Moorhead	5	0	5
1997-A	Dom Talarico	Proctor	3	7	10
1998-AA	Jeff Taffe	Hastings	3	4	7
1998-A	Johnny Pohl	Red Wing	3	8	11
1999-AA	Mike Klema	Roseau	7	2	9
1999-A	Troy Riddle	Benilde-St. Margaret's	7	2	9
2000-AA	Brandon Bochenski	Blaine	3	4	7
2000-A	Todd O'Hara	Breck	3	3	6
2001-AA	Trevor Stewart	Elk River Area	4	5	9
2001-A	Ryan Miller	Fergus Falls	7	2	9
	B. J. Radovich	Hermantown	5	4	9
2002-AA	Kevin Rollwagen	Holy Angels	3	4	7
	Jimmy Kilpatrick	Holy Angels	1	6	7
2002-A	Brandon Harrington	Rochester Lourdes	3	5	8
2003-AA	Josh Frider	Moorhead	4	1	5
2003-A	Shea Walters	Hibbing	3	6	9
2004-AA	Rob Johnson	Duluth East	5	3	8
2004-A	Blake Wheeler	Breck	6	5	11
2005-AA	Matt Overman	Bloom. Jefferson	4	2	6
	Josh Levine	Bloom. Jefferson	2	4	6
	Jay Barriball	Holy Angels	4	2	6
2005-A	Quinn Ellingson	Albert Lea	5	2	7
	Cory Ellertson	Albert Lea	4	3	7
2006-AA	Ben Kinne	Cretin-Derham Hall	3	6	9
2006-A	Karl Gilbert	Hermantown	5	3	8
2007-AA	Matt Reber	Edina	1	6	7
	Tyler Barnes	Burnsville	4	3	7
2007-A	Drew LeBlanc	Hermantown	4	4	8
2008-AA	Ben Goff	Woodbury	5	3	8
2008-A	Ben Hanowski	Little Falls	7	3	10
2009-AA	Anders Lee	Edina	1	8	9
2009-A	Ben Hanowski	Little Falls	7	2	9
2010-AA	Adam Knochenmus	Roseau	1	5	6
2010-A	Brock Nelson	Warroad	6	5	11
2011-AA	Kyle Rau	Eden Prairie	5	2	7
	Brandon Wahlin	White Bear Lake	5	2	7
2011-A	A. J. Reid	St. Thomas Academy	3	4	7
	Zach Schroeder	St. Thomas Academy	3	4	7
	Jared Thomas	Hermantown	3	4	7
	Andrew Mattson	Hermantown	3	4	7
	Jason Samuelson	Rochester Lourdes	1	6	7

Leading Scorers by Year (cont)

YEAR	NAME	SCHOOL	GOALS	ASSISTS	POINTS
2012-AA	Grant Besse	Benilde-St. Margaret	8	3	11
2012-A	Alex Funk	Rochester Lourdes	4	4	8
2013 -AA	Zach LaValle	Hill-Murray	2	3	5
	Grant Weiss	Moorhead	3	2	5
	Aaron Herdt	Moorhead	2	3	5
	Thomas Carey	Moorhead	1	4	5
	Alex Toscano	Duluth East	3	2	5
	Connor Hurley	Edina	3	2	5
	Dylan Malmquist	Edina	3	2	5
2013-A	Matt Perry	St. Thomas Academy	7	3	10
2014-AA	Dylan Malmquist	Edina	4	4	8
	Tyler Nanne	Edina	4	4	8
2014-A	Austin Isaacson	New Prague	3	6	9
2015 - AA	Peter Tufto	St. Thomas Academy	4	5	9
	Nick Poehling	Lakeville North	1	8	9
2015-A	Dixon Bowen	East Grand Forks	3	6	9

MOST POINTS SCORED DURING A TOURNAMENT CAREER

Rank	Name	School	Years	Goals	Assists	Total
1	John Mayasich	Eveleth	1948-51	36	10	46
2	Dave Spehar	Duluth East	1994-96	20	9	29
3	Ben Hanowski	Little Falls	2005-08	19	9	28
	Johnny Pohl	Red Wing	1995-98	11	17	28
5	John Matchefts	Eveleth	1946-49	14	12	26
6	Mike Antonovich	Greenway	1967-69	12	10	22
7	Alex Funk	Roch. Lourdes	2010-13	11	10	21
	Jason Samuelson	Roch. Lourdes	2010-13	5	16	21
9	Aaron Broten	Roseau	1977-79	10	10	20
10	Chris Locker	Duluth East	1995-96	4	15	19
	Ryan Miller	Fergus Falls	2000-02	13	6	19
12	Mike Castellano	Eveleth	1950-53	7	11	18
	Tom Moore	Red Wing	1996-98	12	6	18
	T.J. Oshie	Warroad	2003-05	7	11	18
	Shea Walters	Hibbing	2003-04	7	11	18
	Doug Woog	So. St. Paul	1959-62	11	7	18
17	John Bader	Irondale	1979-80	6	11	17
	Brock Nelson	Warroad	2008-10	9	8	17
19	Todd Lecy	Roch. J.M.	1977-79	8	8	16
	Anders Lee	STA; Edina	2005-09	4	12	16
	Drew Walters	Hibbing	2003-04	7	9	16
	Jared Thomas	Hermantown	2010-12	5	11	16
	Nick Poehling	Lakeville North	2013-15	5	11	16

MOST POINTS SCORED DURING A TOURNAMENT CAREER (CONT.)

Rank	Name	School	Years	Goals	Assists	Total
24	Earl Anderson	Roseau	1967-69	10	5	15
	Jamie Langenbrunner	Cloquet	1992-93	4	11	15
	Tom Peluso	Greenway	1968-70	6	9	15
	Erin Roth	Grand Rapids	1974-76	6	9	15
	John Rothstein	Grand Rapids	1974-75	8	7	15
	Don Voce	Eveleth	1949-51	10	5	15
	Brandon Harrington	Roch. Lourdes	2000-03	9	6	15
	Dixon Bowen	E. Grand Forks	2014-15	5	10	15
32	Jim Amidon	Int'l Falls	1962-63	6	8	14
	Scott Bloom	Burnsville	1984-86	8	6	14
	Ron Castellano	Eveleth	1949-51	4	10	14
	Matt Cullen	Moorhead	1993-95	6	8	14
	Sam Gibbons	Warroad	1948-49	8	6	14
	Drew LeBlanc	Hermantown	2006-07	7	7	14
	Mike Lundbohm	Roseau	1966-68	9	5	14
	Buster Oshie	Warroad	1948-49	8	6	14
	Jake Randolph	Duluth East	2010-12	4	10	14
	Dylan Malmquist	Edina	2013-15	6	8	14

MOST POINTS SCORED IN A SINGLE TOURNAMENT

Points	Name	School	Goals	Assists	Year
18	John Mayasich	Eveleth	15	3	1951
14	John Matchefts	Eveleth	9	5	1948
13	Wally Grant	Eveleth	9	4	1945
	Pat Finnegan	Eveleth	8	5	1945
	Jamie Langenbrunner	Cloquet	3	10	1993 (Tier I)
	Sergei Petrov	Cloquet	6	7	1993 (Tier I)
	Dave Spehar	Duluth East	9	4	1996 (AA)
12	John Mayasich	Eveleth	11	1	1950
	Ray Beauchamp	Williams	5	7	1950
	Aaron Broten	Roseau	6	6	1979
11	John Mayasich	Eveleth	7	4	1949
	Jack Petroske	Hibbing	3	8	1952
	Craig Sarner	No. St. Paul	2	9	1967
	Joe Micheletti	Hibbing	7	4	1973
	Chris Locker	Duluth East	2	9	1996 (AA)
	Johnny Pohl	Red Wing	3	8	1998 (A)
	Blake Wheeler	Breck	6	5	2004 (A)
	Brock Nelson	Warroad	6	5	2010 (A)
	Grant Besse	Benilde-St. Marg.	8	3	2012 (AA)

MOST POINTS SCORED IN A SINGLE TOURNAMENT (CONT.)

Points	Name	School	Goals	Assists	Year
10	Erin Roth	Grand Rapids	3	7	1975
	Jon Bader	Irondale	4	6	1979
	Scott Bloom	Burnsville	5	5	1986
	Mark Amundsen	Lake of Woods	6	4	1993 (Tier II)
	Aaron Novak	Cloquet	7	3	1993 (Tier I)
	Brian Bolf	Hibbing	2	8	1994 (A)
	Jesse Sampair	Mahtomedi	4	6	1994 (A)
	Dom Talarico	Proctor	3	7	1997 (A)
	Ben Hanowski	Little Falls	7	3	2008 (A)
	Brandon Zurn	Mahtomedi	5	5	2010 (A)
	Matt Perry	St. Thomas	7	3	2013 (A)

MOST GOALS IN A SINGLE TOURNEY

Goals	Name	School	Year
15	John Mayasich	Eveleth	1951
11	John Mayasich	Eveleth	1950
9	Wally Grant	Eveleth	1945
	John Matchefts	Eveleth	1948
	Dave Spehar	Duluth East	1995 (AA)
	Dave Spehar	Duluth East	1996 (AA)
8	Pat Finnegan	Eveleth	1945
	Dick Jinks	St. Paul Harding	1954
	Bryan Benedict	Orono	1993 (Tier II)
	Ryan Kraft	Moorhead	1994 (AA)
	Grant Besse	Benilde-St. Marg.	2012 (AA)
7	John Mayasich	Eveleth	1949
	George Jetty	Hibbing	1952
	Oscar Mahle	Int'l Falls	1957
	Mike Antonovich	Greenway	1969
	Joe Micheletti	Hibbing	1973
	Aaron Novak	Cloquet	1993 (Tier I)
	Brandon Sampair	Mahtomedi	1994 (A)
	Ryan Dolder	Hutchinson	1995 (A)
	Mike Klema	Roseau	1999 (AA)
	Ryan Miller	Fergus Falls	2001 (A)
	Ben Hanowski	Little Falls	2008 (A)
	Marshall Everson	Edina	2009 (AA)
	Ben Hanowski	Little Falls	2009 (A)
	Matt Perry	St. Thomas Acad.	2013 (A)

Most Goals in a Single Tourney (cont)

Goals	Name	School	Year
6	Neil Celley	Eveleth	1945
	Rube Bjorkman	Roseau	1947
	Tony Tassoni	Eveleth	1948
	Sam Gibbons	Warroad	1949
	Stu Anderson	St. Paul Johnson	1954
	Dave Frank	Int'l Falls	1957
	Ken Pederson	So. St. Paul	1958
	Dan Cullen	Int'l Falls	1959
	Bob Boysen	Alex. Ramsey	1963
	Earl Anderson	Roseau	1968
	Aaron Broten	Roseau	1979
	Scott Bjugstad	Irondale	1979
	Scott Richart	Irondale	1980
	Jason Miller	Bloom. Kennedy	1987
	Joe Bianchi	Bloom. Jefferson	1992 (Tier I)
	Sergei Petrov	Cloquet	1993 (Tier I)
	Mark Amundsen	Lake of the Woods	1993 (Tier II)
	Joe Lolich	Hibbing	1994 (A)
	Tom Moore	Red Wing	1998 (AA)
	Troy Riddle	Benilde-St. Marg.	1999 (A)
	Ryan Miller	Fergus Falls	2001 (A)
	Dan Kronick	Holy Angels	2002 (AA)
	Blake Wheeler	Breck	2004 (A)
	Scott Kozlak	Duluth Marshall	2005 (A)
	Chris Hickey	Cretin-Derham	2006 (AA)
	Ryan Walters	St. Thomas Acad.	2008 (A)
	Brock Nelson	Warroad	2010 (A)

Most Assists in a Single Tournament

Assists	Name	School	Year
10	Jamie Langenbrunner	Cloquet	1993 (Tier I)
9	Craig Sarner	No. St. Paul	1967
	Chris Locker	Duluth East	1996 (AA)
8	Jack Petroske	Hibbing	1952
	Brian Bolf	Hibbing	1994 (A)
	Johnny Pohl	Red Wing	1998 (A)
	Anders Lee	Edina	2009 (AA)
	Tyson Fulton	Breck	2010 (A)
	Nick Poehling	Lakeville North	2015 (AA)

Assists	Name	School	Year
7	Ray Beauchamp	Williams	1950
	Erin Roth	Grand Rapids	1975
	Sergei Petrov	Cloquet	1993 (Tier I)
	Derek Locker	Duluth East	1995 (AA)
	Dom Talarico	Proctor	1997 (A)
	Jack Stang	St. Thomas Acad.	2013 (A)
6	Ron Castellano	Eveleth	1951
	Bob Miggins	Int'l Falls	1957
	Bob Collyard	Hibbing	1967
	Mike Antonovich	Greenway	1968
	Aaron Broten	Roseau	1979
	John Bader	Irondale	1979
	Tony Kellin	Grand Rapids	1981
	Steve Bianchi	Grand Rapids	1982
	Todd Okerlund	Burnsville	1983
	John Young	So. St. Paul	1987
	Kevin Degel	Bloom. Jefferson	1988
	Andy Hemenway	Mahtomedi	1994 (A)
	Jesse Sampair	Mahtomedi	1994 (A)
	Chris Locker	Duluth East	1995 (AA)
	Josh Heppner	Warroad	1996 (A)
	Matt Hendricks	Blaine	1999 (AA)
	Jimmy Kilpatrick	Holy Angels	2002 (AA)
	Shea Walters	Hibbing	2003 (A)
	Kyle Hardwick	Warroad	2004 (A)
	Ben Kinne	Cretin-Derham Hall	2006 (AA)
	Matt Reber	Edina	2007 (AA)
	Garrett Grimstad	Rochester Century	2007 (AA)
	Conor Rooney	St. Thomas Academy	2008 (A)
	Ben Marshall	Mahtomedi	2010 (A)
	Jack Morrisette	White Bear Lake	2011 (AA)
	Jason Samuelson	Rochester Lourdes	2011 (A)
	Jack Daughterty	St. Thomas Acad.	2013 (A)
	Neal Pionk	Hermantown	2013 (A)
	Austin Isaacson	New Prague	2014 (A)
	Ryan Kero	Hermantown	2015 (A)
	Dixon Bowen	East Grand Forks	2015 (A)

Most Saves by a Goalie
in a Single Game

Saves	Goalie	School	Year/Opponent/Outcome
65	Karl Goehring	Apple Valley	1996/Duluth East/won 5-4 (5 OT)
61	Doug Long	St. Paul Johnson	1970/Greenway-Col./won 4-3 (5 OT)
58	Mason Campion	Marshall	2013/Duluth-Marshall/lost 4-1
54	Murray MacPherson	Edina-Mrnngside	1956/Thief River Falls/lost 3-2 (3 OT)
52	Doug Long	St. Paul Johnson	1970/Edina/lost 2-1 (3 OT)
50	Roger Evenson	Mpls. South	1955/Thief River Falls/won 3-2 (11 OT)
50	Jim Nelson	Roseau	1966/St. Paul Johnson/won 5-3 (3 OT)
50	Alex Kangas	Rochester Cntry	2005/White Bear Lake/lost 2-1
49	Jim Mattson	St. Louis Park	1949/Warroad/lost 10-0
48	Gary Aulik	Edina-East	1978/Grand Rapids/won 5-4 (2 OT)
48	Chris Sall	Duluth East	2005/Moorhead/lost 4-1
47	Tom Moran	Bloom. Jefferson	1985/Minnetonka/won 4-3 (4 OT)
46	Gary Flasch	St. Paul Harding	1972/So. St. Paul//lost 4-2
45	Terry Smith	Bloomington	1965/International Falls/lost 7-0
45	Ted Fresvik	White Bear Lake	1990/Bloom. Kennedy/won 5-4 (2 OT)
45	Nick Malvin	Blaine	2011/White Bear Lake//lost 4-3 (2 OT)
44	Ben Allen	Alexandria	2011/Hermantown/lost 5-1
43	Al Morrison	White Bear Lake	1970/No. St. Paul/lost 1-0 (3 OT)
43	Pat Farrington	Henry Sibley	1975/Grand Rapids/lost 8-3
42	Dick Doyle	White Bear Lake	1949/Eveleth/lost 6-0
42	Jerry Gangloff	Mpls. Roosevelt	1956/International Falls/lost 3-2 (3 OT)
42	Karl Mattson	Hutchinson	1997/Warroad/lost 7-3
42	Matt Klein	Hastings	2000/Edina//won 4-2 (2 OT)
42	Brandon Wigen	Woodbury	2008/Benilde-St. Marg./lost 4-1
42	Jim Kruger	Minnetonka	2010/Hill-Murray/won 2-1 (4 OT)
42	Charlie Lindgren	Lakeville North	2010/Minnetonka/lost 6-1
42	Kendall Meyer	Luverne	2013/Hermantown/lost 6-3

Most Saves by a Goalie
in a Single Tournament

Saves	Goalie	School	Year
124	Doug Long	St. Paul Johnson	1970
119	Jim Nelson	Roseau	1966
109	Murray MacPherson	Edina-Morningside	1956
108	Charlie Lindgren	Lakeville North	2011 (AA)
107	Robb Stauber	Duluth Denfeld	1986
106	Terry Smith	Bloomington	1965
	Karl Goehring	Apple Valley	1996 (AA)
105	Rudy Lindbeck	South St. Paul	1948

Saves	Goalie	School	Year
104	Kendall Meyer	Luverne	2013
99	Bill Bieber	Edina-Morningside	1960
	Len Eagon	Hill-Murray	1976
	Reggie Miracle	Columbia Heights	1983
	Troy Ricci	Lake of the Woods	1993 (Tier II)
98	Matt Klein	Hastings	2000 (AA)
	Chris Sall	Duluth East	2005 (AA)
97	Peter Waselovich	International Falls	1972
96	Jim Boosalis	Mpls. Washburn	1962
95	Bob Lewis	Warroad	1953
	Jim Metzen	South St. Paul	1962
	Mike Dibble	Mpls. Southwest	1972
93	Larry Price	Mpls. Roosevelt	1958
	Carl Bloomberg	Bloom. Kennedy	1976
92	Paul Butters	Roch. John Marshall	1977
	Jon Downing	Irondale	1981
	Alex Kangas	Rochester Century	2005 (AA)
	Mason Campion	Marshall	2013
91	Michael Stumpf	Little Falls	2012
88	Roger Evenson	Mpls. South	1955
	Jim Quirk	South St. Paul	1965
	Keaton Smith	Holy Angels	2005 (AA)
87	Greg Page	St. Paul Murray	1963
	Chris Langenbrunner	Cloquet	1982
	Dominic Wippler	Totino-Grace	2014

Most Tourney Saves Career by Goalie

Rank	Goalie	School	Years	Games	Total Saves
1	Jim Nelson	Roseau	1965-67	8	252
2	Peter Waselovich	Int'l Falls	1971-73	9	241
3	Paul Butters	Roch. J.M.	1977-79	9	241
4	Henry Metcalf	So. St. Paul	1953-55	9	202
5	Willard Ikola	Eveleth	1947-50	12	192
6	Brad Shelstad	Mpls. S.W.	1968-70	9	189
7	Gary McAlpine	So. St. Paul	1959-61	9	188
8	Doug Long	St. Paul Johnson	1970-71	6	184
9	Michael Sperl	Little Falls	2006-09	9	182 (A)
10	Charlie Lindgren	Lakeville North	2010-11	6	171 (AA)
11	Terry Smith	Bloomington	1964-65	5	166
12	Tom Wahman	St. Paul Johnson	1954-56	9	165
	Jim Quirk	So. St. Paul	1965-66	6	165
14	Jim Jetland	Grand Rapids	1976-78	9	161

Rank	Goalie	School	Years	Games	Total Saves
15	Matt Klein	Hastings	1999-00	6	159 (AA)
	Mike Lee	Roseau	2006-08	6	159 (AA)
17	Murray MacPherson	Edina-M'side	1955-56	5	158
	Aaron Crandall	St. Thomas	2006-07	6	158 (A)
19	Derrick Caschetta	Edina	2007-08	6	157 (AA)
20	Kip Myre	Richfield	1963-64	6	155
21	Nick Heimer	Rochester Lourdes	2009-11	8	152 (A)
22	Roger Evenson	Mpls. South	1954-55	6	151
23	Jake Kluver	Little Falls	2005-06	6	148 (A)
24	Jeff Wizner	Bemidji	1972-74	7	146
25	Blake Burgau	New Ulm	2010-11	4	145 (A)
26	Brad Wohlers	Mahtomedi	2009-10	5	143 (A)
27	Rick Horvath	Hill-Murray	1985-86	6	142
	Ron Schuldt	St. Cloud Tech	1950-51	6	142
29	Kevin Powell	Hill-Murray	1991-92	6	141 (one-class; Tier I)
30	Nathan Hardy	Hermantown	2006-07	6	140 (A)
	Jon Michelizzi	Duluth Denfeld	1988-89	5	140 (AA)
	David Zevnik	St. Thomas Acad.	2011-13	9	140 (A)
33	Gary Flasch	St. Paul Harding	1972-73	5	139
	Dean Grindahl	Roseau	1977-78	6	139
	JoJoe Jeanetta	Duluth East	2009-11	8	139 (AA)
36	Jim Wherley	Int'l Falls	1957-59	8	136

JOHN MAYASICH'S STATE TOURNEY RECORDS

Most all-time points scored – 46 (1948-51)
Most all-time goals scored – 36 (1948-51)
Most consecutive games scoring a goal – 12 (1948-51)
Most all-time hat tricks – 7 (1948-51)
Most points one tournament – 18 (1951)
Most goals one tournament – 15 (1951)
Most points one game – 8 (1951)
Most goals one game – 7 (1951)
Most points one period – 5 (1951)

MINNESOTA STATE BOYS HOCKEY TOURNAMENT PARTICIPANTS (1945-2015)

Academy of Holy Angels – 1999 AA, 2002 AA, 2003 AA, 2004 AA, 2005 AA
Albert Lea – 2004 A, 2005 A, 2007 A
Alexander Ramsey – 1963, 1964, 1965, 1971, 1972, 1973
Alexandria – 1992 II, 1996 AA, 2010 A, 2011 A
Anoka – 1985, 1990, 1978 AA, 1998 AA, 2003 AA
Apple Valley – 1981, 1992 I, 1993 I, 1996 AA, 2010 AA
Austin/Austin Pacelli – 1993 I, 2001 AA
Bemidji – 1972, 1973, 1974, 1976, 1985, 1986, 2015 AA
Benilde-St. Margaret's – 1999 A, 2001 A, 2008 AA, 2012 AA
Blaine – 1992 I, 1996 AA, 1999 AA, 2000 AA, 2006 AA, 2007 AA, 2008
   AA, 2009 AA, 2010 AA, 2011 AA, 2015 AA
Blake – 1995 A, 1999 A, 2006 A, 2007 A, 2008 A
Bloomington – 1961, 1964, 1965
Bloomington Jefferson – 1980, 1981, 1982, 1985, 1986, 1988, 1989, 1992
   I, 1993 I, 1994 AA, 1995 AA, 1997 AA, 1998 AA, 2000 AA, 2002 AA,
   2005 AA
Bloomington Kennedy – 1966, 1976, 1983, 1984, 1987, 1990, 1991
Bloomington Lincoln – 1975
Breck – 1994 A, 1996 A, 1997 A, 2000 A, 2004 A, 2009 A, 2010 A, 2011
   A, 2012 A, 2013 A, 2015 A
Burnsville – 1983, 1984, 1985, 1986, 1987, 1990, 1991, 2007 AA
Cambridge – 1992 II
Centennial – 2004 AA, 2013 AA, 2014 AA
Champlin Park – 1995 AA
Chisago Lakes – 1995 A, 2014 A
Cloquet – 1982
Cloquet/Esko/Carlton – 1992 I, 1993 I, 2002 AA, 2008 AA
Columbia Heights – 1983
Cretin-Derham Hall – 1988, 2006 AA, 2009 AA
Detroit Lakes – 1995 A, 1996 A
Duluth Central – 1954, 1996 A
Duluth Denfeld – 1986, 1988, 1989
Duluth East – 1958, 1960, 1961, 1964, 1975, 1991, 1994 AA, 1995-98 AA,
   2000 AA, 2003 AA, 2004 AA, 2005 AA, 2009 (AA), 2010-15 (AA)
Eagan – 2006 AA, 2011 AA, 2012 AA, 2014 AA
East Grand Forks – 1971, 1980, 1982, 1998 A, 1999 A, 2001 A, 2002 A,
   2013 A, 2014 A, 2015 A
Eastview – 2001 AA, 2013 AA
Eden Prairie – 1992 I, 1999 AA, 2001 AA, 2003 AA, 2009 AA, 2011 AA,
   2014 AA, 2015 AA
Edina-Morningside – 1955, 1956, 1957, 1960, 1962

Edina – 1967-72, 1982-84, 1987-89, 1995-98 AA, 2000 AA, 2007-15 AA
Edina-East – 1973, 1974, 1977, 1978, 1979
Edina-West – 1981
Elk River – 2005 AA
Elk River Area – 1993 I, 1999 AA, 2001 AA, 2002 AA, 2004 AA
Eveleth – 1945-56, 1960
Eveleth-Gilbert – 1993 I, 1998 A
Faribault/Bethlehem Academy – 1993 II
Farmington – 1994 A, 2000 A
Fergus Falls – 1997 A, 1998 A, 1999 A, 2001 A, 2002 A, 2003 A
Frank B. Kellogg – 1974
Grand Rapids – 1972, 1974, 1975, 1976, 1977, 1978, 1979, 1980, 1981, 1988, 1990, 1991, 2006 AA, 2007 AA
Granite Falls – 1945, 1946
Greenway-Coleraine – 1962, 1966, 1967, 1968, 1969, 1970, 1987
Greenway-Coleraine/Nashwauk-Keewatin – 1992 I, 2001 AA
Hallock – 1957, 1961
Hastings – 1971, 1985, 1998 AA, 1999 AA, 2000 AA, 2001 AA
Henry Sibley – 1973, 1974, 1975, 1976, 1982, 1983, 1993 I, 1997 AA
Hermantown – 1994 A, 1998 A, 1999 A, 2001 A, 2006 A, 2007 A, 2010 A, 2011 A, 2012 A, 2013 A, 2014 A, 2015 A
Hibbing – 1952, 1967, 1970, 1973, 1974, 1982, 1984, 1985, 1986, 1994 A, 2003 A, 2004 A
Hibbing/Chisholm – 2011 A
Hill-Murray – 1975-80, 1983-88, 1991, 1992 I, 1993 I, 1997 AA, 1999 AA, 2000 AA, 2002 AA, 2006-10 AA, 2012 AA, 2013 AA, 2015 AA
Hopkins Lindbergh – 1975, 1980
Hutchinson – 1995 A, 1997 A, 2000 A
Hutchinson/New Century Charter School – 2009 A
International Falls – 1950, 1956-59, 1962-66, 1968, 1971, 1972, 1973, 1983, 1989, 1995 A, 2000 A, 2002 A
Irondale – 1979, 1980, 1981
Lake of the Woods, Baudette/ Rainy River, Ont – 1993 II
Lakeville – 2002 AA, 2003 AA, 2004 AA
Lakeville North – 2006 AA, 2010 AA, 2011 AA, 2013 AA, 2014 AA, 2015 AA
Lakeville South – 2008 AA, 2012 AA
Litchfield/Dassel-Cokato – 1996 A, 2008 A
Little Falls – 2005 A, 2006 A, 2007 A, 2008 A, 2009 A, 2012 A
Luverne – 2014 A
Mahtomedi – 1992 II, 1994 A, 1997 A, 1998 A, 2001 A, 2009 A, 2010 A, 2015 A
Mankato East/Loyola – 2006 A
Mankato West – 2008 A
Maple Grove – 2012 AA

Marshall – 2013 A
Marshall School (Duluth) – 2001 A, 2005 A, 2006 A 2007 A, 2008 A, 2012 A, 2013 A
Minneapolis Central – 1949, 1950
Minneapolis Edison – 1994 A
Minneapolis Patrick Henry – 1959, 1960, 1964
Minneapolis Roosevelt – 1956, 1958, 1961, 1963, 1966, 1967, 1974, 1978, 1992 II
Minneapolis South – 1950, 1954, 1955, 1957, 1993 II
Mpls. Southwest – 1951, 1952, 1953, 1955, 1965, 1968, 1969, 1970, 1971, 1972, 1973, 1975, 1976, 1977, 1980
Mpls. Washburn – 1948, 1949, 1959, 1960, 1962, 1979
Minneapolis West – 1946, 1947
Minnetonka – 1985, 1990, 1994 AA, 2006 AA, 2010 AA
Moorhead – 1992 I, 1993 I, 1994 AA, 1995 AA, 1997 AA, 2001 AA, 2002 AA, 2003 AA, 2004 AA, 2005 AA, 2009 AA, 2011 AA, 2012 AA, 2013 AA
Mora/Hinckley-Finlayson – 1996 A, 1997 A
Mound Westonka – 1998 A, 2001 A
Mounds View – 1968, 1969, 1976, 1977, 1978 ,
New Prague – 2014 A, 2015 A
New Ulm (New Ulm/New Ulm Cathedral/MN Valley Lutheran – 2010 A, 2011 A, 2012 A, 2015 A
New Ulm/New Ulm Cathedral – 1992 II
North St. Paul – 1961, 1967, 1970, 1981
Orono – 1992 II, 1993 II, 2002-04 A, 2006 A, 2007 A, 2014 A
Osseo – 1994 AA
Owatonna – 1998 AA
Park Center – 1993 I
Princeton – 2002 A, 2003 A
Proctor/Albrook, Saginaw – 1997 A
Red Wing – 1995 A, 1996 A, 1997 A, 1998 A, 1999 A, 2002 A
Richfield – 1962, 1963, 1964, 1976, 1986, 1991
Robbinsdale – 1959
Rochester – 1945, 1946, 1947, 1948
Rochester Century – 2005 AA, 2007 AA, 2009 AA
Rochester John Marshall – 1977, 1978, 1979, 1988, 1989, 1996 AA
Rochester Lourdes – 2003 A
Rochester Lourdes/Stewartville – 2010 A, 2011 A, 2012 A, 2013A
Rochester Lourdes/Stewartville/Chatfield – 2009 A
Rochester Lourdes/Stewartville/Chatfield/Plainview – 2000 A, 2001 A, 2002 A
Rochester Mayo – 1982, 1992 I, 1994 AA, 1995 AA, 1997 AA, 1999 AA, 2000 AA
Roseau – 1946, 1947, 1953, 1955, 1957-69, 1971, 1975, 1977-79, 1981,

1983, 1984, 1990, 1991, 1998 AA, 1999 AA, 2000 AA, 2006 AA, 2007 AA, 2008 AA, 2010 AA, 2014 AA

Rosemount – 1992 II

Roseville Area – 1987, 2002 AA, 2003 AA

St. Cloud Apollo – 1984, 2013 AA, 2015 A

St. Cloud Cathedral – 1993 II, 1994 A, 2004 A, 2008 A, 2009 A, 2014 A

St. Cloud Tech – 1945, 1946, 1947, 1948, 1950, 1951, 1952

St. Louis Park – 1948, 1949, 1953, 1958, 1998 A, 2003 A

St. Paul Harding – 1948, 1954, 1958, 1969, 1972, 1973, 1974, 1979

St. Paul Humboldt – 1952, 1953

St. Paul Johnson – 1946, 1947, 1951-57, 1959, 1961, 1963-68, 1970, 1971, 1984, 1991, 1995 AA

St. Paul Monroe – 1962

St. Paul Murray – 1949, 1950, 1951, 1957, 1958, 1963

St. Paul Washington – 1945, 1956, 1960

St. Thomas Academy – 1999 A, 2005 A, 2006 A, 2007 A, 2008 A, 2011 A, 2012 A, 2013 A, 2015 AA

Sauk Rapids-Rice – 2000 A

Shakopee – 2005 A

Silver Bay – 1999 A

Simley – 1996 A, 2003 A

South St. Paul –1947, 1948, 1950, 1953, 1954, 1955, 1957-62, 1965, 1966, 1968, 1969, 1972, 1977, 1978, 1980, 1981, 1986, 1987, 1989, 1990, 1994 AA, 1996 AA, 2004 A

Spring Lake Park – 2015 A

Staples – 1945

Stillwater – 2014 AA

Tartan – 2004 AA, 2005 AA

Thief River Falls – 1945, 1951, 1952, 1954, 1955, 1956, 1959, 1960, 1965

Thief River Falls/Goodridge – 2006 A, 2011 A, 2012 A

Totino-Grace – 1993 II, 1995 A, 2002 A, 2005 A, 2014 A

Virginia/Mt. Iron-Buhl – 2005 A, 2009 A, 2010 A

Wadena-Deer Creek – 2004 A

Warroad – 1948, 1949, 1953, 1963, 1969, 1970, 1987, 1988, 1989, 1994 A, 1995 A, 1996 A, 1997 A, 2000 A, 2003 A, 2004 A, 2005 A, 2007 A, 2008 A, 2009 A, 2010 A, 2011 A

Wayzata – 1954, 2004 AA, 2013 AA

White Bear Lake – 1945, 1946, 1949, 1951, 1956, 1966, 1967, 1970, 1989, 1990, 1994 AA, 1995 AA, 1996 AA, 1998 AA, 2001 AA, 2003 AA, 2005 AA, 2011 AA

White Bear Mariner – 1982

Williams – 1949, 1950, 1951

Willmar – 1947

Winona – 1952

Woodbury – 2007 AA, 2008 AA

State Boys Hockey Tournament
Head Coaches (1945-2015)

Abram, Terry, Roseau, 1971, 75, 77

Alm, Rick, Minneapolis South, 1993

Almquist, Oscar, Roseau, 1946, 47, 53, 55, 57-59, 61-67

Amundson, John, Lake of the Woods, 1993

Anderson, Dick, St. Paul Harding, 1969, 72, 73, 74

Anderson, Shawn, Farmington, 1994, 2000

Antonovich, Mike, St. Cloud Cathedral, 1994

Armstrong, Kevin, Orono, 1992, 93, 2002, 03

Ashby, Jr., Cliff, Hermantown, 1994

Aslakson, Greg, Mora/Hinckley-Finlayson, 1996, 97

Aus, David, Blaine, 2006-2011

Aus, Erik, Centennial, 2004

Aus, Peter, Blaine, 2009, 10, 11

Aus, Whitey, F.B. Kellogg, 1974

Balfour, David, Detroit Lakes, 1995, 96

Bauer, Arnie, North St. Paul, 1961

Bauer, Pete, Simley, 1966

Bauer, Wes, North St. Paul, 1967

Benson, Tom, Spring Lake Park, 2015

Bergland, Tim, Fergus Falls, 2003; T.RF., 2011, 2012

Bergland, Scott, Thief River Falls/Goodridge, 2006

Bergstrom, Brad, Fergus Falls, 1997, 98, 99, 2000, 01, 02

Bergstrom, Terry, Bloomington Lincoln, 1975

Birrenkott, John, Anoka, 1997, 98

Bjorkman, Rube, Greenway-Coleraine, 1962

Bjugstad, Scott, Blaine, 1999, 2000

Blais, Dean, Roseau, 1990, 91

Boeser, Bob, Bloomington Lincoln, 1965

Bolin, Wes, Woodbury, 2007, 08

Bourdeau, Don, Duluth East, 1975

Boysen, Bob, Henry Sibley, 1973, 74, 75, 76

Bradley, Drey, Eastview, 2013

Bradley, R.P., White Bear Lake, 1945, 46, 49

Braga, Al, Williams, 1949, 1950, 51

Broderick, Bernie, Warroad, 1948, 49, 53; St. Paul Murray, 1957, 58, 67

Broten, Aaron, Roseau, 2000

Brown, Derrick, Luverne, 2014

Brown, Harry, Minneapolis Patrick Henry, 1964

Budge, Rick, East Grand Forks, 1971

Burns, Terry, International Falls, 1989

Burroughs, Charlie, Minneapolis Edison, 1994

Butters, Bill, White Bear Lake, 2001

Campbell, John, Wayzata, 1954

Carlson, Carl, Minneapolis Washburn, 1949, 59, 60

Carroll, Chris, Blaine, 2015

Chapman, Wally, Breck, 1994, 96, 97, 2000, 04

Chiodo, Wade, Bemidji, 2015

Christensen, Rod, Grand Rapids, 1980

Cotroneo, Lou, St. Paul Johnson, 1964, 65, 66, 67, 68, 70, 71

Coudert, Dave, Marshall, 2013

Couture, Tony, Little Falls, 2005, 06, 07, 08, 09, 12

Cullen, Pete, Moorhead, 2013

Cullen, Terry, Moorhead, 1992, 93, 94, 95, 97

Dahlof, Ray, Osseo, 1994

Davey, Merlin, Rochester, 1947, 48

Davis, Carl, Wayzata, 2004

Davis, Jim, St. Paul Harding, 1979

DeCenzo, Mark, Apple Valley, 1992, 93; Hibbing, 1994, 2003, 04, 11

DePaul, Robert, International Falls, 1950

Dillner, M.C., Minneapolis Washburn, 1948

Doig, Tom, Burnsville, 1991

Doman, Matt, Stillwater, 2014

Donahue, Mike, Alexandria, 1992

Donahue, Tim, St. Louis Park, 1998, 2003

Eades, Cary, Warroad, 1994, 95, 96, 97, 2000, 03, 04

Eigner, Trent, Lakeville North, 2013-15

Eklund, Wayne, Eden Prairie, 1992

Ellingson, Lyn, Grand Rapids, 1988, 90-1

Erickson, John, Minnetonka, 1985, 90

Essay, Ken, Mankato West, 2008

Head Coaches (1945-2015)

Esse, David, Cloquet/Esko/Carlton, 2002, 08

Fermoyle, Dennis, Warroad, 2005

Flaherty, Brendan, Duluth Central, 1996, 2001; Marshall School 2005, 06, 07, 08, 12, 13

Franke, Todd, St. Cloud Cathedral, 1993

Frederick, Todd, Princeton, 2002, 03

Freeburg, Clayton, Minneapolis Roosevelt, 1967, 74, 78

Frerker, Bob, Rochester John Marshall, 1988, 89

Froiland, Elly, Columbia Heights, 1983

Frutiger, Bruce, Rochester John Marshall, 1996; Rochester Century, 2005, 07, 09

Funk, Mike, Mounds View, 1978

Gavin, William, St. Paul Harding, 1978

Genz, Gordy, Alexander Ramsey, 1963, 64, 65, 71, 72, 73; Roseville Area, 1987

Gernander, Bob, Greenway-Coleraine, 1967, 68, 69, 70, 87

Gibbons, Mike, Eastview, 2001

Gibson, Paul, Chisago Lakes, 2014

Giles, Curt, Edina, 2000, 2007-2015

Gill, Aaron, Rochester Lourdes, 2009

Gordon, Kevin, International Falls, 1995, 2000, 02

Grafstrom, Myron, Warroad, 1963

Grand, Bryan, Bemidji, 1985, 86

Greer, Ted, Edina-Morningside, 1955, 56

Grillo, Chuck, Bemidji, 1974, 76

Grina, Todd, Hutchinson, 1995, 97, 2000

Grosso, Lorne, Rochester Mayo, 1982, 92, 94, 95, 97, 99, 2000

Rube Gustafson, St. Paul Johnson, 1946, 47, 51-57, 59, 61, 63

Guyer, Pat, Greenway-Coleraine/N.K., 1992, 2001

Guyer, Tim, Henry Sibley, 1997

Guzzo, Mike, Silver Bay, 1999

Halbrehder, Bill, North St. Paul, 1970, 81

Hamre, John, Blake, 2006, 07, 08

Hasbargen, Albert, Warroad, 2005, 07, 08, 09, 10

Haskins, Bob, Rochester Lourdes, 2003

Hayes, Jerry, Apple Valley, 2010

Hendrickson, Gus, Grand Rapids, 1972, 74, 75

Hendrickson, Keith, Virginia/Mt. Iron-Buhl, 2005, 09, 10

Hendrickson, Larry, Richfield, 1976; Apple Valley, 1981, 96

Hokanson, Gary, Roseau, 1978, 79, 81, 83, 84

Homola, Craig, Eveleth-Gilbert, 1998

Houck, D.A., Minneapolis West, 1946

Humphrey, John, Tartan, 2004, 05

Hurt, Steve, White Bear Lake, 1998

Ikola, Willard, Edina (East), 1960, 62, 67, 68-74, 77-79, 82-84, 87-89

Jaskowiak, Blake, Boomington Lincoln, 1961, 64

Jerome, Tom, Alexandria, 1996

Jocketty, Peter, Mpls Washburn, 1979

Johnson, Art, St. Paul Monroe, 1962

Johnson, Bob, Mpls Roosevelt, 1958, 61, 63

Johnson, Curt, Blaine, 1992

Johnson, Eric, St. Cloud Cathedral, 2008, 09, 14

Karn, George, South St. Paul, 1953-55, 57

Kendig, Bucky, St. Paul Johnson, 1991, 95

Kennedy, Bill, Cloquet, 1982

King, Tom, Warroad, 1978, 88, 89

Kivihalme, Janne, Burnsville, 2007

Klein, Dave, Mound-Westonka, 2001

Klein, Tom, Minnetonka, 1994

Kochevar, Bob, Eveleth-Gilbert, 1993

Kogi, Rudy, Minneapolis South, 1954, 55, 57

Koski, Wayne, Staples, 1945

Kottke, Larry, St. Cloud, 1948, 50, 51

Lackner, John, St. Paul Washington, 1945

Lagoo, Jeff, South St. Paul, 2004

LaRoque, Bruce, Grand Rapids, 2006, 07

Larson, Bart, Edina West, 1981; Edina, 1995, 96, 97, 98

Larson, Les, Breck, 2009-13, 15

Larson, Steve, Blaine, 1996, 99, 2000

Laumeyer, Dennis, Austin, 1993, 2001

Lechner, Bill, Hill-Murray, 1999, 2000, 02, 06, 07, 08, 09, 10, 12, 13, 15

Lehn, Lloyd, Willmar, 1947

Lindquist, Jeff, Blake, 1995, 99; Bloomington Jefferson, 2005

Liston, Ed, St. Paul Humboldt, 1952, 53

Loahr, Mark, Totino-Grace, 1993, 95, 2002, 05, 14

Loiselle, Ed, Shakopee, 2005

Lonke, Chris, Simley, 2003; New Prague, 2014, 15

Head Coaches (1945-2015)

Louricas, Pete, White Bear Lake, 1951, 56

Lund, Dave, Hopkins Lindbergh, 1975, 80

Lundbohm, Andy, Roseau, 2010, 14

Macho, Tom, New Ulm/Cathedral, 1992

Macioh, Francis, Roseau, 1968, 69

Magnuson, Rod, St. Paul Johnson, 1984

Manley, Dave, Mounds View, 1979, 80, 81

Manthey, Todd, Anoka, 2003

Markley, Joe, Minneapolis Central, 1949, 50

Matanich, Pete, St. Cloud Apollo, 2013, 15

Matchefts, John, Thief River Falls, 1959; Eveleth, 1960

May, Bob, Minneapolis Roosevelt, 1956

McCarthy, Bill, St. Thomas Academy, 1999

McFadden, Ken, Hallock, 1957

McFarlane, Tom, Cloquet/Esko/Carlton, 1992, 93

McGann, Bill, Proctor, 1997

McLaughlin, Dwight, Minneapolis West, 1947

Menne, Rich, Centennial, 2013, 14

Michaud, Patrick, Mankato East/Loyola, 2006

Miller, Bing, St. Cloud, 1947

Minnelli, Phillip, Granite Falls, 1945, 46

Monsrud, Cliff, Rochester, 1945, 46

Monsrud, Jeff, Mound Westonka, 1998

Morninville, Dave, Moorhead, 2001, 02, 03, 04, 05, 09, 11, 12

Morrison, Vern, St. Cloud, 1945, 46, 47

Moore, Bill, South St. Paul, 1996

Myhrman, Ralph, St. Cloud, 1952

Nataro, Dave, Champlin Park, 1995

Nelson, Jim, Grand Rapids, 1976, 77, 78, 79, 81

Nemanich, George, Red Wing, 1995, 96, 97, 98, 99, 2002

Ness, Jay, Rochester Lourdes, 2000, 01, 02

Nystrom, Roy, Albert Lea, 2004, 05, 07

Odegaard, Andy, Chisago Lakes, 1995

O'Leary, Pat, Wayzata, 2013

Olive, Gene, Richfield, 1962, 63, 64

Oliver, Scott, Roseau, 2006, 07, 08

Olson, Bill, Hibbing, 1984, 85, 86

Olson, Bruce, Roseau, 1998, 99; Warroad, 2007, 08

Olson, Chris, Litchfield/Dassel-Cokato, 2008

O'Neill, Jim Cretin-Derham Hall, 1988, 2006, 09

Orhn, Todd, Faribault/Bethlehem Academy, 1993

Osiecki, Tom Burnsville, 1983, 84, 85, 86, 87, 90

Page, Ralph, South St. Paul, 1947, 48, 50

Palmiscno, Tony, East Grand Forks, 1980, 82

Palmiscno, Tyler, East Grand Forks, 2013, 14, 15

Pauly, Ken, Benilde-St. Margaret's, 1999, 2001, 08, 12; Minnetonka, 2006

Peart, Tom, Minneapolis Roosevelt, 1992

Perpich, George, Hibbing, 1967, 70, 73, 74, 82

Peterson, Dave, Minneapolis Southwest, 1965, 68-73, 75-77, 80

Peterson, Jack, Anoka, 1985

Peterson, Jerry, Bloomington Kennedy, 1976, 83, 84, 87, 90, 91

Plante, Bruce, Hermantown, 1998, 99, 2001, 06, 07, 10-15

Poeschl, Jeff, Mahtomedi, 1998, 2001, 09, 10, 15

Rajanen, Greg, Anoka, 1990

Randolph, Duluth East, 1991, 94-98, 2000, 03, 05, 09, 10-15

Roberts, Dick, Warroad, 1969, 70

Rohlik, Steve, Hill-Murray, 1993, 97

Rolle, Dennis, Thief River Falls, 1951, 52, 54, 55, 56

Rolle, Glenn, Duluth East, 1958, 60, 61, 64

Root, James, Robbinsdale, 1959

Ross, Larry, International Falls, 1956-59, 62-66, 68, 71-73, 83

Rossi, John, St. Paul Harding, 1954, 58

Ryan, Brad, Orono, 2006, 07

Saatzer, Don, Hastings, 1971

Sack, Gene, Thief River Falls, 1960; Rochester John Marshall, 1977, 78, 79

Sager, Tim, White Bear Lake, 2003, 05, 11

Sandberg, Albert, St. Paul Murray, 1949-51

Sarsland, Tony, Elk River, 1993, 99, 2001, 02, 04, 05

Saterdalen, Tom, Bloomington Jefferson, 1980, 81, 82, 85, 86, 88, 89, 92, 93, 94, 95, 97, 98, 2000, 02

Scanlan, Jim, East Grand Forks, 1998, 99, 2001, 02

Head Coaches (1945-2015)

Schey, Martin, Minneapolis South, 1950

Schieff, George, Thief River Falls, 1965

Schmitz, Randy, Lakeville, 2002, 03, 04; Lakeville North, 2006, 10, 11

Schwartz, Mike, White Bear Lake, 1994, 95, 96

Senta, Frank, Rosemount, 1992

Serratore, Tom, Henry Sibley, 1993

Sertich, Steve, Roseville, 2002, 03

Setterholm, Erik, New Ulm, 2010-12, 15

Sharrow, Bob, Bloomington Kennedy, 1966

Shelstad, Jeff, Hastings, 1985

Simpson, Tom, White Bear Mariner, 1982; White Bear Lake Area, 1989, 90

Skrypek, Terry, Hill-Murray, 1975, 76, 77, 78-80, 83-87

Smalley, Jim, Bemidjii, 1972, 73

Smith, Charles (Lefty), South St. Paul, 1958, 59, 60, 61, 62, 65, 66, 68

Smith, Lee, Eden Prairie, 1999, 2001, 03, 09, 11, 14, 15

Smrekar, Bill, Cambridge, 1992

Spaniol, Josh, Rochester Lourdes, 2010, 11, 12, 13

Stanbridge, Connie, Thief River Falls, 1945

Standbrook, Grant, Greenway-Coleraine, 1966

Stefano, Gary, Park Center, 1993; Maple Grove, 2012

Sundin, Michael, Litchfield/Dassel-Cokato, 1996

Taylor, Mike, Eagan, 2006, 11, 12, 14

Telecky, Matt, Hutchinson, 2009

Tutu, Dennis, South St. Paul, 1969, 72, 77

Thomas, Mike, Richfield, 1986, 91

Thompson, Cliff, Eveleth, 1945-56

Thorson, Carl, White Bear Lake, 1966, 67, 70

Trebil, Greg, Holy Angels, 1999, 2002, 03, 04, 05

Turk, Tom, Minneapolis Roosevelt, 1966

Turner, Robert, St. Paul Washington, 1956, 60

Tyler, Stanford, Winona, 1952

Uhrbom, M. J., Hibbing, 1952

Urick, Brian, Minnetonka, 2010

Vannelli, Greg, St. Thomas Academy, 2005-08, 11, 12, 13. 15

Vannelli, Tom, St. Thomas Academy, 2005-08, 11, 12, 13, 15

Voss, Jonathan, St. Cloud Cathedral, 2004

Vucinovich, John, Duluth Central, 1954

Vukonich, Bill, Duluth Denfeld, 1986, 88, 89

Weber, Kurt, Lakeville South, 2008, 12

Wegleitner, Dave, Mounds View, 1968, 69, 76, 77

Weisjahn, Todd, Orono, 2004

Welch, Russ, South St. Paul, 1986, 1987, 1989, 1990, 1994; Hastings, 1998, 99, 2000, 2001

Wellen, Ken, Hallock, 1961

Wentworth, Todd, Duluth East, 2004

Weston, Sheldon, Sauk Rapids-Rice, 2000

Whisler, Jeff, Hill-Murray, 1988, 91; Mahtomedi, 1992, 94, 97

Whitney, Jeff, Rochester Mayo, 1999, 2000

Will, Dennis, Owatonna, 1998

Wohlford, Paul, Minneapolis Southwest, 1951, 52, 53, 55

Woods, Scott, Wadena-Deer Creek, 2004; Alexandria, 2010, 11

Woog, Doug, South St. Paul, 1978, 80, 81

Yackel, Ken, Edina-Morningside, 1957

Yoder, Casey, Orono, 2014

Younghans, Hal, Minneapolis Patrick Henry, 1959, 60

Younghans, Steve, St. Paul Johnson, 1995

Zanna, Peter, St. Louis Park, 1948, 49, 53, 58

Zins, Ed, St. Cloud Apollo, 1984

Zywiec, Joe, Henry Sibley, 1982, 83

State Boys' Hockey Tournament Attendance

1945	8,434	1957	33,041	1969	79,868	1981	100,914
1946	11,035	1958	35,243	1970	83,625	1982	101,006
1947	17,566	1959	36,023	1971	79,362	1983	102,596
1948	19,354	1960	39,488	1972	82,300	1984	100,160
1949	15,471	1961	40,607	1973	84,039	1985	103,096
1950	14,272	1962	41,571	1974	84,210	1986	100,824
1951	18,582	1963	43,061	1975	83,089	1987	100,215
1952	15,523	1964	44,362	1976	92,333	1988	98,718
1953	19,924	1965	43,728	1977	94,772	1989	95,356
1954	25,508	1966	46,016	1978	98,870	1990	97,718
1955	27,213	1967	45,140	1979	100, 902	1991	99,507
1956	30,949	1968	45,369	1980	102,197		

1992 117,573
Tier 1 90,370
Tier 11 27,193

1993 107,030
Tier 1 88,014
Tier 11 19,016

1994 112,846
Class AA 87, 738
Class A 25,108

1995 116,870
Class AA 89,095
Class A 27,775

1996 115,235
Class AA 76,457
Class A 27,3g9

1997 111,800
Class AA 74,729
Class A 26,338
A, AA,Cons. Finals. 10,733

1998 116,155
Class AA 74,902
Class A 29,557
A, AA, cons Finals 11,696

1999 106,307
class AA 12,760
Class A 22,616
A, AA Cons Finals 10,931

2000 106,918
Class AA 74,944
Class A 20,801
A, AA Cons. Finals 11,123

2001 111,273
Class AA 78,551
Class A 21,730
A, AA Cons. Finals 10,992

2002 108,524
Class AA 77,578
Class A 19,937
A, AA Cons. Finals 11,019

2003 115,524
Class AA 81,069
Class A 23,218
A, AA Cons. Finals 11,237

2004 120,114
Class AA 81,879
Class A 26,530
A, AA Cons. Finals 11,705

2005 123,809
Class AA 82,249
Class A 29,475
A, AA Cons Finals 12,085

2006 125,201
Class AA 83,179
Class A 29,929
A, AA Cons. Finals 12,093

2007 124,348
Class AA 82,460
Class A 29,938
A, AA Cons. Finals 11,950

2008 129,643
Class AA 87,355
Class A 30,421
A, AA Cons. Finals 11,867

2009 116,690
Class AA 78,989
Class A 26,750
A, AA Cons. Finals 19,951

2010 118,934
Class AA 81,499
Class A 26,440
A,AA Cons.Finals 10,995

2011 116,662
Class AA 80,214
Class A 25,903
A, AA Cons.Finals 10,545

2012 123,615
Class AA 83,441
Class A 29,127
A, AA Cons. Finals 11,047

2013 116,051
Class AA 80,130
Class A 25,410
A,AA Cons. Finals 10,431

2014 118,249
Class AA 80,028
Class A 26,909
A,AA Cons. Finals 11,312

2015 135,618
Class AA 78,856
Class A 34,147
A,AA Cons. Finals 22,615

The author as a high school senior at Greenway High 1969-70.

Jim Hoey was born and raised in Taconite, Minnesota, on the Mesabi Iron Range. He played hockey at Greenway High School in Coleraine, and appeared with the team in the state tournaments of 1968, 1969, and 1970. He was a captain of the hockey team at St. Mary's University in Winona, where he played from 1970 to 1974, and was later a head coach at Shakopee and Farmington high schools. Now retired after teaching secondary social studies for more than thirty years, Hoey is currently pursuing a second career as a writer. He lives in Eagan with his wife, Ann, and his son, Eddie. His first book, *Minnesota Twins Trivia*, was published in 2010. The first edition of *Puck Heaven* appeared in 2011 and *Minnesota Vikings Trivia* was published in 2013.